# About Island Press

Since 1984, the nonprofit organization Island Press has been stimulating, shaping, and communicating ideas that are essential for solving environmental problems worldwide. With more than 1,000 titles in print and some 30 new releases each year, we are the nation's leading publisher on environmental issues. We identify innovative thinkers and emerging trends in the environmental field. We work with world-renowned experts and authors to develop cross-disciplinary solutions to environmental challenges.

Island Press designs and executes educational campaigns in conjunction with our authors to communicate their critical messages in print, in person, and online using the latest technologies, innovative programs, and the media. Our goal is to reach targeted audiences—scientists, policymakers, environmental advocates, urban planners, the media, and concerned citizens— with information that can be used to create the framework for long-term ecological health and human well-being.

Island Press gratefully acknowledges major support of our work by The Agua Fund, The Andrew W. Mellon Foundation, The Bobolink Foundation, The Curtis and Edith Munson Foundation, Forrest C. and Frances H. Lattner Foundation, The JPB Foundation, The Kresge Foundation, The Oram Foundation, Inc., The Overbrook Foundation, The S.D. Bechtel, Jr. Foundation, The Summit Charitable Foundation, Inc., and many other generous supporters.

The opinions expressed in this book are those of the author(s) and do not necessarily reflect the views of our supporters.

Handbook of Biophilic City Planning and Design

# Handbook of Biophilic City Planning and Design

*Timothy Beatley*

**ISLAND**PRESS

Washington | Covelo | London

Library of Congress Control Number: 2016938091

Printed on recycled, acid-free paper ✹

Manufactured in the United States of America
10  9  8  7  6  5  4  3  2  1

Keywords: Biodiversity, Biophilia, Biophilic Cities Network, bird-safe buildings, Birmingham (United Kingdom), carbon footprint, climate change, ecosystem, garden, greenbelt, green infrastructure, Green Streets Initiative, health, Intertwine, Khoo Teck Puat Hospital, Milwaukee, nature, nature center, Oslo, park, parklet, Portland, resilience, restoration, San Francisco, Singapore, Stephen Kellert, Sutton Park, urban ecology, vertical garden, Vitoria-Gastiez (Spain), watershed, Wellington (New Zealand), Zealandia

*To Anneke, Caro, and Jadie*

# Contents

# List of Case Studies

# Preface

This handbook is about the power of nature to create better, more livable, sustainable, and resilient urban neighborhoods and environments.

It is intended to be useful in several ways. First, it provides a comprehensive guide to biophilic urbanism and urban practice, with a wealth of information about how cities can integrate nature into their planning and design processes and projects.

Second, it offers inspiration for how cities of the future might look, feel, and function. As we move into the urban age, we are desperately in need of new models, examples, and frames of reference for the relationship between urban and natural environments. This book also provides more than a modicum of hope in an age where climate change and global environmental degradation cause concern about the future of human and nonhuman life on Earth. While the tools, ideas, strategies, and emerging urban practices reported in these pages do not represent a complete antidote to these global challenges—indeed, what book could?— they are a considerable step in the right direction.

This book synthesizes and expands on the research conducted by the Biophilic Cities Project at the University of Virginia. Begun in 2011, the Project sought to apply the ideas, principles, and practices of the emerging biophilic design movement to the larger scale of cities and metropolitan areas. Focused initially on seven partner cities within the United States and around the world (later expanded to ten cities included in the 2013 Biophilic Cities exhibition and launch event), researchers, practitioners, and politicians collaborated to develop ideas about what a biophilic city is and what it could be in the future.

Much of the work in the initial years of the project focused on fleshing out the concept of biophilic urbanism, and telling the stories of cities leading the way. In October 2013, the Project expanded with the launch of a global Biophilic Cities

Network, which is intended to help foster a common agenda and a mechanism for sharing insights and collaborating across cultures and geographic boundaries to reimagine a planet of cities that not only value and respect nature but also make it a centerpiece of future design and planning.

Building from the Biophilic Cities Network's efforts, this handbook is intended to advance and solidify some of these nascent ways of understanding and speaking about nature in cities. While we continue to understand and embrace the value of concepts and language—like sustainable cities, resilient cities, regenerative cities—we believe the emphasis on *biophilic cities* is a useful and necessary addition.

Why? Don't we already speak compellingly of green cities and green infrastructure? Yes, but those descriptors fall short in significant ways. *Greening cities* is more often understood in terms of the many ways that buildings and neighborhoods can reduce energy consumption and lower ecological footprints. These are important goals, but they don't tell us much about the kinds of neighborhoods, communities, and cities we wish to live in, and they understand nature as only one of many green design and planning arrows in the quiver.

*Biophilic*, in its emphasis on both the natural world and living things (*bio*) and the connections with and love of nature (*philia*), captures more squarely what cities and city planning and design need today. We need something more than nature that serves as infrastructure—we need to speak compellingly and passionately about the need to nurture, protect, care for, and connect with nature. We need to connect with nature for our health and well-being, as scientific evidence increasingly tells us, and *biophilic cities* captures this importance of urban nature in a way that other contemporary words or language cannot.

What follows are many stories and examples of emerging practice. Part 1 summarizes key ideas, theory, and literature that define *biophilic cities* and *biophilic urbanism*. Parts 2 and 3 represent the bulk of the handbook. Part 2 contains full-length chapters on the main cities that the Biophilic Cities Project research has focused on for several years. These cities are also inaugural cities in the new global Biophilic Cities Network. Part 3 features a rich array of shorter examples of urban biophilic innovation from cities around the world. Part 4 presents reflections and lessons about how to advance urban biophilia and biophilic cities. The book closes with a bibliography and an extensive list of resources, including leading books and online resources.

Together the chapters provide a comprehensive understanding of both the theory and the practice of biophilic cities. It is a practical mix of ideas and principles, current urban practice, and future aspirations. The reader will see that much has already been done, or is under way, in cities around the world.

These are daunting times in terms of the challenges cities face in the decades ahead, but they are also exciting times, when cities are making room for nature, appreciating the importance of nature to health and well-being and to leading meaningful lives.

# Acknowledgments

There are many people to thank for help in writing this book and in conducting the research that went into these chapters and cases. Many specific individuals have helped collect and supply data and information. Special thanks go to our main contacts and collaborators in the partner cities. While this is by no means a complete list, we owe a special thanks to the following individuals in these cities: Lena Chan (Singapore); Mayor Celia Wade-Brown, Amber Bill, and Charles Dougherty (Wellington); Mike Houck, Matt Burlin, and Linda Dobson (Portland); Matt Howard, Erick Shambarger, and Marcia Caton Campbell (Milwaukee); Per Gunnar Roe and Mark Luccarelli (Oslo); Sabine Courcier and Josee Duplessis (Montreal); Scott Edmondson and Peter Brastow (San Francisco); Nick Grayson and Rob MacKenzie (Birmingham, UK); Cecilia Herzog (Rio de Janeiro); Luis Andres Orive and Rebeca Dios (Vitoria-Gasteiz); and Craig Thomas and David Pijawka (Phoenix), among many others. Other individuals who have been very helpful and have lent support to the biophilic cities idea include Julia Africa, Bill Browning, Herbert Dreisetl, John Hadidian, Stephen Kellert, Stella Tarnay, Helena van Vliet, Catherine Werner, and Jennifer Wolch, among others.

Special thanks must also be given to the Summit Foundation of Washington, DC, and to its director of sustainable cities, Darryl Young, who provides extensive financial (and moral) support for the work, and for the emerging global network of cities. Financial support for this research was provided initially under the grant "Biophilic Urbanism: Global Methods and Metrics," and was followed by additional support to develop the project's web page and newly launched Biophilic Cities Network.

Significant financial support for the Biophilic Cities Project and the event launching the global Biophilic Cities Network was also provided by the George Mitchell Foundation. George Mitchell sadly passed away in 2013, but he will be remembered as a leader and catalyst for sustainable, biophilic design, as evidenced in his work with Ian McHarg in designing and building the Woodlands, a green new town ahead of its time. It was a pleasure to get to know George Mitchell, and an honor to have his personal and financial support for the work we have been doing in green urbanism and biophilic cities.

Special thanks are also due Professor Peter Newman, of Curtin University, who has been a partner and close colleague in developing the ideas of biophilic cities and biophilic urbanism. Many of the cities we have examined here, and the projects and people profiled, are due to Peter's suggestions and generous sharing of his immense network of global contacts.

A number of graduate students in the Department of Urban and Environmental Planning, at the University of Virginia, have helped with this project along the way, either working directly on the information and cases presented here, or on some other aspect of the Biophilic Cities Project over the years. These current and former students include Holly Hendrix, Harriett Jameson, Sarah Schramm, Amanda Beck, Mariah Gleason, Briana Bergstrom, Dita Beard, and JD Brown, among others. Special thanks are owed to Carla Jones and Julia Triman who read and edited all parts of this book.

Several of the chapters to follow draw from earlier writing. Some material has appeared earlier in our Biophilic Cities blogs. Several chapters in part 2 draw from earlier published work. An earlier version of the Singapore chapter was published in *SiteLines* (Foundation for Landscape Studies), and a version of the Oslo chapter was published earlier in the book *Green Oslo: Visions, Planning and Discourse* (Ashgate), though both have been substantially modified. Two of Beatley's EverGreen columns written for *Planning Magazine* (longer drafts) make up portions of the chapters on Birmingham and San Francisco.

# PART 1:

# The Background and Theory of Biophilic Cities

This first section of the handbook lays some essential groundwork in exploring evidence of the need for biophilic cities, their different features and dimensions, and the ways in which they help advance resilience and sustainability.

Chapter 1 describes the history of biophilia and its application to buildings and cities, and reviews the emerging and growing evidence about the benefits and value of nature (health, psychological, economic). Chapter 2 explores more specifically what a biophilic city is, or could be—since this field is still young—and its various features and dimensions. Chapter 3 considers the different kinds of nature in cities and the ways in which nature might be experienced and enjoyed in cities. It introduces the idea of the urban nature diet as a framework for thinking about the kinds and extent of nature needed in urban environments. Finally, chapter 4 makes the explicit argument that the actions and strategies we undertake to make cities more biophilic will also help to make them more resilient and sustainable. It presents a model of the different pathways, direct and indirect, by which biophilic design and planning interventions can influence health and resilience.

# 1

# The Power of Urban Nature:
## *The Essential Benefits of Biophilic Urbanism*

Human beings need contact with nature and the natural environment. They need it to be healthy, happy, and productive and to lead meaningful lives. Nature is not optional, but an absolutely essential quality of modern urban life. Conserving and restoring the considerable nature that already exists in cities and finding or creating new ways to grow and insert new forms of nature are paramount challenges of the twenty-first century.

We know, moreover, that creating sustainable, resilient cities will necessitate the design qualities of compactness and density. To achieve those urban qualities that allow us to walk, to invest in and use public transportation, to reduce our energy and carbon footprints, cities will definitely need to be denser and more compact. That presents challenges to integrating nature, and finding ways to ensure that all urban residents have the daily, ideally hourly, contact with the natural world that they need.

We live in the age of cities, this is clear. Some 54 percent of the world's population now lives in cities, and that percentage is already much higher in American and European cities. Globally we have seen spectacular growth in urban population in a mere few decades. The number of people living in cities, according to the United Nations, has increased from 756 million in 1950 to nearly 4 billion in 2014. The percentage of the world's population living in cities is expected to approach 70 percent by 2050 (United Nations, 2014).

Cities and metropolitan areas represent governmental entities and geographical scales of concern that best match the global times we are in. As Parag Khanna, writing in the journal *Foreign Policy* (Khanna, 2010) observes: "The 21st century will

**Figure 1.1.** A major task for modern cities is to become more compact and dense, but at the same time foster closer connections to nature. Cities like Singapore have done much to show how this is possible, and to imagine a dense city immersed within nature. Singapore, shown here, has recently changed its city motto from "garden city" to "city in a garden." Credit: Photo by Tim Beatley.

not be dominated by America or China, Brazil or India, but by the city. In an age that appears increasingly unmanageable, cities rather than states are becoming the islands of governance on which the future world order will be built. This new world is not—and will not be—one global village, so much as a network of different ones."

Cities will need to take significant steps to enhance and regrow local and regional nature (fig. 1.1), but also serve as leaders in helping other cities to do the same and to provide leadership in global conservation.

### Biophilia

The concept of biophilia is the foundation for what follows in this handbook. Although the term was originally coined by German social psychologist Erich Fromm, Harvard entomologist E. O. Wilson deserves much credit for this idea, and for his career of tirelessly working on behalf of the natural world. Wilson famously defines *biophilia* as "the innately emotional affiliation of human beings to other living organisms. Innate means hereditary and hence part of ultimate human nature"

(Wilson 1984, 31). Innate connections and affiliation are hardwired in us, though Stephen Kellert, emeritus professor at Yale and a major figure in the development of the idea of biophilia, believes them to be "'weak' genetic tendencies," essentially needing cultural reinforcement and exercising (rather like a muscle)(Kellert, 2005).

Biophilia argues that we carry with us predispositions to certain things in our modern landscapes that, over evolutionary history, helped with our survival. Prospect and refuge theory holds that we are predisposed to prefer or desire wide-vista landscapes (prospect), because they delivered survival advantages, and refuge (caves and cliffs, for instance) for similar reasons. We also prefer water and coastal environments for these reasons (more about this later).

Stephen Kellert along with others, notably Judith Heerwagen, Roger Ulrich, and Bill Browning, have done much to advance and further expound on the idea of biophilia. Their work has helped cultivate and stimulate the application of these ideas in architecture (Kellert, Heerwagen, and Midor 2008).

### Increasing Evidence of the Healing Power of Nature

While there is a long history of celebrating and emphasizing the value and benefits of parks and nature (from Frederick Law Olmsted to Ian McHarg), the last decade has seen an explosion of scientific evidence and scholarly research documenting and demonstrating the various ways exposure to nature helps us. Dr. Kathleen Wolf, at the University of Washington, has analyzed an impressive 2800 articles describing research on the relationship between green space and health and concludes that the vast majority of this literature is from the 2000s and 1990s. Relatively few articles were published on this topic in the 1970s or 1980s, showing just how recent this trend in scholarship has been (Wolf and Flora 2010).

There is considerable and growing research, then, showing that contact with nature provides a wide range of positive mental and physical benefits. Exposure to nature helps reduce stress and boosts our cognitive performance. The early work of Rachel and Stephen Kaplan, on the Attention Restoration Theory (ART) emphasizes the important role that nature plays in helping us recover from the stress and emotionally taxing aspects of so-called directed attention (where we are concentrated and focused on accomplishing a task [see Kaplan and Kaplan 1989]).

Roger Ulrich's study of the healing power of nature is a watershed study for many in the biophilic design world. His study of patients' recovery from gallbladder surgery was one of the first to show in an empirically rigorous way that natural features could have recuperative power. More specifically, this research found that patients with hospital rooms that looked out on trees, compared with those with rooms that had only a brick wall view, recovered faster, with less need for painkillers. Since that time many similar studies have come to similar conclusions.

Japanese researchers have done extensive studies on what they refer to as forest bathing, or Shinrin-yoku in Japanese (shinrin = forest, yoku = bathing, basking). They have recorded significant positive biophysical benefits of a walk in a forest—a reduction in the stress hormone cortisol and a boost to the immune system. In large part this is due, it is believed, to the natural chemicals, phytoncides, that are emitted by evergreen trees. The Japanese government is so convinced by the evidence that they have established a series of Forest Therapy Bases in and around Japanese cities (Wang, Tsunetsugn, and Africa 2015).

Trees and forests, and other forms of urban nature, then, deliver important mental health and stress-reduction benefits. Biophilic theory and research suggest other elements of nature, especially water, are often highly valued and preferred. Michael Depledge and his team have produced significant research that shows this. In one large study of residents in the United Kingdom they found that reported health was strongly related to proximity to coastal environments (Wheeler, White, Stahl-Timmons, and Depledge 2012).

Proximity to green space for residents of a city has also been shown to correlate to lower stress hormone levels as well as lower self-reported levels of stress. Ward Thompson et al. (2012) and Roe and Aspinall (2011) demonstrate this through innovative studies where participants monitor their salivary cortisol levels over the course of a day, allowing the researchers to track the diurnal patterns of cortisol and to understand how stress might affect the circadian cycle of cortisol. Both these salivary cortisol levels and self-reported stress are found to be inversely related to levels of green space, controlling for socioeconomic variables.

A 2009 study by Dutch researchers published in the *Journal of Epidemiology and Community Health* found that the greenness of a neighborhood was predictive of a variety of maladies. Maas et al. (2009) conclude the following:

> The annual prevalence rates for 15 of the 24 investigated disease clusters is lower in living environments with more green space in a 1 km radius. Green space close to home appeared to be more important than green space further away…It appears that for the prevalence of these more specific diseases green space close to home is more important. This study differs from other studies, which mainly focused on the relation between green space and self-perceived measures of physical and mental health. This is the first study to assess the relation between green space and specific diseases, derived from electronic medical records of GPs. (p. 971)

Similarly, a recent study by Feda et al (2015) found a strong association between proximity to parks and lower perceived stress in adolescents. A number of recent studies are showing how walks in nature can positively improve mood and outlook, as well as provide other physical and mental benefits. Perhaps the benefits from physical exercise are obvious, as so much of the modern lifestyle involves sitting (especially during the workday). It has been said that sitting and sedentary lives represent "the new smoking" (Perinotto 2015). Walking in nature can, it seems, also change the brain in very positive ways. New research by Gregory Bratman and his colleagues at Stanford suggests that walks in nature help to curtail brooding or rumination, a likely precursor to depression (Bratman et al. 2015; Reynolds 2015). Other studies come to similar conclusions about the positive mental and mood enhancements of nature walks. More research is necessary, however, as scientists at the National University of Singapore recently highlight the potential negative influence of climate—heat and humidity—on human enjoyment of being outside (Saw et al. 2015).

Having nearby nature is an important antidote to the stresses of modern life and delivers immense emotional and physical health benefits. There are a number of new studies that show compellingly the health benefits and value of trees and tree-planting in the city. These have shown, for instance, an inverse relationship between trees and low birth weight (Donovan et al. 2011), and the impact of planting trees in vacant lots in reducing crime rates and gun violence. Troy, Grove, and O'Neil-Dunne (2012) found an inverse relationship between tree cover and crime in neighborhoods, leading to the conclusion that a "10% increase in tree cover would be associated with an 11.8% decrease in crime rate, all else equal." A study of more than 30,000 residents of Toronto found a strong association between urban tree density and perceived health and reported cardiometabolic illness (and after controlling for socioeconomic variables, such as education and income). The more trees on a city block, the less likely are residents to report ailments like hypertension and the more likely they are to report feeling healthier (fig. 1.2). In neighborhoods with just 10 more trees on the block on average, residents, the study authors conclude, are likely to feel 7 years younger or $10,000 richer (Bullen 2015; Kardan et al. 2015).

### New Technologies and Techniques for Understanding the Role of Nature in Cities

Changes in technology are now making it possible to understand and gauge the power of nature as experienced by individuals in the field. Jenny Roe and her colleagues in the United Kingdom have been some of the first to utilize portable electroencephalography (EEG) caps, which allow researchers to monitor brain activity while

**Figure 1.2.** San Francisco has pioneered the creative repurposing of small spaces in the city for nature. There are spaces that can help to lower urban stress and enhance quality of life. Credit: Photo by Tim Beatley.

a subject is mobile, exploring outside the hospital environment. In a study published in the *British Journal of Sports Medicine*, University of Edinburgh students wearing EEG caps went on a roughly 30-minute walk, following a consistent route that took them through various urban segments of that city, including a shopping area, a busy commercial street, and a segment that included parks and green space, all the while sending streaming data of brain scans. The results of this study are consistent with restoration theory, and "showed evidence of lower frustration, engagement and arousal, and higher meditation when moving into the green space zone; higher engagement when moving out of it" (Aspinall, Mavros, Coyne, and Roe 2013).

As these studies suggest, there is a trend in utilizing brain scans to better and more rigorously understand the positive power of nature. In the Bratman study mentioned earlier participants engaged in walks in nature (and those walking in a nonnatural setting) were administered a brain scan both before and after the walks, yielding clear evidence about effects on the subgenual prefrontal cortex, the area of the brain associated with brooding. Brain science will, it seems, be increasingly employed in understanding nature's effects on urbanites.

The value of nature is further reconfirmed when people are asked where and when they are happiest, a real possibility given the growing ubiquity of cell phones.

With the emergence of smart phones everywhere there are new abilities to gauge how nature in daily life matters and matters immensely. The Mappiness Project based in the United Kingdom is one such example. More than 60,000 British citizens participate in the Mappiness Project (an iPhone app), which asks participants to indicate the extent of their happiness when "pinged." The responses are geocoded to a physical location and setting and include other variables. Participants indicate that they are happiest when they are in nature, and this is one of the main conclusions of the project (MacKerron and Mourato 2013).

That we are more productive in work environments that include even a modicum of natural elements has been demonstrated in a series of recent studies. Another interesting study looked at the impact of natural light in hospitals, this time focusing on the mood and well-being of nurses. Published in the *Health Environments Research and Design Journal*, this study found that access to natural light in hospitals had a dramatic effect on the work environment for the nursing staff. Rana Zadeth, of Cornell, quite creatively measured differences in things like blood pressure, and how much nurses talked to one another. Nursing work stations with greater amounts of daylight were associated with lower blood pressure readings and greater interaction between nurses, and, especially interesting, she found more laughter observed at these daylit nursing stations. Happier nurses must be associated with more effective nursing and presumably these positive feelings filter down to patients and many others working in these spaces (Osgood 2014).

## Creativity, Humanity, and Taking the Long View

It is increasingly evident that exposure to nature helps us to be better, more caring and compassionate human beings. Several recent studies have documented that we are more likely to exhibit generous behavior in the presence of nature (e.g., Weinstein, Przybylski, and Ryan 2009).

Recent work by van der Wal et al. (2013) shows that humans, in the presence of nature, tend to value and care for the future more. A series of experiments showed that participants were less likely to discount the future, and showed a greater willingness to delay gratification, after exposure to scenes of nature (as compared with scenes of urban landscapes). Precisely why this results is not clear, but it does seem consistent with what we would expect from exposure to nature—a sense of health and abundance that nature conveys, and perhaps the uplifting feelings of optimism seem a reasonable assumption.

We are also likely to be more creative in the presence of nature. There is now evidence that we are also more likely to be cooperative when nature is around (Zelenski,

Dopko and Capaldi, 2015). Researchers from the University of Utah and the University of Kansas found that study participants who had been immersed in nature performed better on creativity problem-solving tasks (Atchley, Strayer and Atchley 2012). Even exposure to the color green (just a brief glimpse) leads to better performance on creativity tasks (Lichtenfeld , Elliot, Maier, and Pekrun 2012). If we are concerned, as we should be, about responding effectively to the immense global environmental challenges we face as a species, it seems that having nature all around us (as in fig. 1.3) will likely result in the most generous, cooperative, and creative responses possible.

### The Economic Benefits of Biophilic Cities

There is a long and extensive body of economic literature that demonstrates the economic benefits and wealth bestowed by nature. We know, and there are many studies that confirm, that trees pay back manyfold the upfront costs of growing and planting them. Natural daylight, fresh ventilation, and greenery in schools and offices lead to beneficial improvements in learning and working environments (e.g., increased test scores and learning ability in schools, reduced absenteeism in offices) that carry with them considerable economic values.

Having a nearby park adds to the market value of a home, for instance, as does the presence of trees on one's urban or suburban lot. Recently, the Trust for Public Land has been calculating the considerable economic value bestowed by parks, and the numbers are strikingly high. For San Francisco alone they calculate annual economic benefits (revenues generated, economic cost-savings to citizens and the city, and wealth creation) of around $959 million (Trust for Public Land 2014).

A number of studies demonstrate that investing, individually or collectively, in nature, adds to urban wealth and value. Donovan and Butry (2010), for instance, in their study of trees in Portland, Oregon, conclude that the presence of trees adds thousands of dollars in value to homes. Extrapolating to the larger city, they conclude: "applying the average tree effect to all houses in Portland yields a total value of $1.35 billion" (Donovan and Butry, 2010, 81).

The consulting firm Terrapin Bright Green has produced reports calculating many of the economic benefits of cities with biophilic qualities and estimating them for New York City. Reduced absenteeism in New York schools would save hundreds of millions of dollars, as would improvements in the biophilic working conditions of offices. Crime reduction resulting from new green elements would have even greater economic value. The conclusions of this study provide a sense of the immense economic value: "This sampling of economic impacts of biophilia in New York City adds up to over $2.7 billion per year in 2010 dollars." The report

**Figure 1.3.** Wildness is often close by in cities. Richmond, Virginia, is a good example, where efforts are under way to enhance physical access to the James River, what the city now refers to as its "Central Park." Within a few hundred feet of downtown there are class IV rapids, a heron rookery, and, at certain times of the year, migrating shad. Credit: Photo by Tim Beatley.

continues, "Though the costs of creating vegetated spaces can seem high, the enormous value of a biophilic city has the potential to outweigh the costs by far" (Terrapin Bright Green 2012, 23).

There are few investments in a city, public or private, that would outperform investments in nature. A recent economic analysis of the economics of completing Houston's ambitious Bayou Greenway Initiative supports this claim. The costs of land acquisition are estimated at $480 million, a considerable sum that might quickly discourage completion of this bold regional trail and park network. Estimating the physical and mental health benefits of the green spaces and the enhancements to quality of life also yields a high number: conservatively these benefits are estimated at more than $117 million per year. The authors conclude, "There is unlikely to be any other $480 million investment the greater Houston area could make that would generate such an extraordinary annual return" (Crompton and Marsh Darcey Partners 2011, 12).

## Conclusions

There are many good reasons to have nature all around us, and the empirical evidence has been mounting over the last decade especially. We are happier, healthier, and more productive when we have nature nearby. We are likely to be more generous and more creative and to think longer term when we have nature all around us. We are healthier and more likely, then, to be better, more caring and compassionate human beings. This is not surprising given the basic premise behind biophilia—that we have coevolved with the natural world. No wonder we are more relaxed, more at home, more comfortable in natural settings. These are all very good reasons to aspire to and work to become a greener, more biophilic city. And the economic research and evidence provide even more reasons—as investing in trees, parks, green rooftops, and trails delivers large benefits and large returns. Biophilic design and planning in cities makes good sense from many perspectives.

# 2

# Understanding the Nature
# of Biophilic Cities

Nature takes many different forms in cities, and it can be experienced in many different ways. To a certain degree, however, nature is a social construct. In this book we argue that nature comprises all the life and living systems in and around cities, from the birds and mammals we can see to the immense populations of invertebrate and largely invisible nonhuman life around us. Increasingly, the nature in and around cities takes the form of green rooftops, green balconies, or vertical facades and gardens on high-rise buildings. These are human-designed and constructed, of course, yet we also respond to them in positive ways, and they do provide an element of nature in an otherwise gray and asphalt urban world. This book focuses mainly on the impact of outdoor spaces in cities, but we acknowledge that there is an important role for indoor nature as well. This chapter details important new ways of seeing and understanding cities as places of nature.

## Cities Are Ecosystems and Habitat for Many (Other) Species

There is an immense amount of nature in and around cities—more than is popularly thought. In many parts of the world where industrially farmed landscapes lie beyond city boundaries—often monocrops carefully monitored and treated with pesticides—comparitively, cities harbor greater biodiversity within their parks, yards, and rooftops. Increasingly we recognize the role that cities play and must play to an even greater degree in the future, as biodiversity hotspots, and as urban arks protecting, restoring, harboring nature that is under global assault. My early book *Biophilic Cities* (2011), describes the many places where nature and biodiversity can be found in cities—from fungi and lichen on the tops of tree branches, to the bacteria wafting by on clouds, to the immense diversity of life found in the soil beneath our feet. It is everywhere we look, above, below, around us.

Recent discoveries of new species in cities are evidence of the extent of the nature found in an urban environment, often much more native flora and fauna than people realize or appreciate. The year 2014 saw the discovery of a new species of leopard frog in New York City (Feinberg et al. 2014), and not that long ago a bioblitz in Central Park resulted in the discovery of a new species of centipede (Stewart 2002). Many cities are perched on the edge of the marine world, where significant amounts of biodiversity can be found. Singapore has embarked on a comprehensive inventory of its marine life and has already discovered some 14 species previously unknown to science (Hoh 2013). The age of biodiscovery is anything but over and much of the action is happening in cities today.

The growth and development of cities has had a profound effect in altering the natural landscape in which they are situated. But, as with hydrology, we know that much of these remnant patterns of nature and biodiversity remain if we search for them. The ecosystems, flora, and fauna present in cities are experiencing changes as a reaction to stimuli from urban locations. Research suggests that some species of ants are heartier in cities, birds are changing the frequency of their calls in response to urban noise, and there are new and different assemblages of plants and animals that are adapting to and thriving in the urban conditions of cities. Nature in cities is dynamic and changing (fig. 2.1).

## Nature in Cities Is Multisensory

We experience nature in many different ways, especially in cities. We see it and watch it, and enjoy visual connections with nature. But we also experience nature through other senses, especially through sound. A natureful city is one that recognizes the importance and value of natural soundscapes. In my own life, the summer evening sounds of katydids, grasshoppers, tree frogs, and other species are important qualities of place and immensely enhance the quality of living. Cicadas and bird song during the day, moreover, are also part of the sweet music that urbanites can, under the right conditions, enjoy. Especially when we recognize the sounds of nature, we appreciate the sense of not being alone, but sharing the spaces of cities with many other forms of life.

Sound ecologist Bernie Krause has devoted his life to recording and analyzing sounds of nature, and increasingly we recognize the psychological and other values these sounds bring. Krause says that part of the challenge is for us to simply be quiet

**Figure 2.1.** The Chicago skyline, with the Lincoln Park Zoo in the foreground. All cities are a dynamic intertwining of natural systems and built environments. Credit: Photo by Tim Beatley.

and listen. This is difficult when the sounds of nature are obscured by the sounds of cars and highways, airplanes and helicopters, jackhammers and other construction noises, so part of the agenda of a biophilic city is to seek to integrate quiet areas, to restrict the mechanical and loud noises in cities that are themselves quite unhealthy.

Research is emerging about the beneficial effects of nature sounds and soundscapes. Hedblom et al. (2014) examined the reactions of young urbanites to a combination of images and bird sounds. They found that participants were more likely to rate images positively when the bird songs were heard, and more likely still when there were multiple birds singing. "From our test, we conclude that participants generally liked passerine song, more so when provided by several species than by a single species, and that song often improved the rating given to urban settings in residential areas. We interpret these data as support for the idea that bird song enhances people's experience of urban environments" (2014, 472).

Of course there are other important senses at work that can help connect us to nature. Sight and sound are key, but so are smells and tastes, and the many opportunities to touch and feel the natural world. Holding a smooth pebble in one's hand or stroking the bark of a tree undoubtedly delivers benefits. Experiencing the fragrance of flowers and flowering trees, or the aromas of such things as fruit picked in the garden, are things that connect us to place and to Earth's bounty, and are profoundly biophilic experiences as well. Efforts at appreciating smells in a city (not all natural and not all of them pleasant) have led to the creation of smell maps, similar to more commonly developed sound maps in cities (Logan 2009).

### Nature in Cities Is Both Large and Small

Nature in the biophilic city can be found in forms that are both large and small. There is plenty of remarkable, dramatic nature in and near cities. In the 3300-hectare Tijuca National Park in the center of Rio de Janeiro, there are maned three-toed sloths and channel-billed toucans. In Nairobi National Park one famously sees zebras, lions, and giraffes, with the city's skyline in the background. I remember well the experience of seeing gray-headed flying foxes (large fruit bats) in Sydney and Brisbane. And there are spectacular marine organisms living near cities, from gray whales in San Francisco to orcas in Wellington Harbor.

The patterns of geology, hydrology, and landscape create the larger environmental context of cities, the rivers and mountains and canyons that provide the physical and visual backdrop to urban life. Every city has unique landforms, topography, weather, and climatic conditions that make that city and region unique and different and set the larger stage for urban nature.

Biophilic cities should consider nature at all levels, from the microscopic to the bioregional and continental. I have been inspired by the long history of scientists (professional and amateur) learning and writing about the microbiological world of cities. I think especially of writers in the Victorian era, like Agnes Catlow, whose 1851 book *Drops of Water* described compellingly the micro-organisms that would likely be found in four drops of water, as might be collected from the Thames River or a freshwater pond. The illustrations are fascinating and wondrous and depict common organisms that few even today would recognize or know about. Catlow describes them in the subtitle of the book as "marvelous and beautiful inhabitants" ("displayed by the microscope") (Catlow 1851). These remarkable organisms look and behave in ways foreign to us in the nonmicroscopic world. Keeping with the practice of the day they're described as *animalcules*, a charming, accessible word that describes these very small creatures. As Catlow argues so eloquently, there are many clear and wonderful pleasures to be found in looking at these small life forms, nearby nature we may often neglect.

There is equally abundant life to be found in the soil beneath our cities, and there is newfound appreciation for the ecological (and economic) benefits it provides. A 2014 study of soil biota in Central Park in New York uncovered a remarkable extent of microbial diversity. The authors conclude that "Central Park's soils harboured nearly as many distinct soil microbial phylotypes and types of soil communities as we found in biomes across the globe" (Ramirez et al. 2014).

There is, of course, a healthy invertebrate life in cities, and, thanks to new research by people like Rob Dunn and his lab at North Carolina State University, and Amy Savage of Rutgers University, we are beginning to understand better the ways that small critters function and live and increasingly adapt to cities. Research on the diversity of ants in New York City is especially telling in this regard. Dunn and Savage, and their colleagues, have published the first comprehensive study of ants in that city and found an impressive 42 species overall (Savage, Hackett, Youngsteadt and Dunn 2015). They surveyed more natural forested parts of the city, where ant diversity was found to be highest but also more "stressed" urban settings, such as median strips, and found considerable diversity there as well. This ant diversity is impressive, especially given the density and extent of urbanization—70,000 people per square mile; the densest city in the United States can still harbor such remarkable life.

## Nature in the City Is Seen Around Every Corner, Through Every Window

A biophilic city takes full advantage of the nature in and around it. Nature is ever present, and efforts are made to ensure physical and visual access to natural features and qualities. Many of the cities described in this handbook have made efforts to restore rivers and waterways and to design new points of access and connection. Cities like New York, and Richmond, Virginia, for instance, have sought in their planning to emphasize new connections with riverfronts through different means—new shoreline parks, new trails and access points. Similarly, many cities have sought to ensure visual connections to the nature around them, whether a river, ocean, or mountain range. There is pleasure and stress-reduction value when one catches a glimpse of nature—large or small—from a window, rooftop, or stairwell.

The many benefits of contact with water are increasingly understood (Nichols 2014), and biophilic cities seek at once to maximize these benefits, while also balancing the associated dangers (e.g., from sea level rise). Many cities (e.g., Baltimore, Oslo, and Boston) have invested in waterfront trails or promenades that provide pedestrian access. One example of the health benefits can be seen in the relocation of the Spaulding Rehabilitation Hospital, in Boston, to a site along the Boston harbor with physical access to the Boston Harborwalk, as well as efforts to design the structure to maximize views of the water (e.g., through lowering windows so those in wheelchairs can adequately see out). Water can be included in many other ways in urban environments, of course, from fountains and water features to stream-daylighting, and few would deny the positive solace and solitude provided by even very small water elements, such as the waterfall at Paley Park, a very small urban space in New York City (see the case to follow in part 3 of the book).

### Nature Is Often Hidden in Cities but Is Still Knowable

Much of the immense biological diversity in and around cities is hidden in one way or another. It is the biodiversity of soil and micro-organic life of the city, but also many other forms of hidden nature. These include marine and aquatic nature, where organisms are underwater and beyond the typical visual and physical access of residents. Developing an awareness of and emotional caring for and connection with this nature may require some unusually creative strategies, but this is a key dimension of a biophilic city (fig. 2.2).

Cities making progress toward a biophilic agenda today employ a variety of techniques to unearth and educate about these more hidden forms of nature. Whether it is efforts to guide urban residents to places where the wonder of local nature can be seen and experienced at different times of the year (salmon viewing areas in Seattle and the Northwest, for instance), or a phone app that indicates a lost river underfoot, knowing about and engaging with these elements of nature in cities that may be harder to see or find is important.

### Nature in the City Is Both Human Designed and Preexisting in Wild or Semiwild Conditions

Increasingly, biophilic urbanism is expressed in the many ways that buildings and built environments can integrate new green elements or features. From ecological rooftops to vertical gardens and facades to skyparks and eco-bridges, there is an increasingly larger and robust toolbox of design techniques, ideas, and technologies that can be applied. And, with increased research and monitoring of these human-designed features, we recognize the tremendous amount of biodiversity that can be harbored and fostered in these features. These spaces add much to preexisting wild and semi-wild spaces in the city, such as a remnant prairie, a natural stretch of an urban stream, or an ancient tree.

Today we recognize that it is possible to live in a high-rise tower in a dense, vertical city, and still find ways to connect with the natural world. These designed natural elements can harbor much biodiversity. Research in New York City green rooftops, for instance, shows remarkable fungi and lichen diversity, different from,

**Figure 2.2.** Parks, trees and green spaces of various sorts provide opportunities for respite, contemplation, and active recreation. Here, London's Hampstead Heath is a beloved (and wild) space close to where many residents live. There is much more nature here, of course, than we realize: from microorganisms in soil to lichen on tree branches. Credit: Photo by Tim Beatley.

yet complementary to, the biodiversity found on ground-level parks in that city. A study of green rooftops in London found not only an abundance of invertebrate life but many that were "nationally rare or scarce" (Kadas 2006).

Much of this new nature then will be in the vertical realm. Techniques and design strategies that seemed fanciful only a few years ago are being tried and tested; as a result we have evidence that confirms their practicality and feasibility. In Milan, the twin towers that make up the project Bosco Verticale are illustrative. Here, "forests in the sky" are literally a reality now, as these towers near completion. Designed by Italian architect Stefano Boeri, these high-rise residential towers are wrapped with balcony-integrated trees from floor to roof, including some 900 trees as well as thousands of plants. Not long ago the aspiration of a vertical forest might have seemed a pipedream, depicted in architectural renderings that bore little connection to engineering and building reality. Fanciful renderings are still common, but today they are more likely to be achievable or realistic in a way they perhaps weren't just a decade or two ago. Cities in the future will necessarily entail a rich mix of designed nature, such as this, with more traditional forms of (ground level) nature.

**Nature Is Mostly Outside but Is Also Found Inside**

The reality of modern life is that much of our day—by some estimates more than 90 percent—is spent indoors, in offices and homes. There is now a growing body of research that suggests that fresh air, full-spectrum natural daylight, greenery, and growing nature of all sorts will boost productivity and mood in indoor environments. Biophilic design of the interior spaces of buildings, then, is another important dimension of a biophilic city and an important part of the agenda of creating healthy spaces and places in cities. There are now a host of off-the-shelf commercial products and systems (from terraria to small interior green walls), and a growing number of examples of inspiring green interior designs that demonstrate what is possible. Indeed in many climates the barriers (often as much psychological as physical) between inside and outside are being broken down, with the result being much more intimate and extensive connections with nature. While much of the planning and design techniques in this book will focus on outdoor strategies, biophilic urbanism acknowledges that enjoyment of nature *inside* is important, underscoring the need for "room to region" strategies.

Biophilic cities recognize the importance of creative strategies for bringing nature into the interior spaces of homes and offices. Interior green walls, natural ventilation, daylit interior spaces, and interior forest atria are among the many ideas that can be embraced, and biophilic cities understand the health benefits of encouraging such features, not as substitutes, but as necessary supplements, to outside nature. One small personal example can be seen in the glass terrarium we commissioned for the Biophilic Cities Network launch. While relatively small and compact, the visual effect served to bring an intense and important element of nature into the exhibition spaces of the University of Virginia School of Architecture. Designed by a San Francisco Bay Area firm called Crooked Nest, the terrarium quickly became known as the biophilic bubble, and continues to deliver a small element of natural delight to interior office space. Candace Silvey, one of the principals in the design firm, tells me that they have designed around 50 of these terraria, and she often hears stories about their beauty and how these "living assemblages" positively engage their owners. Each one is unique, each a special design that combines handblown glass with mostly local species of plants.

There is of course a long history of interior terraria and other structures that seek to bring an element of nature to the indoors. The so-called Wardian cases were some of the first—invented by a physician, Nathaniel Bagshaw Ward, in the early 1800s, as a response to the abysmal air quality of London, so bad in fact that outdoor gardens and flowers would simply not grow. Today, there are a host of interior greening strategies and off-the-shelf growing systems—from interior green walls to water features in courtyards to potted trees and plants—there are many ways to create nature indoors that complements outside environments.

One of the continuing design challenges is how to effectively overcome or at least minimize the indoor–outdoor bifurcation through creative use of sliding doors and windows, plazas and green areas that extend partially indoors, sunscreens, and many other techniques. Efforts to reduce the drone of air conditioning through biophilic plantings can help reduce outdoor barriers as well.

## Nature Can Be Created in Cities through Biophilic Design

The biophilic cities movement builds on and benefits from much of the work of biophilic design that has focused more on the building scale. In the last decade especially, there has been much progress and innovation around biophilic design. New books have been published (e.g., Kellert, Heerwagen, and Mador 2008) and biophilic design principles have now been included in several major green and healthy building certification systems, including the Living Building Challenge and the WELL Building Standard. These certification systems and a growing body of design practice demonstrating how biophilic principles can manifest are useful, and our notion of biophilic cities is one that seeks more buildings—homes, office towers, hospitals, etc.—as places of nature. Cities of nature must be cities where buildings of various sorts contain abundant nature.

The biophilic design movement has also generated very helpful thinking and guidance about the qualities and conditions of nature that we would like to see. Boxes 2.1 and 2.2 contain two complementary versions of guidelines for nature. Box 2.1 puts forth a highly useful, applicable, and readable set of 14 patterns of biophilic design, written by Bill Browning and Catie Ryan of the consulting company Terrapin Bright Green. Box 2.2 summarizes the biophilic design ideas put forth by Yale professor Stephen Kellert, a leading thinker and writer in this area. Both are excellent summaries of some of the main aspects and features of nature that we desire to see and experience not only in homes and buildings but in the larger urban cities and regions in which these structures lie—water, daylight, trees and greenery, and the sounds of nature, among others.

Both of these sets of biophilic design principles also highlight the value of the shapes and forms of nature, something I have discussed as well in earlier books (Beatley 2011). While the evidence is less clear about the therapeutic and mental health benefits of such references to nature, I am convinced that they add to comfort and pleasure of cities and stand as important symbols and recognition of our natural

## Box 2.1. 14 Patterns of Biophilic Design

Biophilia is humankind's deep-seated connection with nature. It helps explain why crackling fires and crashing waves captivate us; why a view to nature can enhance our creativity; why shadows and heights instill fascination and fear; and why gardening and strolling through a park have restorative healing effects.

Biophilic elements have demonstrably real, measurable benefits for human performance metrics, such as productivity, emotional well-being, stress, learning, creativity, and healing. As the world population continues to urbanize, these qualities are ever more important. Theorists, research scientists, and design practitioners have been working for decades to define aspects of nature that most impact our satisfaction with the built environment. Terrapin Bright Green, a strategic planning and consulting firm based in New York City, has codified this research into *14 Patterns of Biophilic Design*, a book and design tool that begins to articulate the relationships between nature, human biology, and the design of the built environment so that we may experience the human benefits of biophilia in our design applications for the healthful advancement of individuals and society as a whole.

1. Visual Connection with Nature—A view to elements of nature, living systems, and natural processes
2. Nonvisual Connection with Nature—Auditory, haptic, olfactory, or gustatory stimuli that engender a deliberate and positive reference to nature, living systems, or natural processes
3. Nonrhythmic Sensory Stimuli—Stochastic and ephemeral connections with nature that may be analyzed statistically but may not be predicted precisely
4. Thermal & Airflow Variability – Subtle changes in air temperature, relative humidity, airflow across the skin, and surface temperatures that mimic natural environments
5. Presence of Water—A condition that enhances the experience of a place through the seeing, hearing, or touching of water
6. Dynamic and Diffuse Light—Leveraging varying intensities of light and shadow that change over time to create conditions that occur in nature
7. Connection with Natural Systems—Awareness of natural processes, especially seasonal and temporal changes characteristic of a healthy ecosystem
8. Biomorphic Forms and Patterns—Symbolic references to contoured, patterned, textured, or numerical arrangements that persist in nature
9. Material Connection with Nature—Material and elements from nature that, through minimal processing, reflect the local ecology or geology to create a distinct sense of place
10. Complexity and Order—Rich sensory information that adheres to a spatial hierarchy similar to those encountered in nature
11. Prospect—An unimpeded view over a distance for surveillance and planning

*Box 2.1 cont.*

12. Refuge—A place for withdrawal, from environmental conditions or the main flow of activity, in which the individual is protected from behind and overhead

13. Mystery—The promise of more information achieved through partially obscured views or other sensory devices that entice the individual to travel deeper into the environment

14. Risk/Peril—An identifiable threat coupled with a reliable safeguard

Terrapin Bright Green offers free public access to *14 Patterns of Biophilic Design* (2014), *The Economics of Biophilia* (2012), and other publications. Visit TerrapinBrightGreen.com /publications for more information.

## Box 2.2. Attributes of Biophilic Design

I. Direct experience of nature
    Light
    Air
    Water
    Plants
    Animals
    Weather
    Natural landscapes and ecosystems
II. Indirect experience of nature
    Images of nature
    Natural materials
    Natural colors
    Simulating natural light and air
    Naturalistic shapes and forms
    Evoking nature
    Information richness
    Age, change, and the patina of time
    Natural geometries
    Biomimicry
III. Experience of space and place
    Prospect and refuge
    Organized complexity
    Integration of parts to wholes
    Transitional spaces
    Mobility and wayfinding
    Cultural and ecological attachment
        to place

Source: Kellert and Calabrese (2015).

embeddedness, and that we share a world with many other creatures. There are many examples in the cases to follow—from the fish and aquatic nature referenced in the architecture of Oslo to the fern frond–shaped bollards employed in the streets and public spaces of Wellington, New Zealand. These shapes, forms, and references to nature also help to make up a biophilic city.

## What Are the Qualities of a Biophilic City?

Once you understand how to be aware of the complex dimensions of nature that can exist in urban areas, the next step is to understand them in the context of the entire city. What does it mean to live in, or work to create, a biophilic city?

The main dimensions of urban biophilia can be described in several different ways. One approach is to describe a biophilic city in narrative and poetic ways: to articulate in words

**Box 2.3. Biophilic Cities Pledge**

"I hereby commit my city, organization, university, or self to helping my community become a Biophilic City, and to join together with other cities in the global Network of Biophilic Cities. I understand that a Biophilic City is a city of abundant nature, where citizens, young and old, have rich daily (if not hourly) contact with the natural environment; where citizens have nature nearby, where larger natural areas and deeper nature experiences are an easy walk, bike or transit ride away; and where the urban environment allows for and fosters connections with diverse flora, fauna, and fungi; a city where citizens recognize, are curious about, and actively care for the nature around them; a city where citizens spend extensive time outside, learning about, enjoying and participating in the natural world; a city where leaders and elected officials place nature at the heart of their decision making, and where every major planning and development decision is judged by the extent to which nature is restored and connections with the natural environment enhanced.

Declaring my intention to become a member of the global network of Biophilic Cities means that I commit to working diligently to protect and restore nature and to creating opportunities for new nature and connections to the natural world wherever possible; sharing information and insights about what tools, techniqes, programs and projects have been successfully applied in our city; assisting other cities to become more biophilic, offering help in data collection and analysis, sharing technical expertise and knowledge, and other forms of political and professional support for efforts to protect and expand urban nature; meeting periodically as a group to share experiences and insights and to provide mutual support and guidance in advancing the practice of biophilic urbanism.

I pledge to actively further the Biophilic Cities Mission and commit to protecting and enhancing opportunities for citizens to connect with nature in my city."

what makes a biophilic city. Box 2.3 presents one version that has been frequently used by the Biophilic Cities Project. Box 2.4 is a summary listing of some of the key qualities and attributes of biophilic cities. The list that follows in the text is a brief discussion of what compromises the vision of biophilic cities. Should you be interested in more detail, you'll find it in *Biophilic Cities* (Beatley 2011).

## Natureful Cities, an Abundance of Nature

In the most basic sense, a biophilic city is a city that has abundant nature. Often we are using the word *natureful* to describe these conditions. Nature is ever present, ever nearby, really all around, in a variety of forms—trees and forests, streams and rivers, meadows and wildflowers, birds and urban wildlife of many kinds. We know when we visit a green, biophilic city, because we often see and notice this abundant nature (and we often feel better and happier in these places).

Many of the chapters to follow in this handbook are about the numerous creative ways in which cities can protect, restore, and grow new forms of nature.

## Engagement with Nature

A biophilic city is not just a city that has lots of nature in and around it, though that is an extremely important dimension. It is also the engagement with, the enjoyment of, the celebration of that nature. How much time do individuals in the city spend enjoying outside nature? For example, do they walk, hike, swim, ponder, gaze, clean up and care for, actively explore and learn about the nature around them in cities. Some of this

---

### Box 2.4. What Are Biophilic Cities?

1. Biophilic cities are cities of abundant nature and natural experiences.

2. Biophilic cities are biodiverse cities—places with rich flora, fauna, fungi.

3. Biophilic cities are multisensory cities.

4. Biophilic cities are cities of interconnected, integrated natural spaces and features.

5. Biophilic cities immerse us in and surround us with nature; in biophilic cities one does not visit nature, one lives in nature.

6. Biophilic cities are outdoor cities.

7. Biophilic cities embrace the blue as well as the green; the marine and aquatic as well as the terrestrial.

8. Biophilic cities celebrate the small and large; the microscopic to the celestial.

9. Biophilic cities are cities where citizens care about and are engaged with nature; residents of all ages are actively involved in enjoying, watching, learning about, and participating in the nature around them.

10. Biophilic cities foster a profound curiosity; they are cities of awe.

11. Biophilic cities care about and nurture other forms of life; they are cities that value inherent worth and the right for other species to exist.

12. Biophilic cities care about nature beyond their borders.

13. Biophilic cities invest in nature.

14. Biophilic cities are inspired by and mimic nature.

15. Biophilic cities exhibit and celebrate the shapes and forms of nature.

16. Biophilic cities seek an equitable distribution of nature and natural experiences.

Source: Based on and expanded from Beatley (2011).

can and will happen without much intervention, design, or planning—having trees and greenery nearby creates a passive experience during the normal course of one's urban life—on the way to work or to the store or to the metro. But there are more intensive experiences—participating in birding clubs and attending events that require a more in-depth engagement and commitment. These voluntary activities often activate a level of learning about an aspect of nature that deepens awareness and personal connection to urban nature. A biophilic city has a robust and extensive number of clubs, organizations, and programs that encourage these deeper connections—some municipal and public, but others organized by private and community organizations.

A certain infrastructure is associated with fostering these different forms of engagement and connection. Chapter 6 discusses the innovative urban ecology centers in Milwaukee, Wisconsin. These are privately funded centers, largely neighborhood focused, and they provide many services that make it easier to learn about and engage with nature—from hosting school visits to sponsoring nature walks to providing some equipment one might need but not own to fully enjoy the natural environment (e.g., cross-country skis, snowshoes).

### Integrated, Multiscaled Natural Systems

As mentioned earlier, even the interior spaces of offices and homes are places where nature can be cultivated. A biophilic city has nature at many interconnected scales and levels. The Biophilic Cities Project describes a biophilic city as a place where an individual or a family has nature where they live and work, and then allows for movement to larger systems of nature. It is a city where one can see and experience nature from the start to the end of one's day, and as much or as long an experience of nature as a day and schedule permit.

From new residential towers that include forests, such as the *Bosco Verticale* in Milan, to the many examples of public institutional designs that include nature, such as the new Healy Family Center at Georgetown University, and hospitals and healthcare facilities, such as Boston's new Rehabilitation Hospital, are many and growing. Much nature can and should be integrated into the building scale, and today there is no reason why every building cannot be a biophilic building, at least in some small way.

### A Humane and Caring View of the Life around Us; an Ethic of Coexistence

As we've discussed, there is considerable evidence about the physical, emotional, and economic benefits of nature in urban environments. But a biophilic cities framework takes the relationship a step further, acknowledging that nature has inherent moral worth and value, irrespective of its value to humans. *Homo sapiens* as a species owes its survival to the intricate web of life on Earth, and we must acknowledge a profound ethic of respect for the other forms of life—from blue jays to mountain lions to ants and arthropods—with which we share urban spaces.

A key part of the philosophy of biophilic cities, then, is that urbanites share spaces with many other forms of life. This is not just an empirical fact but a beneficial and desirable condition. We seek in biophilic cities to understand and appreciate this nature around us, and see an obligation to proactively work for coexistence. Many cities in the United States and elsewhere are confronting the presence of new urban occupants in the form of species such as coyotes.

An important dimension to this coexistence is understanding the complexity and sophistication of the life forms around us in cities. This is perhaps most apparent when it comes to sentient life, but even here we are wholly underappreciative of the abilities and unique biology of fauna especially. The work of John Marzluff, at the University of Washington, has provided new understanding of the intelligence of American crows, for instance, testing their ability to recognize individual human faces, and to remember these faces over a relatively long period of time (Marzluff et al., 2010). Professor Con Slobodchikoff, of Northern Arizona University, has been studying the danger calls and vocalization of black-tailed prairie dogs, and concludes that their language is much more complex and sophisticated than was previously thought (e.g. see Slobodchikoff, Perla, and Verdolin, 2009). Prairie dogs, he is finding, have very specific words for predators and are able to create new words to describe specific features (height, color) of predators (humans in the case of the experiments he has conducted; this is a language skill known as productivity). Prairie dogs also have the capability to communicate about things not present (a language skill known as displacement).

These new insights provide a window into the fascinating and complex life forms that co-occupy the world, and increasingly cities, with us. We are perhaps too often evaluating other forms of life according to human rubrics and biases of "intelligence," and that is something to be careful of. On the other hand there is value in noting how impressive the fellow creatures are who co-occupy cities with us, perhaps suggesting we do more to both learn about them and give them their due respect.

There are many ways in which city design can take wildlife and biodiversity into account. New research shows the impact that artificial lighting has on bats, for instance, with potentially effective methods for creating more bat-friendly cities by reducing such lighting and by ensuring adequate trees and other ecological connections for bats, which help to overcome the lighting impacts (Freeman 2015).

## Curiosity about the Nature around Us; Cities of Awe and Wonder

Occupants of a biophilic city pay attention to the nature around them. They are curious about the sights, sounds, and other evidence of fauna in their neighborhoods. They seek to identify common species of birds, insects, and trees, and they celebrate the diversity of life and the complexity of the natural systems around them.

There is much to be curious about here, and our understanding of urban nature is rapidly advancing. We are discovering new species in urban settings, such as the so-called Central Park centipede (*Nannarrup hoffmani*), discovered in the leaf litter during a bioblitz there. An impressive recent example is the discovery of 30 new species of flies in the single genus *Megaselia*, found in the backyards of Los Angeles homes. Many species are modifying their behavior in response to city life, including a number of studies showing that birds have changed the pitch and frequencies of their songs in cities (e.g., Jha 2009), and are changing their behavior toward predators (Science News 2012). Some species, such as coyotes, have adapted well to life in urban settings, and we are only now beginning to fully understand these different urban biologies. So, in many respects, we are in an era in which it is possible to see evolution and adaptation unfold in a remarkably brief time frame.

There are many examples, moreover, of new blendings of the natural and the built realms, and new opportunities to experience the wonder of nature in cities. Notable examples include the 1.5 million Mexican free-tailed bats that take up residence each summer under the Congress Avenue Bridge, in Austin, Texas. Or the flocks of Vaux's swifts that make dramatic stopovers in Portland, Oregon, where they roost in the chimney of a school, drawing large crowds to watch these spectacular visits. For cities perched on the marine realm much of this wondrous nature arrives by sea, for instance, the migrating gray whales off the coast of San Francisco, or the orcas that visit the harbor of Wellington, New Zealand (nearly bringing the day to a halt in that city).

While not all urban nature elicits a sense of wonder or awe, much of it does. In some of the cities profiled in this book these opportunities for awe are found in places that permit viewing of larger animals, such as orcas or dolphins or other whales, as in cities like Wellington or San Francisco. In other places it might be peregrine falcons or the evening emergence of bats, but of course a sense of wonder is also possible in observing the many smaller forms of nature from the insect world to the microscopic. These are all potentially awe inspiring (fig. 2.3).

What it means to experience awe is an open question. Researchers have tried to define it; Keltner and Haidt have identified two characteristics: vastness and

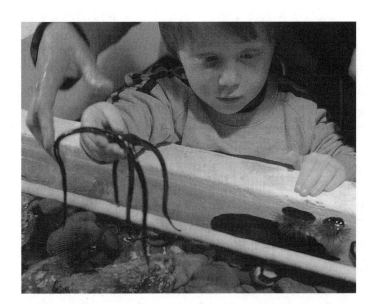

**Figure 2.3.** Fostering a sense of awe and wonder on the part of children is a key goal of a biophilic city. Here children enjoy the touch tanks at the Island Bay Marine Education Center in Wellington, New Zealand. Credit: Photo by Tim Beatley.

accommodation. They define vastness as "anything that is experienced as a being much larger than the self, or the self's ordinary level of reference." Accommodation involves the mind-shift that is brought about as we attempt to assimilate these new experiences into our view of the world. It involves, then, what Keltner and Haidt describe as adjusting mental structures (Keltner and Haidt 2003).

### Nature Is Not Something to Visit

Many cities and towns have a long heritage of urban parks and parks planning that holds that it is important to have such places near neighborhoods and business districts. This is true, but sometimes contributes to a bifurcation in cities themselves—a sense that "nature is over there," a specific place in the city to be visited.

A deeper, more ambitious vision of biophilic cities suggests that we must really begin to reimagine urban life in much more profound ways. Conventional green planning in many cities now focuses on the provision of parks within a certain distance. Having adequate access to parks and having a neighborhood park nearby are important goals. But our notion of a biophilic city here goes much further, to begin to understand the city as itself an ecosystem and larger place of nature. Why should one have to *walk to* the park or *visit* the park—rather, shouldn't the city be situated *in* a park, that is, *be* the park?

This suggests the idea that a biophilic city might serve as a nest, as an immersive experience and context of nature for its inhabitants (humans and nonhumans alike). Many of the cities in the Biophilic Cities Network aspire to this bolder vision.

Wellington, New Zealand, already speaks of itself as a city in a forest, and Melbourne has developed an ambitious urban forest plan that expresses a similar vision. Partner city Singapore not long ago changed its city motto from "Singapore, a Garden City" to "Singapore, a City in a Garden" (see chap. 5). This seems like a nuanced change in language, but it is really quite a significant shift in goal. It seeks in many ways to overcome the nature/city dichotomy that exists within cities.

Melbourne, Australia, an emerging biophilic city, has taken similar steps in shifting mental frameworks. It has embarked on an ambitious program to grow its urban forest, and has adopted a goal of doubling its forest canopy coverage (from 22 to 44 percent by 2040). The city is explicitly aspiring to a shift from just seeing itself as a city with trees, to "a city in a forest rather than a forest in a city" (Lynch 2015).

One of the most interesting examples of this idea can be seen in London, where there is a proposal to designate that city as the world's first "national city park." It is a bold move to re-imagine this city, and its considerable green space and nature as itself a national park. It is the brainchild of Daniel Raven-Ellison, a self-described guerilla geographer, who believes such a national park city could help to "conserve London's ability to be dynamic, to innovate, and evolve. The park's leadership role would be to inform and inspire, help coordinate and promote London's biodiversity and recreational opportunities while helping to tackle some of the city's biggest challenges" (Raven-Ellison, 2014).

The arguments are pretty compelling in favor of the idea, and when the statistics about nature in the city are marshalled it begins to look more like a national park: 47 percent of the metro area is covered by green space, including some 3.8 million gardens. The city's 13,000 species, 3000 parks, and 8 million trees make it, Raven-Ellison argues, the world's largest urban forest (Usborne, 2014). We will see how far the idea goes in the United Kingdom (there is an online petition campaign currently under way that will be submitted to the Mayor of London). It has garnered the support of the Royal Society for the Protection of Birds and the London Wildlife Trust. But whether legally or officially designated, it is an idea with potential to shift the very way citizens and elected officials see the city in which they live.

### Cities That Provide Leadership on Behalf of Global Nature

Biophilic cities, consistent with a profound ethic of care for nature and other forms of life, are also cities that exhibit global leadership in nature conservation. They have programs and policies in place that facilitate understanding and modification of the negative impacts of their own patterns of global consumption on nature (e.g., from a city's complex metabolic flows, typically gathering global resources—water, energy, building materials, food—from hundreds or thousands of miles away), as well as advocating for and acting on behalf of nature at a global scale. The latter is still a nascent and emerging sense of what urban biophilia means, and there are as yet relatively few examples.

There are many ways that a biophilic city could give expression to this responsibility for global leadership and action—organizing, hosting, attending international fora on conservation; signing intercity agreements to aid and assist other cities in conserving the nature they have; and signing international agreements or treaties (in a world of growing city-states perhaps much more of this will happen), among many others.

## Biophilic Cities Idea Gaining Traction

In an era when there is little good news on the global environmental front, the vision of and movement toward biophilic cities is encouraging. Though the terminology isn't always used, there are very positive signs that nature in urban areas is understood as something important and essential.

Two or three decades ago the installation of green or ecological rooftops, for instance, was a building practice that could be found in Germany, the Netherlands, and parts of Scandinavia and was viewed curiously in North American cities. In the last decade, green rooftops have gained currency and are increasingly viewed as a mainstream urban building practice. A recent study of ecological roofs in central London is telling. Undertaken by the Greater London Authority utilizing aerial photographs, almost 700 green rooftops were identified (GLA, 2014). An impressive map of these central London green roofs can be found online, and the number will likely increase as citizens and building owners add some that have been missed in this process. This remarkable number of green roofs and similar counts could likely be made in other European and North American cities. Equally true, while only a handful of cities had programs to encourage such green elements only a few years ago, many more today do, and some, like the City of Toronto, are now mandating these green elements.

There are other positive trends. While in almost every culture, in every country, we spend too much of our time indoors and away from nature, there are impressive new ways that we are finding to enjoy the nature in cities. We continue to see considerable efforts to reconnect cities with their rivers and waterfronts. Some partner cities in the Biophilic Cities Project, including Portland, Milwaukee, and Singapore, have undertaken impressive efforts to restore the natural qualities of rivers, to enhance their habitats and to reconnect citizens to them (e.g., the Big Float event in Portland each summer!). Many cities, such as Copenhagen and Berlin, have developed areas for public swimming in harbor and river environments that were formerly too polluted to permit these activities. London has seen the development of plans for public swimming in the Thames River, though water pollution there remains a concern.

Many cities are, moreover, aspiring to more comprehensively green and natureful visions. The City of Vancouver, British Columbia, has declared its intention to be the world's greenest city by 2020 and has published an impressive action plan. Other cities around the world have expressed similar aspirations. On the European scene, many cities are actively competing for the designation of European Green Capital (Vitoria-Gasteiz received this designation in 2012, and more about this can be found in chapter 12).

There are other encouraging trends. The emergence of citizen science, with many new initiatives and technologies (especially smart phones), permits many more individuals to participate directly in making observations about nature, and in engaging with the nature around them. The Globe at Night program, for instance, run by the National Optical Astronomy Observatory, enlists citizens to take measures of how bright the night sky is where they are. This program has engaged a remarkable number of people in the 8 years or so it has been running— some 100,000 measurements have been uploaded to an "interactive data map" in 115 countries (see www.globeatnight.org/about.php). These are but a few of the many new opportunities for residents of cities to be directly involved in learning about, studying and (hopefully) emotionally connecting with the environments and nature around them. From counting birds and butterflies, to snapping images of marine life, above and below the water, there are numerous ways to directly engage that did not exist just a few years ago.

## Conclusions

While there are many different forms of nature in cities—some preexisting and remnant, such as forest fragments and native flora, fauna, and fungi; others newly designed, such as green rooftops and vertical gardens—we increasingly recognize the essential need to merge the urban and natural. And we should recognize as well the importance of the larger geological, hydrological, and ecological settings in which cities sit and their value as opportunities to connect (e.g., physically, visually) with the nature around them—the mountains and shorelines and rivers that define our lives on a larger scale and that are so central to shaping and defining place. This chapter has identified some of the emerging qualities and characteristics of biophilic cities. They are places of abundant nature, profoundly natureful, and their residents are engaged with and care deeply about the nature around them. Biophilic cities also care about the nature, the flora, fauna, and fungi beyond their boundaries, and are expected to give expression to biophilic values through global leadership on conservation.

# 3

# The Urban Nature Diet:
## *The Many Ways That Nature Enhances Urban Life*

The nature we experience in cities can be understood in many different ways. This leads to some important questions about how much exposure to nature we need to feel healthier and happier, and what forms promote these positive responses. We might refer to this as the urban nature diet.

What we need from nature may depend on our particular life circumstances. If we are working inside a building, we may need a certain kind of nature. If we are sick, then the dose of nature we need may be more about the power to heal or calm or promote a speedy recovery. The sights, sounds, and experiences of nature seem especially potent in hospital settings.

The length of time we engage in or enjoy these activities is a significant factor in our nature experiences. In cities we are able to seek out and visit nature— hiking along a waterfront promenade, picnicking in a park, spending a Sunday birdwatching. But very often we experience nature in much smaller "doses"— the flash of a bird in flight or a snippet of bird song. We may glimpse nature from a window of a high-rise apartment, or from the window of a bus or train. These briefer interludes can still be powerful and enjoyable experiences. And the more natureful a city is, the greater the likelihood that these daily and hourly experiences, ones that are perhaps more accidental, add up to something special and important.

To promote biophilic interactions, a city must have an extensive tree canopy or a high degree of biodiversity within its borders. But for nature's presence to be meaningful, residents must be aware of it, care about it, and engage with it in some way—seeing and hearing it, actively enjoying it, working on its behalf (fig. 3.1). These are all important dimensions of how we experience nature in cities.

Bratman, Hamilton, and Daily (2012) offer a useful framework for categorizing nature experiences (and organizing studies about them) by combining the types of exposure (images, window views, physical presence), the types of environment (urban green, water bodies, forests, etc.), and the duration of time spent experiencing this nature (box 3.1).

## How Long Is Enough Time to Spend in Nature?

How long does one have to experience nature—listening to a bird singing, sitting under a tree in a park, hiking along the water—to receive desirable benefits? This is an important and open question. The urban nature diet is likely to be less about immersing oneself in the sights, sounds, and experiences of a pristine forest or coast-line, and more about a *series* of nature experiences over the course of the day—the

**Figure 3.1.** There are many different ways to enjoy and experience nature in cities. Physical con-nections are important, but so also are visual connections, as the design for the new Healy Family Center, at Georgetown University, shows. Here a student works outside on the building's terrace, with a clear and beautiful view of the Potomac River. Credit: Photo by Tim Beatley.

Box 3.1. Some of the Many Ways to Experience Nature in the City
- Watching, seeing, listening to actual nature outside
- Hiking, camping, spending time out of doors
- Feeling the wind, rain, mist on one's body
- Purposeful enjoyment of outdoor nature—gardening, tree planting, cleaning up garbage from a stream or beach
- Participating in a nature club or organization
- Watching nature through a window
- Experiencing indoor nature (e.g., looking at a terrarium, aquarium, indoor green wall)
- Watching images of nature on a computer screen
- Reading about nature; attending a lecture about nature
- Contemplating nature or a memory of a previous experience

glimpse of a bird, the view of the skyline, and perhaps a green swath of trees. What do these different, discrete experiences add up to? And are they enough to deliver the positive benefits and values we argue for in this book?

This book, and the work of the Biophilic Cities Project, argues for the value and importance of physical presence in nature, spending time outside being surrounded by nature, hiking, swimming, sitting under a tree. But there is considerable evidence about the therapeutic and other benefits of having views of nature through an office or apartment window. Researchers at the University of Oregon found that workers with a view of nature took 11 hours fewer sick leave hours than workers without (Elzeyadi, 2011). And a study by the Heschong Mahone Group found workers at a call center were 6 to 12 percent faster in processing calls when they had a view of nature through a window near their desk than workers without such a few (Heschong Mahone Group, 2003). There is a long tradition of limiting building heights and locations to preserve views (e.g., Denver's protection of views of the Rockies from prominent public parks), and siting hospitals and other facilities to maximize views of nature.

Visiting a park or greenspace once a week, or twice a week, will likely have considerable value. Danielle Shanahan and her colleagues at the University of Queensland, have been exploring the positive role of nature on depression and high blood pressure, utilizing a nature-dose frame. In their study involving more than 1,500 residents of Brisbane, they conclude that a visit to a green space for an average of 30 minutes in high blood pressure (Shanahan, et all 2016). Depression is a debilitating and costly illness, of course, and abundant nature in cities can play a major role in reducing its severity and prevalence.

There is some research to suggest that even very brief encounters with nature have significant positive effects. These effects are often spoken of in terms of "dose responses." Barton and Pretty (2010), for instance, examined the effects of green exercise (activities such as walking or bicycling in the presence of nature) on self-esteem and mood. They found that the greatest changes can be seen for 5-minute activities (additionally, 10- to 60-minute and half-day activities had lower but also positive impacts, and full-day activities delivered benefits close to the 5-minute activities). How long these improvements in self-esteem and mood will last is unclear, but this research suggests the power of even small snippets of natural experience. "Such doses of nature," these researchers conclude, "will contribute to immediate mental health benefits. As with smoking, giving up inactivity and urban-only living results in immediate and positive health outcomes, even from short-duration and light activity such as walking" (2010, 3951). A biophilic life may be made up of many small, but potent, doses of nature.

Ward Thompson (2014), in her study of green space and stress reduction, speculate about this: "The association between high green space levels and lower stress found in our study may be the result of many minor but nonetheless significant episodes of contact with the natural environment" (2014, 227).

A recent study by Kate E. Lee, and her colleagues at the University of Melbourne, found that even a 40-second green "micro-break," where participants were able to view a simulated flowering green roof, showed positive results (lower omission errors on a task, and higher perceived restoration) (Lee et al. 2015). Lee is quoted in the *Washington Post* highlighting the potential importance of green roofs, and other forms of nature, for those working in office environments in cities: "Modern work drains attention away throughout the day, so providing boosted 'green micro-breaks' may provide mental top-ups to offset declining attention" (quoted in Mooney 2015). One hopes that a day is filled with many micro- (and not-so-micro) breaks that will be beneficial to all who are living, working, or visiting cities. Even very small temporal doses, it appears from this work, will make a significant contribution.

## Direct and Indirect Experiences

Stephen Kellert has distinguished between direct, indirect, and symbolic contact with nature (Kellert 2002). For Kellert, *direct nature* is nature that "involves actual physical contact with natural settings and nonhuman species." Kellert elaborates: "Direct contact . . . involves a young person's spontaneous play or activity in a backyard, in a nearby forest, meadow, creek, or neighborhood, park, or even an abandoned lot.

In each case, the natural setting, though influenced by human manipulation and activity, includes creatures and habitats that function largely independent of human intervention and control" (2002, 118).

Exposure to more direct forms of nature is preferable for maximum biophilic effects, and the greater the ability for urbanites to touch, feel, see wild nature—birds, trees, insects—in outdoor settings, so much the better. But other more indirect forms of contact are also valuable.

"Indirect nature," on the other hand, "involves actual physical contact but in far more restricted, programmed, and managed contexts," in Kellert's view. "Indirect experience of natural habitats and nonhuman creatures is typically the result of regulated and contrived human activity. Nature in these situations is usually the product of deliberate and extensive human mastery and manipulation. Examples might include children encountering plants, animals, and habitats in zoos, aquariums, botanical gardens, arboretums, natural history and science museums, and nature centers" (2002, 118).

Experiencing indoor nature, through gazing at a terrarium or aquarium, would certainly fall into this category (fig. 3.2). And there is growing evidence about

**Figure 3.2.** An important goal is to work to creatively bring nature into the interior spaces of houses and work environments. Here is a verdant terrarium designed by the San Francisco firm Crooked Nest, for the University of Virginia School of Architecture. Credit: Photo by Tim Beatley.

the power of watching fish in aquaria, for instance, helping to calm us, to reduce heart rates, as recent studies show (e.g., Cracknell et al. 2015). This is real nature, experienced in real time, though it is more visual, less tactile, and mediated through the glass of a tank.

Finally there is the nature that Kellert refers to as vicarious or symbolic nature. This form of nature "occurs in the absence of actual physical contact with the natural world. What a child encounters instead are representations or depicted scenes of nature that sometimes are realistic but that also, depending on circumstance, can be highly symbolic, metaphorical, or stylized characterizations." (2002, 119).

Some of the most wonderful images of nature in cities are ones that are drawn or painted onto building spaces and facades. I think of the marvelous whale murals, for instance, painted in many American cities by artist Robert Wyland (part of the 100 so-called Whaling Walls see Wyland Foundation, n.d.). Television, the Internet, and experiencing nature through various forms of virtual or electronic means, from phone apps to computer games, would also fall into this category.

### Diversity of Experiences

Structuring urban life in ways that maximize contact with various forms of nature is a key goal. It begins even with the green and natural elements in the more interior spaces of one's life. In office environments, we need to break out of the cubicle designs and windowless and greenless work environments that are stifling and dampen worker productivity. Corporate and business leaders have a special role to play here, recognizing that the design of work environments profoundly influences the health and quality of the work experience, and makes good business sense as well when productivity and health expenses are taken into account.

In residential settings, we need homes that contain a variety of natural elements. Conditions for healthy plants, which include abundant daylight and natural ventilation, are also healthy for most people. The space around homes is also fertile ground. Early work in the United Kingdom examining the biodiversity of gardens, showed remarkable amounts of nature here, very close to where many people live (discovered through the Biodiversity in Urban Gardens [BUGS] initiative undertaken by researchers at the University of Sheffield, e.g., Gaston et al. [2007]).

Overcoming the barriers between the inside and the outside worlds has been a perennial challenge to designers and architects—and very important in shaping the biophilic city. In many dense cities, it will be essential to rethink the transitional spaces, such as courtyards and balconies, to create more livable, sustainable urban areas. We are inspired by cities like Singapore (more about this in chapter 5) that have helped to create new forms of vertical nature, skyparks and green elements that serve as these important transitional zones.

And we are also impressed by new design work of firms such as Cook+Fox architects. Their newly unveiled design for 300 Lafayette, a housing project in the Soho Cast Iron District of Manhattan, represents a new and innovative approach to green balconies. Working with Eric Sanderson, of the Wildlife Conservation Society, to identify native species of plants to employ, the project includes some 11,000 square feet of green balconies and planter boxes. The renderings depict wonderful green outdoor spaces that wrap around the large daylight-drenched apartments. Every structure designed and built offers an opportunity to increase a little bit of residents' urban nature diet. (More about this case can be found in short cases in Section 3).

One framework that we have found useful in thinking about these different elements of urban nature is what we have been calling the Nature Pyramid (fig. 3.3). Modeled after the food pyramid, used for many years to guide decisions about our food consumption, the Nature Pyramid is similarly intended to help us think, individually and collectively, about what might or should make up a healthy urban

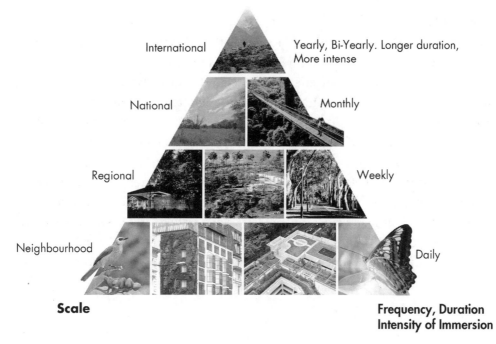

**Figure 3.3.** The Nature Pyramid is one way to begin to understand what might make up a healthy urban nature diet. This a specific version of the pyramid developed for Singapore. Credit: Concept by Tanya Denckla-Cobb, further developed by Tim Beatley. Image prepared by the Singapore National Parks Board.

nature diet. Like things at the top of the food pyramid (salt, meat) things at the top of the Nature Pyramid (intensive visits to faraway nature) are valuable and rewarding, but can't make up the bulk of our nature diet (and we can't as a planet sustain the carbon footprint associated with this). As with the food pyramid, we need to think about all of the forms of nature and nature experiences nearby and all around us, the everyday nature that must make up our diet (for more about the Nature Pyramid, see Beatley [2012]).

The food analogy is a useful one, and we might also ponder what constitutes even a "serving" of urban nature—is it the sight of a bird, the sight and song of that bird, or perhaps a flock of birds flying by, and what combination of these servings will constitute the minimum daily requirement of nature? Is it two birds, some trees, and a green wall, or some other combination? These are interesting questions to consider, and it is important to recognize that what will make up the discrete elements of an urban nature diet will, of course, vary by climate and location (the natural elements, indigenous and designed, will necessarily vary in a desert city like Phoenix, as compared with, say, Helsinki or Rio de Janeiro).

## Conclusions

Two key questions for advocates of biophilic cities are: what kinds of nature do we need and want in cities, and what are the various experiences of nature that are possible in a city? The answers are affected by each individual city's offerings, revealing virtually an endless spectrum—from walking in a remnant forest in Nairobi, to viewing a mountain on the horizon in Seattle, to even just contemplating or thinking about nature. There is a rich and interesting research agenda here, and clearly there are many different variables that will influence what constitutes a healthy urban nature diet. Climate, ecology, the different bioregional characteristics of a city's location will determine to a considerable degree what might constitute this diet (e.g., green roofs work in many cities, but are less appropriate to arid desert settings).The impact and positive health-enhancing effects of nature will also be influenced by other variables, such as gender, age, baseline health conditions, and more.

# 4

# Biophilic Cities and Urban Resilience

Cities in the United States and around the world face many challenges. Some are relatively new, such as climate change and food and water scarcity. Other challenges are cyclical but common—poverty, adequate and affordable housing, provision of jobs, and economic activity, including adapting and responding to economic downturns. Investing in nature, it turns out, helps in addressing almost all of these challenges and contributes to more resilient cities and urban citizens in several ways.

With worries about climate change and the need to adapt to sea-level rise, hotter weather, increasing bouts of drought, and more extreme weather events, it is little wonder that resilience as a concept resonates today. The goals of a biophilic city often complement goals for resilience as well.

There is a considerable, growing literature on the topic of resilience and many different ways to define it and conceptualize it. Some frequently cited definitions of resilience are reviewed in box 4.1. Some consistent emphases include the need to adapt, to learn from change, to weather storms and shocks in ways that maintain the quality of life.

Biophilic urbanism prioritizes many of these same city attributes,

> **Box 4.1. What Is Community Resilience?**
>
> "The capacity of a system to absorb and utilize and even benefit from perturbations and changes . . . and so persist without a qualitative change in the system's structure"
>
> —C. S. Holling (1973, 9)
>
> From the Latin *resilire*, meaning "to jump back" or "rebound."
> Common meanings include durability, flexibility, adaptability, to bend but not break.

and is similarly broad and complex. As figure 4.2 indicates, there are many different ways in which nature in cities can influence urban conditions and urban populations. These Biophilic City Causal Pathways suggest that there are both direct and indirect paths of influence that relate urban nature and resilient city outcomes.

The causal pathways model is also instructive in making the point that there are many different kinds of outcomes and ways that we might judge the value and success of biophilic urbanism and biophilic city programs and interventions. Projects are concerned with personal and public health, but also with creating the conditions for collective urban resilience, and the ability of a city's infrastructure and economy to rebound, to spring back from major stressors and shocks.

### Physical Connections between Biophilic and Resilience Goals

Higher temperatures in cities is a significant challenge, one that will only grow more serious in the years to come. For decades cities have experienced the urban heat island phenomenon, the fact that urbanized and built cities are significantly hotter than surrounding rural areas. These urban–rural temperature differentials have been increasing in recent years, and with the effects of climate change, cities can expect to see even higher summer temperatures.

Climate Central's recent study of the urban heat island effect in the 60 largest US cities is very telling (Kenward, Yawitz, Sanford, and Wang, 2014). The authors found that these cities were on average 2.4°F hotter than surrounding rural areas. But there is quite a variation between the 60 cities in the study. The top 10 have *much* higher temperature differentials than the other 50: Las Vegas tops the list—7.3°F hotter than its surrounding rural areas. Other hot cities include Albuquerque (5.9°F), Denver (4.9°F) , Portland (4.8°F), Louisville (4.8°F), and even Washington, DC (4.7°F).

The study authors also found that the number of really hot days is increasing and also that there is a correlation between these high temperatures and bad air quality (as measured by ground-level ozone). It is fairly clear that as cities warm up there are other significant implications, including unhealthy urban air.

The good news is that there are steps cities can take to moderate or address these heat risks. Many involve the biophilic design and planning methods advocated in this book. The Climate Central study states, "Research suggests that urban planning and design that incorporates more trees and parks, white roofs, and alternative materials for urban infrastructure can help reduce the effects of urban heat islands. But rising greenhouse gas emissions are projected to drive average US summer temperatures even higher in the coming decades, exacerbating urban heat islands and their associated health risks" (Kenward, Yawitz, Sanford, and Wang, 2014, p. 4).

**Figure 4.1.** Urban forests provide essential ecological services, such as retaining stormwater and helping to cool the city, and in many other ways they add to the resilience of cities. Credit: Photo by Tim Beatley.

Similarly, there are serious resource limitations looming, nationally and globally, for instance in the areas of water and food. Biophilic design and planning can help to address these issues as well. Few problems are as pressing as the provision of potable water, and there are many cities, especially in more arid settings, where scarcity is already a serious concern. With climate change, drought will be a concern to cities virtually everywhere. These new water realities have already forced many cities to adopt aggressive water conservation programs, and there is a growing realization of the need to employ additional measures, such as strategies for reuse of water.

Many of the plants and planting schemes applied in cities will by necessity need to incorporate xeriscaping and use of drought-tolerant plant species. In this way, planting trees, plants, and greenery in cities can, if it replaces water-intensive landscaping, help to make these cities more water resilient.

New designs of biophilic features, such as green walls and green rooftops, suggest the potential for these to make a significant contribution to the challenges concerning water reuse and supply. The large green wall installed at the Parc de la Tabacalera, in Terragona, Spain, is one example. Designed by Alex Puig of the plant nursery

Vivers Ter, this large, 11,000-square-meter green wall filters and treats gray water, from showers and bathrooms (and, in turn, saves an estimated 26,000 liters of water daily). It uses a green wall system called Babylon, made of prefabricated plant boxes that are installed by stacking and connecting. The wall has birds' nests designed in and is also Cradle to Cradle[1] certified.

Another good example can be seen in the new Bullitt Center in Seattle. The brainchild of Bullitt Foundation director and Earth Day organizer Denis Hayes, the structure has been designed to function as the Douglas-fir forest would have before the city of Seattle existed. The third floor of the building has a green roof that serves as a constructed wetland, filtering and cleansing the gray water from the building's sinks and showers (via a 500-gallon holding tank in the building's basement). A further example can be seen in the living machine incorporated into the new headquarters building of the San Francisco Public Utilities Commission. The system treats not only all gray water but black water as well from the 13-story building. Some of this treatment system is inside the structure, but its most dramatic element is a lush sidewalk wetland, providing a beautiful biophilic feature for passersby.

### Emotional Connections between Biophilic and Resilience Goals

Urban nature, in its many forms, can help to foster social relationships and networks, and even build friendships that in turn yield significant health benefits and contribute to emotional resilience. Researchers at the University of Michigan, following nearly 7,000 people, found significantly lower risks of stroke and heart attack for those living in neighborhoods that were self-perceived as socially cohesive, controlling for other variables (Kim, Park and Peterson, 2013; Kim, Hawes and Smith, 2014).

Respondents in the study were presented with a series of questions and statements as a way to determine the cohesiveness of their neighborhoods, including "If you were in trouble, there are lots of people in this area who would help you" (Goodyear 2013; Kim, Park, and Peterson 2013). Greater social cohesion means better health, and greater resilience.

Merging physical and emotional elements of a city, the physical design and qualities of space influence the extent of this social capital. A recent study of walkable neighborhoods in two New Hampshire cities is indicative. Involving some 700 participants in 20 neighborhoods, the researchers found that in more walkable neighborhoods (determined by asking respondents how many places in their neighborhood

---

[1] Cradle to Cradle is a product certification system developed by William McDonough, based around the principles of his book by the same name. For more information see www.C2ccertified.org.

they could walk to) there were higher levels of trust and community involvement, "whether that is working on a community project, attending a club meeting, volunteering, or simply having friends to one's home" (Rogers, Halstead, Gardner, and Carlson 2011, p. 209). Residents of walkable neighborhoods were more likely to indicate having excellent health and being happy.

Urban nature also provides many opportunities for urbanites to become involved in ecological restoration and cleanup activities. A study by Miles, Sullivan, and Kuo (2000) of volunteers participating in prairie restoration programs in the Chicago area documents well the "psychological benefits of volunteering." Reporting on the results of a survey of 300 volunteers, the researchers sought to understand the ways in which volunteering enhanced life satisfaction. Overall, the survey results show the high degree to which volunteering and participating in such programs delivers personal benefits and satisfaction. Of the specific categories of satisfaction explored by the researchers, "meaningful action" and "fascination with nature" were the highest rated among the respondents. These survey results are consistent with other studies that demonstrate the value of participating in nature through volunteering.

Public space in a city is also very important to resilience and biophilic city goals. The elements of a biophilic city, from green alleys in cities like Montreal and Austin, to parklets and sidewalk gardens in San Francisco, to waterfront promenades in coastal cities like Oslo and Toronto, have the potential to contribute much to the creation of new public spaces in the city. These are spaces and places that permit socializing and intermingling, where in many ways the public ethos of a shared city comes together.

In many cases, expanding and growing the nature in cities can positively influence multiple direct and indirect pathways simultaneously. Urban tree planting and other steps that can be taken to address the urban heat island phenomenon carry the potential to both directly reduce temperatures and strengthen the social networks and social capital that will help to enhance the ability of individuals, families, and neighborhoods to respond to and cope with major heat events.

## Health and Resilience: The Different Constituencies in Biophilic Cities

It is important to recognize that the benefits of nature in cities will accrue differently, and nature will have different impacts on different social groups and constituents. Children, for instance, are an especially important group to consider, as are older residents on the other end of the age distribution.

There has been much discussion, especially thanks to Richard Louv, of the disconnect from nature that children growing up today feel. There is often a fear of nature, and a fear of the outside world (Louv 2008, 2012).

The evidence in support of the positive value of nature seems especially compelling when it comes to children. School-aged kids, of course, will benefit the most from contact with, for instance, natural, full-spectrum daylight and fresh air and greenery in schools. Test scores go up in schools with full-spectrum daylight, and outdoor classrooms and learning pay great dividends. Other studies, such as those of Cornell environmental psychologist Nancy Wells, have shown the cognitive benefits, especially to disadvantaged youth, of views of nature (Wells 2000). There is evidence, moreover, that time spent in nature reduces the symptoms of ADHD, and can help to treat autism.

Roe and Aspinall (2011), in their study of time spent outside compared with conventional indoor classrooms, show clear positive impacts for adolescents from time outside. Positive impacts were seen in the form of improved mood (on four measures—energy, hedonic tone, stress, and anger) and in perceived effectiveness in reaching personal goals. The positive change brought about by time spent in nature was most significant for children with behavioral problems (poor behavior). Children benefit immensely from nature, and there is little doubt that access to trees and green space, and sustained contact with outdoor life, will contribute positively to individual and family resilience.

### Urban Poverty and Resilience

A focus on cultivating nature in cities can also address resilience in many ways (fig. 4.2) by addressing poverty and jobs, and in bringing new forms of economic and social opportunity to those especially challenged neighborhoods in our cities.

Many of the most innovative programs and initiatives described in this handbook are aimed at addressing the circumstances of poverty and disadvantaged neighborhoods and social groups. Edible landscapes and parks, for instance, add to the nature of cities while providing affordable and healthy foods in cities. Community food initiatives like the Philly Orchard Project aim to increase trees and greenery in the city but also focus on food-insecure neighborhoods. Similarly, efforts to design food production into new dense urban neighborhoods and buildings (e.g., Via Verde in the Bronx in New York City), and the emergence of permaculture projects, such as Seattle's Beacon Food Forest, address these elements of neighborhood resilience.

Biophilic cities offer the possibility of new forms of employment from the work required to green these places. Organizations like Sustainable South Bronx, started by Majora Carter, have created new jobs and job training, aiming to uplift both individuals and neighborhoods economically at the same time as making these places more natureful. Tree planting, nursery work, and designing and planting ecological rooftops can be an important source of green jobs, leading to economic resilience.

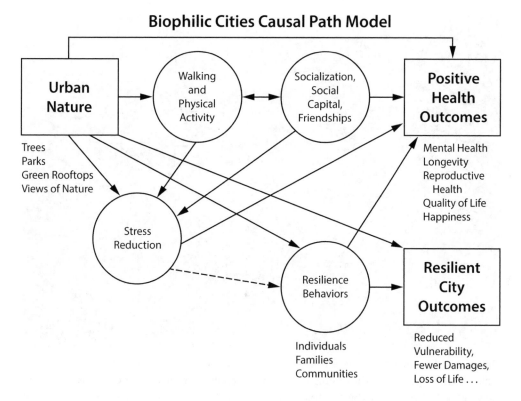

**Figure 4.2.** Biophilic Cities Causal Pathways. There are many potential causal pathways by which nature can influence health, sustainability. and resilience. This diagram shows some of the most important direct and indirect impacts. Solid arrows are meant to indicate known causal effects between variables, while the dotted line indicates hypothesized or possible causal effects.

More broadly, it is important to recognize the pervasive poverty found in cities of the developing world, and the potential of biophilic urbanism to address these conditions. Can favelas and slums in such cities benefit from nature—from trees and edible landscaping and improvements in the water quality of streams and rivers? The answer is a definitive yes, and on a host of issues from food, energy, and potable water to healthy homes and buildings, efforts to creatively insert and grow nature will often represent the best possible and most effective course of action.

### Conclusions

This chapter has made the case that biophilic cities are essentially resilient cities. Virtually every action, project, and policy intended to integrate nature into cities—from urban tree planting to green rooftops and walls to edible landscaping and gardens (fig. 4.3)—will help a city to become more resilient.

**Figure 4.3.** Expanding ways to grow food in cities will help them become more biophilic and resilient. Here a portion of the rooftop of the Khoo Tech Puat Hospital in Singapore is devoted to growing food. Credit: Photo by Tim Beatley.

Greening cities has the potential to make them profoundly less resource intensive, using less water, better adapting to conditions of chronic drought, reducing heat, consuming less energy, and producing at least some of the food that urban neighborhoods need. Biophilic qualities—trees, green space, parks, wildlife—will all contribute, moreover, to the health and well-being of individuals and families in cities and in this way help to make them more resilient. Promoting physical exercise, enhancing mood and mental health, and reducing long-term chronic stress are all important ways in which the agenda of biophilic cities complements resilience efforts.

# PART 2:

## Creating Biophilic Cities: Emerging Global Practice

The chapters in part 2 describe emerging examples of cities that are advancing biophilic urbanism. These cities, for the most part, have been participating in or have been studied as part of the Biophilic Cities Project at the University of Virginia. The natural, social, and political contexts differ among cases, but together these cases show a compelling picture of cities that have elevated nature's importance to their planning and policy goals.

Each case describes a journey toward a more biophilic urban place, the planning and design tools that are used, the exemplary biophilic projects and innovations that are under way, the successes to date, and the obstacles and challenges faced. Some cities have clearly embraced biophilic urbanism as an aspiration and a way of describing their cities—for instance, Birmingham, UK, and Wellington, NZ. In other cities, the biophilic label is less used but still fits the philosophy and the ongoing efforts to preserve, restore, and connect to nature.

None of these cities yet represents a complete model of what a biophilic city is— but, together with the short cases and global survey presented in part 3, they capture much of the current knowledge and excitement of the shift to thinking differently about nature in cities, and the promise and potential of biophilic urbanism.

# 5

# Singapore City, Singapore:
## *City in a Garden*

The island city-state of Singapore occupies a relatively small space—about 700 square kilometers (270 sq. mi.)—on the southern tip of the Malay Peninsula, and is home to some 5.4 million people. Designing and planning for a dense living environment is critical and the vast majority of the population lives in high-rise buildings. And yet this city is remarkably green and full of nature, creating a new model of Asian vertical green living that may represent a compelling model for other cities and parts of the world. As Poon Hong Yuen, the CEO of the National Parks Board, or NParks, told me on a recent visit, this is simply a matter of necessity for this dense, land-scarce city.

Singapore is a difficult country to generalize about—it has a highly diverse mix of religions, cultures, and languages living harmoniously together, and has been able to achieve a level of first-world economic and social development in a short period of time. The social and health statistics are impressive: Singapore has now the fourth-highest life expectancy in the world and the fourth-lowest infant mortality rate (far surpassing the United States). But while the US State Department calls it a "parliamentary republic," with a constitution, the government has been largely controlled by one party (the People's Action Party) since British independence in 1959.

For much of the political history of this young nation Lee Kuan Yew served as its prime minister. He exercised a remarkable influence on the development of the country, and his strong interest in gardens and gardening has shaped the biophilic aspects of the city in important ways. Lee Kuan Yew started the national tree planting campaign in 1963—a highly circulated black-and-white photo shows him planting the very first tree. It is hard to underplay the importance of Lee Kuan Yew. Upon his

51

death in March 2015 the outpouring of emotion from all quarters of Singaporean society was indicative of the sway he held.

While Singapore does not feel like an authoritarian country, it is clear that its government exerts a significant degree of control over daily life. The shaping and implementing of a green vision for Singapore, then, certainly becomes easier to achieve when it is a priority of a strong government. And from its earliest beginnings as an independent nation, its natural qualities were central. Efforts at fusing population density and nature date back to the 1960s, when the city's motto was "Singapore—Garden City," since, as mentioned previously, greening the city was a personal passion of Lee Kuan Yew. Recently, the city has put forth a new motto, "Singapore—City in a Garden." This may be a small, nuanced difference in language, but it signifies something quite important—that the city is not simply a place of gardens, it *is* a garden, in which all current and future development and building are nestled (fig. 5.1).

Although Singapore's verdance is partly a function of a tropical environment in which everything seems to grow well, there is also much conscious intention here. It begins with the impressive protection of much of the interior of the island in nature reserves, and an extensive system of parks, tied together with a 300 kilometer (186 mi.) Park Connector Network. These connectors are in some cases conventional trails and bike paths, but are often dramatic walks in and through, and in some cases above, the extensive greenery of this city.

One of the most impressive stretches can be seen in a series of parks called the Southern Ridges, where much of the connector is an elevated canopy walk through the forest, providing dramatic vistas and perspectives of both the natural and the built setting, and only a few hundred meters from extensive high-rise development (fig. 5.2).

I walked this portion on my visit in 2012, and it is a memorable trail. Although one is never far from a view of a building or road, the experience is nevertheless a green and natural one. Along the way, one encounters quite a lot of nature—including on that day many butterflies and a giant monitor lizard. Several bridges allow the pedestrian to float above the roads and car traffic below. Especially striking is the Henderson Waves bridge, the tallest in the city at 36 meters (39 yd.). It is in itself an embodiment of the ways in which Singapore is creating new public spaces in the vertical realm—the bridge is quite wide, and on that day there were groups picnicking on it.

There is a stretch of the Southern Ridges trail route where the government, in partnership with Sembcorps (a group of energy and water companies), is planting some of the largest species of trees native to Singapore, imagining a "Forest of Giants." Some of these trees—Tualong and Kapur Paji—could tower as high as 80 meters (87 yd.) and 70 meters (77 yd.), respectively.

**Figure 5.1.** Singapore combines urban density and lush nature, and aspires to be a "city in a garden." Credit: Photo by Tim Beatley.

**Figure 5.2.** Singapore can now boast some 300 kilometers (186 mi.) of park connectors. Some stretches, like this one along the Southern Ridges, carry visitors through the forest canopy. Credit: Photo by Tim Beatley.

The park connectors provide ecological connectivity but also importantly tie major housing areas and population centers to the parks. The network of trails and pathways provides exceptional access to nature, and opportunities for alternate transit, for Singaporeans. This system provides a remarkable opportunity for Singaporeans to walk, stroll, and hike the city, with dramatic pedestrian bridges (such as the Henderson Waves) that prevent walkers from having to cross busy boulevards and roadways.

Tree planting and expansion of the city's beautiful and multilayered tree canopy cover is another key strategy. Because it provides important shading benefits to residents, there has been a special effort to create a nearly closed canopy along major roadways. Rain trees are a common (though not native) species, with beautiful sweeping canopies, dripping with epiphytes, and themselves serving as small complex ecosystems. And everywhere in this city, it seems, leftover space is planted with trees and greenery—under highway and transit overpasses, median strips, the small sometimes odd-shaped parcels that surround buildings.

**Vertical Gardens: How to Grow a Green High-Rise City**
Singaporean innovations are especially impressive in the area of vertical greening, since most future growth will by necessity be accommodated by high-rise buildings. NParks has a Skyrise Greening section that provides generous subsidies for the installation of green walls, green rooftops, sky parks and terraces, and vertical green features of various sorts. They will cover up to half the cost of installation, and in some parts of the city a mandatory green spaces replacement standard applies. And there are many other ways in which vertical greening gains support, including through support for research and development (e.g., the NParks sponsored green walls being monitored and tested at HortPark, discussed later in the chapter), and through an annual skyrise greening awards competition, among others. NParks has also created a Centre for Urban Greening and Ecology (CUGE) that trains landscape workers and generally promotes greening in the city (and produces beautiful publications, such as its magazine *CityGreen,* which profiles urban greening practice and thinking in cities around the world).

The vertical greening takes many different forms. Much of the private sector has taken leadership with new and creative vertical green designs. These include, for instance, the 36-story residential tower Newtown Suites, with a long green wall and external garden terraces that jut out every fifth floor. Another example is 158 Cecil Street, the location of a dramatic 7-story green wall, made from a system of irrigated pots, that creates a verdant indoor (and partially outdoor) space. Still other examples include the Singapore School of Arts building with extensive facade trellising, and the Solaris building, dramatically wrapped in a series of linear forests every few floors.

The Solaris, designed by green skyscraper guru Ken Yean, is a remarkable structure. Fifteen stories at its tallest, it combines a number of ecological design features, including extensive daylight and, for an office building of its size, a relatively low energy usage. But most visually dramatic is the way the building is wrapped by a continuous ribbon of green. Referred to in the architect's write-up as an "ecological armature," and a "continuous spiral landscaped ramp," it provides nature and walking space and also cools the building (thus reducing its energy consumption). In total it is some 1.5 kilometers (almost a mile) in length, and together all the green features exceed the square footage of the building's footprint (with an estimated 95 percent of the landscaping above ground level). According to the firm's literature, "The continuity of the landscaping is a key component of the project's ecological design concept, as it allows for fluid movement of organisms and plant species between all vegetated areas within the building, enhancing biodiversity and contributing to the overall health of these ecosystems" (Yeang and Hamzah n.d.).

This creative vertical greening in Singapore has been advanced through several important policies, notably the Skyrise Greenery Incentive Scheme, and the Landscape Replacement Policy, which mandates that new buildings (in many parts of the island) must at least replace the nature lost at ground level. Yeang's Solaris does this, and increasingly newer buildings are going considerably beyond this requirement. Under the Incentive Scheme, NParks provides up to 50 percent of the cost of vertical greening investments, and both residential and nonresidential projects are eligible.

The annual Skyrise Greenery Awards, organized by NParks, has also helped to give visibility to many of these best projects and to educate about and build interest (among the public and the building industry) in vertical greening.

Commitment to support for research and development on biophilic urbanism can be best seen at HortPark, where NParks, in collaboration with the Building and Construction Authority and the National University of Singapore, has been monitoring and testing several different vertical greening technologies. It is a dramatic part of the park where eight different 4- by 6-meter walls (13 by 19.5 ft.), plus a control wall, demonstrate different vertical wall systems. Each wall has a different type of support structure (e.g., carrier vs. support systems) and thickness. Long-term monitoring has included measuring surface temperatures on the walls as well as experimenting to gauge the abilities of the different wall types to dampen sound (Chiang and Tan 2009).

The signals on many levels suggest that creative vertical greening is valued by consumers and policy makers alike. It seems clear that the urban housing market

**Box 5.1. Skyrise Greening—New Projects Pushing the Envelope**

Several new building projects in Singapore show what is possible and how nature can find a place in the vertical realm. An office and retail complex, called Jem in the Jurong District, rising to 17 stories, includes nature in four different zones: Active Laneways, Cascading Skypark, Sky Terraces, and Sky Sanctuary. Together these green features encompass 122 percent of the area of the building site. Designed by SAA Architects, the project has been awarded the Green Mark Platinum Award. In addition to the vertical greening the project includes a number of other sustainability features, including water and energy conservation, that significantly reduce its environmental impacts.

More ambitious in terms of the amount of greenery is the new PARKROYAL on Pickering. Recent winner of the Hotel of the Year Award, the 367-room hotel includes 15,000 square meters of greenery in various forms—most spectacularly in a series of vegetated terraces that provide both physical access but also views of nature from rooms. There are also waterfalls and planters and a 300-meter garden walk on one level. Designed by the architectural firm WOHA, the 16-story project has other biophilic features: "Nature-inspired materials and textures such as light and dark wood, pebbles, water and glass are used throughout the design of the hotel." (Park Royal Hotels, 2013). It is quite aptly described as a "hotel in a garden."

The design team Wong Mun Summ and Richard Hassell, together making up the design firm WOHA (a combination of their last names) have done much to push the nature envelope in Singapore. Hassell recently spoke with me about these projects, noting the very positive reactions their clients, and the general public, have to them. The hotel's occupancy rates have been much higher than predicted, and the room rates have been doubled. These natural elements are enjoyed by hotel guests but also by residents on the street. "People are drawn to the building," Hassell tells me, and "respond very emotionally to seeing this kind of landscape building."                    —Tim Beatley

has also caught on to the importance of green elements in these higher-density projects. A casual perusing of the weekend edition of the *Straits Times*, the major local paper, provides strong evidence of the increasing importance of green features in the purchase or rental of properties in the city, as greenery and nature are offered as important amenities. One full-page advertisement in a recent edition screams, "Welcome home to Eco-Blissfulness," and boasts a new project's green credentials, including vertical farming, rainwater harvesting, and a 5-minute walk to the MRT (the city's metro system). Other advertisements speak of access to nature and the outdoors, and "nature revealed" in one case, with balconies looking over a dense tree canopy. In another case the mantra is "creation sits at your doorstep."

That designers and developers are pushing the vertical green to new heights can be seen in a number of planned or newly constructed buildings. These include, for instance, the new mixed-use complex called Jem designed by SAA Architects. The total amount of greenery to be contained in the project is estimated at 122 percent of the ground space lost, but perhaps most impressive is the extent of the design detail and the various ways that new nature is included. Greenery is included in four distinct zones: the Active Laneways, the Cascading Skypark, Sky Terraces, and the Sky Sanctuary. These features together create an integrated green project where nature is not an afterthought but designed in creative and careful ways from the beginning (box 5.1).

And the trend in new high-rise structures appears to be to see how much more greenery can be designed in. A new hotel called PARKROYAL at Pickering shows what is possible. A 2013 winner of the Skyrise Greenery Award, this office and hotel complex replaces some 215 percent of the nature lost on site. It dramatically incorporates natural features—some 15,000 square meters (18,000 sq. yd.) (fig. 5.3).

**Figure 5.3.** A View from the street of the PARKROYAL at Pickering Hotel in Singapore. This building incorporates more than 200 percent of the site in the form of vertical greening. The green features have done much to make this an attractive hotel to stay at, and the hotel has been able to double the projected room rate almost from the date the hotel opened. Credit: Photo by Tim Beatley.

### Hospital in a Garden, Hospital as an Ark

Singapore is also a leading innovator of promoting biophilic principles in hospital and healthcare settings, with truly impressive examples of how greening the city also translates into more healthful, healing environments. I visited with Mr. Liat Teng Lit, who runs the Khoo Teck Puat Hospital (KTPH), perhaps the greenest, most biophilic hospital in the world (certainly the best example this author has seen). For Mr. Liat, the story began with an older hospital, the Alexandra, where the potential to enhance healing through nature was dramatically illustrated. Liat tells the story of allocating a few hundred dollars to some of his staff interested in planting flowers and greenery and the impact this made on the environment of this hospital. Eventually he designated Mondays as planting days, setting the goal of planting sufficient host plants to accommodate some 100 species of native butterflies, an interesting and unusual measure of performance and success for a hospital. In 2 to 3 years' time 102 butterfly species were calling the hospital home. And then Liat was called in to take charge of a new hospital, where biophilic ambitions have been even greater.

Liat believes that every building should be an opportunity to restore and repair nature, something strongly reflected in the design philosophy of the KTPH. Liat now serves as its CEO and in many ways sets the tone and the decided emphasis on nature there. Liat argues in favor of setting a national goal: "Just as the rest of the world is chopping down all the rain forest, we declare ourselves as the Noah's Ark of tropical rain forests. That means we consciously with every single project bring back a few species of tropical rain forest." He imagines an audacious goal of coinhabiting the space of the hospital with a family of river otters, and, though that has not happened, the new KTPH consciously harbors and provides habitat for an amazing array of biodiversity. There are many butterflies and birds to be seen in and around the hospital, and prominent wall placards keep track of the running total of species sighted there. There are some 92 species of native fishes in the hospital's pond system (no nonnative koi to be found!).

And there is food production as well. Liat and the hospital offered to make the rooftop available to a local community gardening group that had lost some space to new development. The farming operation has grown and now occupies much of the rooftop. And it turns out the patients with windows looking out on the farm enjoy seeing it, adding to the healing landscape (fig. 5.4).

There is so much greenery here that it pervades the environment. And the healing value of this nature for those who come to the hospital is undeniable. Liat says the healing concept is primary to the hospital's design: "Our definition is when

**Figure 5.4.** The Khoo Teck Puat Hospital has become a model for hospitals seeking to enlist the healing powers of nature. There are many different elements of nature designed into this facility, from window boxes to a central waterfall. This image shows how the roof of one of the buildings has become the site of an urban farm. Credit: Photo by Tim Beatley.

you come in here your blood pressure and your heart rate go down, not up." There are window gardens, and a major interior green courtyard with a waterfall. Most of the rooms in the hospital, including all the intensive care unit rooms, have a view of this green environment.

The hospital has become a community space as well; we heard repeatedly that students come to the green spaces to study. And the hospital was designed from the beginning to be connected with the surrounding neighborhood (which has gone through its own greening process). Mr. Ng, of NParks notes that on "weekends and evenings this place is bustling with people."

The positive experience with KTPH has led to a commitment on the part of the Singapore government to build all future hospitals with similar green and healing features. A notable recent example can be seen in the newly opened Ng Teng Fong General Hospital (NTFGH). Here the design includes extensive trees and greenery on the balconies, and each patient bed, even on the ward floors, has its own window.

**Rethinking Water**

One of the most impressive steps has been to begin to reimagine the city's stormwater collection system as an opportunity to restore nature. The city's new Active, Beautiful, Clean (ABC) Waters Program, is a joint effort of the NParks and the city's Public Utility Board. The premier pilot project, Bishan-Ang Mo Kio Park, was converted from a straight-as-an-arrow concrete drainage ditch to a beautiful, meandering natural stream (box 5.2). German designer Herbert Dreiseitl was commissioned to undertake the transformation, and the result is breathtaking—3.2 kilometers (2

**Box 5.2. Bishan-Ang Mo Kio Park**

In 2006, Singapore's Public Utilities Board (PUB) initiated a new Active, Beautiful, Clean (ABC) Waters Programme, intended to update outdated water infrastructure in an effort to capture every drop of rainwater on the island, and raise public awareness about the importance of water for the land-scarce nation. One of the first pilot projects for the new program was Bishan-Ang Mo Kio Park. Originally created in 1988 around the same time as nearby Housing Development Board high-rises, by 2006, the park was in need of some updating.

Landscape architect Herbert Dreiseitl worked with stakeholders from the National Parks Board (NParks) and PUB to develop a culturally sensitive vision for the park. At the beginning of the design process, Dreiseitl and his team spent 1 week on site at the park, drawing diagrams and having conversations with NParks and PUB staff about what would make the park work. At the end of the week, the group presented their ideas to the CEOs of NParks and PUB, and they agreed to combine funds for updating the park with funds for renaturalizing the Kallang River, which, at the time, was flowing through a 20-meter-wide (66 ft.) monsoon drain, which had been in place for flood control since around the time the park opened in the late 1980s. Through this collaborative effort , the park, formerly 52 hectares (about 128 acres) managed by NParks, adjacent to 10 hectares (about 25 acres) of concrete canal separately managed by PUB, became a 62-hectare (153-acre), jointly managed entity between the two agencies.

The most dramatic change in the park is the conversion of the former concrete drainage canal into a new riverbed. The concrete was excavated in favor of a wide new path for the Kallang River, creating a new, naturalized course for the water and reconnecting residents in the Bishan neighborhood with the river and the park. All of the concrete was reused on site, in the form of stepping stones and stabilization material for the new riverbanks, and for a park feature known as Recycle Hill.

A major part of reconstructing the river was testing and incorporating bioengineering techniques, common in Western nations but never before used in a tropical city. Dreiseitl and his team conducted a 9-month "test reach" of 11 bioengineering techniques to determine which would perform best in an urban tropical setting. According to Singapore's director of Riverine Parks, while the selected bioengineering techniques, including fascines, riprap with cuttings, and gabions, among others, were largely successful, the river is a living water body that changes every day, so park staff continue to monitor the efficacy of the techniques and experiment with different ways to manage the river's new flow.

Local schoolchildren were also involved in redesigning the park: during the test reach, students were invited to attend a workshop to explore the Kallang River. Afterward they created their own artistic interpretation of the river. Their artwork is now embedded in the bubble playground at the center of Bishan-Ang Mo Kio Park.

*Box 5.2 cont.*

The reconstructed Kallang River now meanders for about 2.7 kilometers (1.7 mi.) between still-existing monsoon drains. This vision of unearthing the river from its former concrete confines and revitalizing natural spaces, in proximity to a high density of local residents living in high-rise apartments, represents a significant transformation of the park itself as well as a larger cultural shift toward reinventing and reconstructing nature's role in the city (fig. 5.5). The redesigned park has fostered significant increases in biodiversity, including many butterfly species, birds, and even a rare smooth-coated otter spotted in May 2014 (Lay 2014). Park staff indicate that human visitorship has also increased, and that people appear to be making longer visits to the park than before the renovations.

As of 2016, the PUB has completed 32 ABC Waters projects, and private developers and other public agencies have completed an additional 54 projects (PUB, 2016). Bishan-Ang Mo Kio Park was on the leading edge of what has become a significant transformation in water recreation, aesthetics, and management on the island nation of Singapore, and serves as inspiration for future projects, both within and beyond the city.

—*Julia Triman*

mi.) of nature, a ribbon of life surrounded by 40-story residential towers (fig. 5.5). The biodiversity in the park is remarkably visible.

There are reportedly 22 species of dragonflies sited in the park, for instance, and 59 species of birds, including kingfishers, egrets, drongos, and cuckoos, among others (World Landscape Architecture, n.d.). It is becoming an important place to come to birdwatch and see wildlife. While the park already boasted some 3 million visits a year, this number has only increased, and now nature will be the main attraction.

## Engaging Citizens

Singapore is doing many other things to foster a culture that connects with and cares about nature. These include a program for supporting gardens throughout the city, called Community in Bloom—some producing food, others flowers and butterflies—and the number, now at 480, continues to rise. A visit to the Hougang Primary School revealed an incredible degree to which nature is inhabiting these spaces. The school has multiple gardens integrated into its courtyards—a vegetable garden, a fernery, an orchid garden, among others, and one of the most beautiful green walls this author has ever seen, designed and constructed by the students here (and supported by the city's Skyrise Greenery program). This is a school I would wish every child could attend.

**Figure 5.5.** A former concrete drainage channel has been converted to a meandering Kallang River at Bishan-Ang Mo Kio Park. Credit: Photo by Tim Beatley.

Singapore's nature and immense native biodiversity also extend to coastal and marine areas, and nature conservation efforts here have been growing in importance. This is a different way perhaps of thinking about the "garden" in which the city lies. Much has been lost—mangroves and coral reefs—to the extensive land reclamation and shoreline development that occurred, especially in the 1960s, but there are many positive signs that Singapore now has a different view of its coastal and marine environments. A key turning point was the public opposition that emerged in 2001 to the proposed land reclamation project at Chek Jawa, an area of wetlands and intertidal flats on Palau Ubin (one of the larger islands that surrounds Singapore) that boasts a remarkable abundance of marine life, from longhorn cowfish to orange sea stars, antibacterial sponges to carpet anemones (Ng, Corlett, and Tan 2002). A new visitor's center there, and a 1-kilometer-long (half-mile) boardwalk herald different views of these habitats, and Chek Jawa has become a beloved and popular area to visit. Among the most popular activities today are the intertidal walks run by NParks guides, which allow Singaporeans a firsthand view of this exotic marine life during low tides. Ria Tan, who runs the website Wild Singapore and who has had a role in organizing citizen support for marine conservation, believes finding ways to connect this vertical city to its amazing marine life is critical. She says, "I really believe that people need to see it, taste it, feel it; then when the time comes they will stick up for it" (R. Tan, pers. comm., February 1, 2012).

The marine biodiversity that remains in Singapore waters is truly remarkable in light of the fact that the city is one of the most active ports in the world. There are some 255 species of hard corals (zooxanthellates), for instance (Huang et al. 2009), and more than 100 species of reef fishes.

There is more to do in the marine realm, but here Singapore represents another exemplar, giving needed attention and emphasis to understanding and managing nature here. Most impressively, it is nearing completion of a 2-year Comprehensive Marine Biodiversity Inventory, that has already yielded considerable new appreciation for what lies beneath and below, and rather nearby! The marine survey, spearheaded by NParks, has engaged a number of international scientists as well as hundreds of citizen volunteers. There have been two extensive expeditions, and the extent of the marine life uncovered is remarkable. Some 100 new species (new to Singapore waters) have been identified, as well as 14 marine species thought to be new to science. These included some remarkable discoveries, such as a "lipstick" anemone, an orange-clawed mangrove crab, and a small goby fish.

Owing much to the Blue Plan developed in 2009, the city/nation is moving forward in better protecting and managing this marine nature, and in 2015 it created its first marine park, the Sisters' Islands Marine Park. While not especially large (comprising about 40 hectares [99 acres]), it protects extensive marine biodiversity, including coral reefs, and species of special interest, such as the Neptune's cup sponge (*Cliona patera*), thought to have gone locally extinct.

The marine park represents a major opportunity to educate and engage the public about the amazing marine world nearby. There is a new Sisters' Islands Marine Park Public Gallery on St. John's Island, which will serve as a major facility for public education. Among other things, there will be guided walks at low tide, and two new underwater dive trails (complete with underwater educational signage). The Gallery will also serve as a focal point for citizen science projects and for research as well as a variety of habitat restoration efforts.

There have also been efforts to explore and test new techniques and technologies that would enhance marine habitat along the shore edge, for instance, a new tile, described by Lena Chan, director of the NParks Center for Biodiversity, that could be attached to new seawalls to provide habitat to marine organisms.

### New Forms of Urban Nature

Singapore has received much international press for the opening of its new Gardens by the Bay Project, an area redeveloped along the city's harbor front, and especially its so-called supertrees. Supertrees are larger than life, visually dramatic metal structures in the shape of massive trees, covered with plants and vegetation and providing, essentially, many of the positive functions of natural trees—shading and cooling as well as habitat.

There are 18 of the supertrees in all, 12 clustered in a supertree grove. According to Gardens by the Bay, more than 160,000 plants have been used in planting the supertrees, including more than 200 species "and varieties of bromeliads, orchids, ferns and tropical flowering climbers." In the evening the trees light up, and there are dramatic light shows.

The supertrees are immense. The tallest of the supertrees are as high as a 16-story building. There is a restaurant atop one of them and an elevated skyway connecting several others. Seven of the supertrees incorporate solar panels and produce energy (again, not unlike real trees). There are also two large, glass-domed conservatories in addition to the supertrees.

### Prospects and Success

Has the city been successful in creating a city in a garden? Has it been able to grow a green culture at the same time that it has accommodated dramatic population growth in recent years? The evidence seems to point to yes. Landsat imagery comparing green areas in 1986 with those in 2007 shows that, while development increased substantially, green areas went from 36 percent of the island to 47 percent; this despite an increase in nearly 2 million residents during that period (NParks 2009). It is not a perfect story, certainly: there is continued loss of ground-level nature and green space, too much some believe, and some of its newest and densest development areas (e.g., the new eco-district of Punggol) are not especially green. Still there is much to laud in this Asian model. And the city is exercising leadership in other ways, as NParks has spearheaded the development of a City Biodiversity Index (CBI), known as the Singapore Index, and has worked hard to make biodiversity conservation important to the other agencies and offices of government there. Increasingly Singapore's pioneering brand of green urbanism will be relevant in other cities, within Asia and beyond, and its vertical innovations will show that greenery and density can be coupled to effectively protect biodiversity and improve living conditions. Singapore increasingly demonstrates what Lee Kuan Yew believed, that greening the island, creating a city in a garden, would lay the foundation for the economic prosperity and high quality of life that Singaporeans today enjoy.

Singapore offers many impressive lessons on how to think about and move in the direction of creating a biophilic city. One lesson is the importance of public support for biophilic urbanism through a number of different, mutually reinforcing strategies—regulatory mandates (e.g., as seen in the landscape replacement policy), financial incentives, technical assistance, and support for research and development, have all played a role. Enlisting the private sector in the vertical greening innovations has been key, and it is clearly now the case that private developers there understand the importance of including vertical greening elements (as a way of enhancing market-ability and the quality of living and work environments they create).

Singapore shows as well the value of both investing in citywide biophilic infra-structure—the park connectors, for example, and efforts to green and restore its rivers and waterways—at the same time as more discrete facilities and buildings, such as the KTPH. The reconceptualizing of the KTPH as a "hospital in a garden" and more recent buildings like the new PARKROYAL on Pickering as a "hotel in a garden" shows the important ways in which the framing of a larger city as biophilic and natureful can in turn shape and frame individual buildings and smaller-scale urban interventions.

Singapore has innovated a new way of understanding cities in the process—an understanding that to accommodate future population growth will require parks and greenery and nature in the sky, as well as on the ground. Equally innovative are the ways in which Singapore is exploring new hybrids of real and built nature, most notably with the unveiling of supertrees (fig. 5.6).

Singapore offers other lessons as well. Few coastal cities have done more to

**Figure 5.6.** The supertrees at the Gardens by the Bay. Credit: Compliments of Gardens by the Bay.

embrace marine nature than Singapore, and in many ways this represents one of the most important new areas of opportunity for urban nature. Connecting land-based urbanites with their amazing nearby ocean environments and organisms remains, for many reasons, a significant challenge, but Singapore is taking this on in a serious way that other coastal and marine cities should understand and follow.

# 6

# Milwaukee, Wisconsin:
## *From Cream City to Green City*

Milwaukee is perhaps best known for its beers and its brewing history. While most of its breweries are now gone, it is a city innovating in many other areas, particularly in forging new models for urban sustainability and greening. Settled where three rivers come together, and perched on the shores of Lake Michigan, it is a city with considerable natural assets and beauty.

### A Former Industrial City Rethinking Its Future

Milwaukee has indeed made considerable strides in urban sustainability, which is now a priority issue for current mayor, Tom Barrett. Barrett has established a "green team" to advise and guide the preparation of the city's new sustainability plan. Barrett created the city's Office of Environmental Sustainability in 2006, to help advance this agenda. Much has already been accomplished as it transitions from "cream city to green city." There are new stormwater management efforts under way in the city, including the installation of a number of green rooftops (including one on the roof of the city's central library), and the planting of thousands of trees. There is a very successful home energy retrofit program, and a new bold plan called HOME GR/OWN that reimagines the city's some 3000 vacant parcels as the basis for a new community renewal. Mayor Barrett, in a recent op-ed article in the *Milwaukee Journal Sentinel*, described this latter plan as an effort to "knit the city back to the land" (Barrett 2012).

In many US cities there has been a marked recent uptick in gun violence and homicides. After years of declining homicide rates, this is alarming to be sure. It is a renewed recognition of the challenges of growing up in high-poverty neighborhoods where there are few opportunities and much despair.

For Milwaukee much of the epicenter of this is the North End, where it turns out most of the city's vacant lots, more than 2400 of them, are found. Mayor Barrett developed the HOME GR/OWN initiative as a cornerstone of his efforts as mayor, with intentions to convert many of these vacant lots into community spaces and opportunities to grow food.

Twenty of these pocket parks and community orchards were completed in 2015, at a relatively low cost. With a grant from the Greater Milwaukee Foundation, and design help from the University of Wisconsin–Milwaukee, these new community growing spaces have at least the promise of providing healthier food and reshaping the look, feel, and promise of these hardscrabble environments. According to the city's HOME GR/OWN website, the effort aims to transform these vacant lots into "community assets that spark new economic opportunities around local, healthy food production and distribution, and new, green community spaces." One recent example is the Eze-kiel Gillespie Park, created by combining two vacant lots, and planting 15 fruit trees (apple and pear) and hundreds of edible berry bushes and native perennials.

Some neighbors have reacted cautiously to the plans for orchards, as Eric Sham-burger, the city's new sustainability director, notes, and they express some concerns about messy fallen fruit. The number of fruit trees to be planted has been scaled back somewhat in response to these concerns.

Milwaukee is already quite well known for its innovative work in urban agriculture and community food production. It is notably home to Will Allen's nonprofit *Growing Power*, and more recently the aquaponics company Sweet Water Organics (inspired by Allen's work, and highly publicized, though not without a few hiccups along the way).

Some of the other community food and urban agriculture stories are less well known outside Milwaukee. One of the more impressive of these is Alice's Garden, a large growing space and virtual beehive of community-based activities. Located in one of the city's poorest neighborhoods, Lindsay Heights, this garden aims to do many things at once—provide jobs and income for young adults in the neighborhood, create new educational programming for school kids (the Brown Academy School lies adja-cent to the site), and provide important green space for the community. Creating and growing Alice's Garden has been a collective effort, helped along through partnerships with a number of organizations in the community, including the Milwaukee Food Council, the University of Wisconsin, and the Center for Resilient Cities.

I had the chance to see the Garden, on a visit to Milwaukee, on what turned out to be a fairly hot summer day. There were so many things happening, so much activity, so many projects to hear about, and so many young people zipping by, that it was a bit dizzying. It is hard to envision a spot of urban ground more intensively programmed: there are many classes offered at the Garden, it is the site of storytelling and theater arts, and a horticulture club meets there, among many other programs.

All of this happens on only 2 acres of land (about 0.8 hectares). This creates a fertile layering of energy and meaning, as organic and as complex as the soil itself. The Garden is a staging ground and home-ship, it seems, for many other activities in the community—there is a Healthy Corner Store Initiative, with two stores already stocking produce from the garden, and at least two farmers markets in the neighborhood (including the Fondy market) where food from the garden is sold. I met on that day two amazing individuals that make the garden run and hum: Venice Williams, who is the Garden's executive director, and Fatuma Emmad, the urban farm manager (fig. 6.1). Their energy and passion both for gardens and for positive social change were palpable.

An especially unusual aspect of the garden is the emphasis on food heritage, in particular for African Americans. Through its Fieldhands and Foodways Project, there

**Figure 6.1.** Alice's Garden has become an important neighborhood space in the Lindsay Heights neighborhood of Milwaukee. Here are two key leaders who keep the garden running: Fatuma Emmad, Urban Farm Manager (left), and Venice Williams, Project Director (right). Credit: Photo by Tim Beatley.

is an effort to educate citizens about the role of food during the period of slavery—as Williams explained, not to diminish the hardships and terror, but to show another dimension. There is a master's kitchen garden here, and also a slave allotment garden. Through these gardens many stories related to slavery are told—including the fact that some African communities were targeted by slavers for their specific agricultural knowledge and skills.

There are important place-making aspects of the garden as well. There are walking paths and a shared pavilion for community meetings. A labyrinth is used for contemplative walks and classes.

Another unusual feature we happened upon as we walked around that day was a distinctive-looking elevated "box," which I soon discovered was the first of the Garden's three "little free libraries." Their motto, "Take a book, leave a book," is meant to help tackle at once literacy and community engagement. The brainchild of Wisconsin natives, Todd Bol and Rick Brooks, the idea has now made its way around the world (with several thousand built to date).

Whether Alice's Garden will be able to stitch together this neighborhood is unclear, but there is evidence of progress. The site of the garden was actually intended to be a highway—the Park West Freeway—before it was stopped in the 1970s. But not before many homes were bought and razed. Replacing some of that lost housing would be a positive move, and though hard to do in the present economy, the amenity value of the Garden could be a helpful asset.

## A River Success Story

Alice's Garden is just one of many exemplary community-building efforts in Milwaukee, undertakings that uniquely combine food production, community building, and contact with the natural world. The city's efforts at urban river renewal and river restoration are an especially important part of the Milwaukee story, one already known to many urban planners. Few biophilic features are more important and can have more direct impact on quality of life in cities than efforts to restore and daylight rivers and streams. Water figures prominently in the Milwaukee story. Dating back to Mayor John Norquist is the creation of the city's highly successful Riverwalk along the Milwaukee River. While not yet completed it already covers a 24-block area in the city.

A more recent chapter in this urban river story can be seen in the city's work to restore the Menomonee River, which has been the location for much of the city's industrial base over the years. Much of this area of brownfields has been redeveloped, and through the work of the Menomonee Partnership, new companies have been relocating here. But vacant and underutilized land remains.

## Education and Engagement through Urban Ecology Centers

The Urban Ecology Center is another unique organization in Milwaukee that is playing a key role in the restoration of the Menomonee River. It's a hands-on learning center, aimed at teaching about the environment and ecology of the city. In fact Milwaukee has not just one Urban Ecology Center, but *three*, with the third opening in September 2012 along the Menomonee River. A former tavern, the building has been retrofitted with a number of green elements, including Solatube skylights and a rainwater collection system (fig. 6.2). The Center also encompasses not only the structure but the restoration of a nearby 24-acre abandoned rail yard along the Menomonee River (fig. 6.3). This site will gradually be restored and converted into an outdoor classroom, with new pedestrian and bicycle bridges and new community gardens.

Indeed, Milwaukee leads the nation in creatively engaging kids and adults in hands-on learning about nature and science. The Urban Ecology Center is organized as a 501(c)(3) nonprofit that, according to its literature, "fosters ecological understanding as inspiration for change, neighborhood by neighborhood." The main branch is at Riverside Park, with another at Washington Park, in addition to the new Menomonee location. These ecology centers do impressive work, and are locations for extensive family programs, from monarch larvae monitoring to bluebird house building, adult learning, and interest groups, such as an urban ecology photo club, urban stargazers, and those interested in early morning bird walks. These centers host many school visits and are highly embedded in the neighborhoods where they are located. Some 80,000 visits a year have been logged to the ecology centers (before the addition of the Menomonee branch). These centers have also developed strong partnerships with neighborhood schools.

These urban ecology centers are veritable hubs of community activity. There are summer camps for kids and programs of various kinds—bird walks and lectures and summer concerts—for adults and kids alike. The annual report shows the extent of the impact in a year: more than 200,000 visitors came to the centers, including some 28,000 students. More than 3700 individuals volunteered for the centers, providing much-needed assistance and planting thousands of trees and plants. There are a number of opportunities to participate in one of the Center's citizen science programs about bats, frogs, birds, and many other species, leading to insights about urban ecology in the Milwaukee region. There is also equipment available for residents to borrow, including camping equipment, cross-country skis, gardening tools, ice skates, snowshoes, sleds, and fishing equipment—a service local residents used some 2500 times in 2013 (Urban Ecology Center 2014). The service to local schools is a most impressive part of the benefits the Center provides through its Neighborhood

**Figure 6.2.** Milwaukee's third branch of the Urban Ecology Center opened in 2013 near the Menomonee River. A former tavern, this adaptive reuse boasts many green features, including Solatube skylights and a rainwater collection system. Credit: Photo by Tim Beatley.

**Figure 6.3.** The Milwaukee story is one of rediscovery and reconnecting with its rivers. Much of the recent work has focused on the city's Menomonee River, shown here. Credit: Photo by Tim Beatley.

Environmental Education Project. Some 53 schools are now participating in this program. Schools participate not just in a single visit but throughout the year, "transforming the experience from just another field trip to a permanent outdoor classroom where you can reinforce science concepts taught in class with hands-on outdoor activities during multiple visits" (Urban Ecology Center n.d.).

In 2016 the Urban Ecology Center is participating in an innovative pilot project aimed at reducing violent crime among at-risk high school students. Called Youth Works Milwaukee, and based on a model used in Chicago, one of the paid jobs is at the Urban Ecology Center. The evidence suggests that, when high schoolers have a paying job, the likelihood of violent crime goes down. Although still a pilot project, the experience suggests the promise of organizations such as the Urban Ecology Center to provide jobs and livelihoods through environmental education and outreach, and through biophilic urbanism.

Another interesting initiative connected to the Urban Ecology Center at Riverside Park is the Children's Forest, which opened in 2013. It is one of only three urban examples of a "children's forest," a special program and designation established by the US Forest Service. More formally known as the Milwaukee Rotary Centennial Arboretum, it consists of 40 acres (16 hectares) along a portion of the Milwaukee River. There are paved and unpaved trails and a canoe launch. A dramatic stone arch marks the gateway to the arboretum. Intended to help connect kids and families to nature, and forests in particular, some 70 native species of trees have been planted on the site, as well as thousands of native bushes and flowers. With several outdoor learning areas and volunteer docents providing tours, the Children's Forest has become a major destination for school visits. A unique set of information stations, called ImagiNature Stations, which are denoted with a specially designed leaf emblem, serve as a kind of scavenger hunt for kids.

The forest represents the spirit of collaboration needed in biophilic cities. It is the result of a collaboration between several organizations, including the US Forest Service, Eastern Branch, the Urban Ecology Center, the County Parks Department, the River Revitalization Foundation, and the Rotary Club, which raised much of the funding for the Arboretum (some $400,000, described as catalyst funding for the project).

The arboretum is connected with and viewed as the gateway to the larger 878-acre (355 hectare) Milwaukee River Greenway. The greenway is a terrific story of a river's renaissance and restoration, with steadily improving water quality and increasing biodiversity (River Revitalization Foundation n.d.). The Greenway connects a number of existing county and city parks (12 in total, including Lincoln Park to the North) and has been the site of a number of ecological restoration projects, notably the removal of the North Avenue Dam in 1997. A Milwaukee Greenway Master Plan was prepared in 2010, and the City of Milwaukee has adopted a special zoning overlay to control development along the Greenway. The Master Plan "sets forth a vision for a unique urban wilderness containing restored natural communities and shared recreational opportunities," and identifies future investments, projects, and management, to be guided by a newly created Milwaukee River Greenway Coalition (River Revitalization Foundation 2010). Building support for and between community groups on behalf of river conservation and working to revise zoning and development codes to better protect and allow access are both important steps toward river conservation.

**A Watery Nature**
In many ways, then, water is a key biophilic asset and condition in Milwaukee, and connecting residents to that water is a goal being pursued in different and creative ways. There is now a 35-mile Urban Water Trail for canoes and kayaks (referred to in some of the city's literature as a *liquid parkway*) that encompasses parts of the city's three rivers, including the Milwaukee River. And the importance of the Lake Michigan shoreline cannot be forgotten, with unique opportunities to swim, boat, and sail here. Milwaukee is home to one of the few nonprofit community sailing clubs in the United States—the Milwaukee Community Sailing Center—with more than 80 boats available and sailing classes offered year round.

Few cities are doing more to advance both urban sustainability and connections with the natural world. Milwaukee is a city that has strongly embraced the role nature can play in reframing and reshaping its image and the perception of the city (from both inside and outside) and its long-term vision. The city's efforts demonstrate the power of understanding and taking full advantage of the ecological assets present in an urban environment—in Milwaukee's case especially its rivers and shoreline—and of working with private organizations, such as the Urban Ecology Center, to cultivate and strengthen a community citizenry curious about and committed to the natural world around them.

# 7

# Wellington, New Zealand:
## *From Town Belt to Blue Belt*

Wellington, the capital of New Zealand, is a city of around 200,000 people. It has a long history of progressive environmental plans, policies, and initiatives, and in recent years it has been further extending and developing these commitments to becoming a city of nature.

The establishment of parks and green spaces goes back almost to Wellington's founding. The Town Belt wraps the central city in a U-shape of trees and greenery and has its beginning in the town's 1841 town plan. And while the Town Belt has been nibbled away at over the years, it is mostly intact, with prominent elements including Mount Victoria, Mount Albert, and the Botanic Gardens. In more recent history the city has established an extensive outer greenbelt, a mix of private and publicly owned land. Wellington has an extensive network of nature trails, both within and outside the city, following ridge tops and connecting major parks, and providing spectacular views of the landscape and seascape (fig. 7.1).

### Wellington as a Living City
The city has a number of programs aimed at enhancing and restoring nature in the city. These include an extensive tree-planting initiative, and the goal of planting 2 million new trees by 2020 (already with considerable progress made), and an effort to gradually replace its stock of nonnative trees with native species. This is partly a matter of resilience, as the nonnative species seem less able to adapt to and cope with the strong (and famous) winds of Wellington. The city has also helped to establish

**Figure 7.1.** Downtown Wellington, the capital of New Zealand, has a long history of protecting nature near to the city, beginning with its Town Belt, which encircles downtown and dates to the city's original 1841 town plan. Credit: Photo by Tim Beatley.

a network of community nurseries growing native tree and plant stock for use in neighborhood plantings.

Wellington has relatively little of its original native forest left (estimated at less than 5 percent remaining broadleaf and 1 percent remaining coastal forest). But there are significant remnant bush habitats in the Otari-Wilton's Bush and the Botanic Gardens, important natural spaces in the city. It has also become a priority to plant native species of trees and vegetation, including nationally threatened plants, in many of the interstitial spaces of the city, such as along roadsides and verges and traffic islands.

The city also financially supports the Wellington Zoo, which occupies space in the Town Belt. The Nest Te Kōhanga is a veterinary care facility within the zoo, which emphasizes care for native wildlife species. In its first 5 years in existence, the facility treated some 2000 native animals, from white kiwi to endangered Kākāpō (Wellington Zoo 2014).

The Outer Green Belt consists of a series of Wellington City Council–owned parks and reserves, with the vision being to bring about a "continuous green belt following the ridges west of the city from the south coast to Colonial Knob, in which indigenous vegetation is restored and an informal recreation network is widely accessible" (Wellington City Council 2015). These parks provide residents and visitors unusual ability to hike and bike, with spectacular views. One of the most important hiking and biking trails is the Skyline Walkway, a 12-kilometer (7.5 mi.) route opened in 2006.

The larger regional landscape provides other unusual opportunities. The city and region's commitment to renewable energy can be seen in the 62-turbine wind park, Project West Wind, located in the northwest. Taking advantage of the city's special wind resource, these 2.3 MW turbines generate enough power essentially to cover the domestic energy needs of Wellington's population (enough power to supply an estimated 70,000 average New Zealand homes). And the location, run by Meridian Energy, is also a sheep farm and recreational park providing hiking trails for public use.

In the last several years, and with the strong leadership of recently reelected mayor Celia Wade-Brown, the city has developed a new initiative called Our Living City. Wade-Brown is a strong voice in support of nature in the city and the importance of connecting urban residents with the spectacular nature around them. The primary goal of Our Living City is to "improve Wellingtonians' quality of life by strengthening urban–nature connections and building economic opportunities from a healthy environment" (Wellington City Council 2015). The city has taken many steps to give meaning to the Our Living City philosophy, from tree planting to piloting the installation of living walls to establishing a new healthy homes program, among others. A Living City grants program has provided funding for a variety of local projects, with NZD$80,000 made available each year.

In 2015 the city adopted a new Biodiversity Strategy and Action Plan (building on an earlier 2007 action plan). This plan lays out the principles and philosophy and a variety of specific steps and actions the city intends to take to protect and expand biodiversity. The plan's title, "Our Natural Capital," is at once a play on words and a clear commitment to organizing policy and life in the city around the abundant nature there (Wellington City Council 2015). The plan provides an important statement of the critical importance of nature to the lives of Wellingtonians: "Wellingtonians are connected to nature. They are knowledgeable and passionate about Wellington's biodiversity and want to live in a city of abundant nature that is in close proximity to them" (2015, 15).

While the Biodiversity Strategy contains a variety of specific restoration and management actions, attached to short, medium, and long time frames (such as carrying out integrated pest management in specific areas of the city), much of the plan has to do with further building connections with and access to nature. One proposed action, for instance, is to "investigate the use of live feed cameras on bird nests (e.g., kaka and/or little blue penguin, and/or underwater environments in the inner harbor) and promote these images to the public" (2015, 49). Promoting such things as community gardens and green roofs in the city is suggested, along with every citizen having access to nature within a 10-minute walk or bike ride. There is also a strong endorsement of the concept of water-sensitive urban design, something the city has been supporting.

The terminology of "water-sensitive urban design" is the New Zealand (and Australian) equivalent to what would in North America be referred to as low-impact development, and decentralized, on-site stormwater collection. There are already some impressive projects in the city that show great potential, especially Waitangi Park, a 6-hectare (15-acre) park designed by landscape architects Wraight and Associates. This unique park sits right on the harbor, and an innovative reconstructed wetland system and bioretention features help to cleanse stormwater from streets and upland sites as it flows to the harbor (fig. 7.2). Much of the park comprises a series of "thickly planted sloped terraces," planted with native plants and providing a beautiful and colorful spot of nature in the city (Wright + Associates n.d.). There are also bioretention treepits (belowground structures that hold the roots and allow collection of stormwater) along a walking promenade and a rain garden that collects and treats stormwater flowing from the streets and parking lots. And there are numerous public uses available at the park—a skate park, a playground, and a grassy picnic area.

### Returning the Birdsong to Wellington

The science officer aboard Captain James Cook's first voyage to the Pacific and to New Zealand reported on the deafening "dawn chorus" of birdsong they found there. Many of these birds were decimated in the decades to follow, with the introduction of European and Australian mammals, such as stoats, possums, and rats.

Wellington has helped to pioneer a new and bold conservation strategy of bringing back these native bird species. One of the biggest urban biodiversity success stories in Wellington is Zealandia (previously known as the Karori Wildlife Sanctuary), a former water supply catchment facility that has now been encircled with a mammal-proof fence in order to allow native bird species to recover.

The eco-sanctuary, 225 hectares (556 acres) in size, takes up an important valley a mere 10 minutes from downtown Wellington. The sanctuary serves a number of other important nature-enhancing functions in Wellington. There are trails inside and around the preserve, and a range of educational programs available

**Figure 7.2.** The Waitangi Wetlands Park, Wellington, New Zealand, is 6 hectares (15 acres) of sloped terraces adjacent to the city's harbor. Planted with native plants, the wetlands collect and treat stormwater runoff and provide new water-adjacent public spaces. Credit: Photo by Tim Beatley.

to residents. The preserve is run by a trust and has embraced a remarkable 500-year plan for restoring the nature there, back to the "dense multi-tiered lowland podocarp/broadleaf forest" that existed before the arrival of Europeans (Zealandia, "Forest Restoration" n.d.; Zealandia, "Progress to Date" n.d.). The task is one that is expected to take that long.

A focus in the shorter term has been removing nonnative and invasive species and gradually reintroducing many species that were native. In recent years, for example, the park has reintroduced tuatara (a large lizard-like species, though actually not a lizard) and giant wētā (a kind of very large cricket), among others.

The design of this predator-proof fence is impressive—it is more than 8 kilometers (5 mi.) long, 2.2 meters (7 ft.) tall, with a "curved top hat" on the top (fig. 7.3). It extends another 400 mm (16 in.) into the ground to guard against burrowing mammals (see Zealandia, "Our Groundbreaking Fence," n.d.). Completed in 1999, the fence and the approach taken in Zealandia have spurred similar fences in other parts of New Zealand and the world (in at least 14 other places).

After only little over a decade many local threatened species have rebounded

**Figure 7.3.** Zealandia is a bold effort to restore native habitat and fauna, especially birds, to Wellington. This natural reserve in the center of the city is surrounded by a tall (2.2 meters [7 ft.]) predator-proof fence, intended to allow native species, such as the native kaka parrot, to propagate and rebound. Credit: Photo by Tim Beatley.

in the park, and the park has now become a kind of propagation site, sending bird species, such as kakas, out to the surrounding neighborhoods of the city. The case of the kaka, a native species of parrot, is telling. In 2002 only a small number of kaka (six from the Auckland Zoo) were introduced to the Zealandia valley. Ten years later, the numbers are estimated at around 180 to 250, with many of these birds visiting and inhabiting the neighborhoods surrounding the preserve and increasingly the city as a whole ("Kaka numbers recovering in Wellington" n.d.).

Zealandia's tagline, "returning the birdsong to Wellington," conveys one exemplary way of imagining the future of a biophilic city. We know that hearing birdsong is beautiful and therapeutic (and biophilic), and ensuring that Wellingtonians live in neighborhoods where they can delight in these sounds is an admirable measure of urban progress.

Much thinking in recent years has been focused on how to protect birds after they leave the safety of the preserve. This is often discussed as the "halo," those bands of neighborhoods and space that emanate out from the sanctuary and bring birds in contact with homes and residential neighborhoods (and dangers such as domestic cats). Victoria University professor Charles Daugherty, a member of the Zealandia Trust Board, describes this halo effect:

> Most people think of the Halo Effect as an increase in numbers of tui, and other native bird species moving beyond the relative safety of the sanctuary's mammal exclusion fence, to occupy adjacent suburbs such as Karori and more widely across the city. To the new Trust Board, the Halo concept embraces a far larger set of benefits to Wellington than the dawn chorus. Key goals for us include not only ecological restoration of our valley and spill-over benefits to surrounding areas, but also environmental education programs for the region's youth, world-leading conservation research, constructive engagement with our local community, and an eco-tourism destination that supports the Wellington economy. (Daugherty 2013)

There is more that can be done outside the fences of Zealandia. An organization called Enhancing the Halo has been formed, aimed at working with and educating neighbors and homeowners outside the park, and enlisting them in monitoring and caring for these bird species. As founder Gareth Morgan has been quoted as saying, "By providing safe haven in our backyards, we can also allow our native birds to spread right across Wellington" (Stewart 2013). "Halo Households" register online and receive an info packet and decal to affix to their window. They also receive advice and guidance about how to make their yards more bird-friendly, and are encouraged to take steps to control and manage the biggest bird killers—domestic cats—by attaching bells, keeping them indoors, or building outdoor enclosures for them.

## An Emerging Model of Blue Urbanism

Perhaps Wellington's most impressive urban nature innovation can be seen in its efforts to grow a new, more marine-oriented nature sensibility to match the land-based efforts. To complement its greenbelts, the city is now proposing a blue belt, which would consist of its harbor, marine conservation area, and all the shorelines and offshore marine habitats that encircle this peninsular city.

The marine life in this city is often spectacular, with orcas frequently coming into the harbor (often following the stingrays) and near to shore, and other species, such as little blue penguins, nesting in the city. It is a very diverse marine environment, with arguably much greater diversity than more terrestrial environments.

The Taputeranga Marine Reserve lies on the city's south coastline and is its pride and joy. It encompasses a large rectangular area—about 4 kilometers (2.5 mi.) of shoreline, extending more than 2 kilometers (1.3 mi.) into the Southern Ocean. Managed by the New Zealand Department of Conservation, it feels more like the city's own. It is a marine reserve and is a fishing no-take zone. Encompassing three oceanic currents, it is a place of tremendous biodiversity, boasting some 400 species of seaweeds, many species of invertebrates, and fascinating creatures, such as the pot-bellied seahorse. Boating, diving, and snorkeling are permitted, however, and there is even a designated snorkel trail.

The proximity of the reserve is a major amenity for Wellingtonians—only about 6 kilometers (3.7 mi.) from downtown. The Island Bay Marine Education Centre is a wonderful marine education facility that exists at the marine conservation area, which includes aquaria and a series of touch tanks. It is operated by the Wellington Marine Conservation Trust, a registered charity created in 1999. At low tide residents can explore the rock pools nearby, and there is even a snorkel trail by which to experience the marine world. Schools in Wellington make regular trips to bring classes to the marine education center.

Years ago Wellington became the site of the world's first marine bioblitz—an effort to comprehensively inventory this immense marine life. It occurred over 30 days, rather than 24 or 48 hours, which is more common with a land-based bioblitz, a nod to the difficult environment and the immense challenge. Overall more than 550 marine species were counted, including a southern right whale and an orca. As in Singapore, several new species were discovered. Specifically, four new marine species were discovered: a tube anemone, a sea slug, a bryozoan, and a diatom (Harper, Patterson, and Harper 2009; Royal Forest and Bird Protection Society 2007).

Establishing a blue belt is partly a planning task but partly a task of changing perceptions and mental maps of citizens as well as public officials. A local diver, Steve Journee, has been a key individual in creating this change, and someone who dives the Wellington harbor almost daily. He is also a photographer and has recently published a fascinating book documenting the marine life of the harbor with the terrific title, *Wellington Down Under* (Journee 2014). Such efforts are hard to evaluate in terms of their impact but can be significant.

Mayor Wade-Brown, herself a diver, has also been a key advocate for blue urbanism. She speaks passionately about the role that the marine world can and should play in the lives of Wellingtonians.

**Figure 7.4.** Wellington is famous for its wind, an important element of place and environment there. A number of wind art projects have been commissioned in recent years, including this wind sculpture called Akau Tangi, by artist Phil Dadson. Credit: Arts Foundation.

## A City with Biophilic Features Throughout

Few cities in the world have natural environment as wondrous and magical as Wellington's. There is a closeness to nature that is discernible to visitors. And Wellington is, in many ways described here, working to strengthen human–nature connections. Taking full advantage of its natural environment Wellington also harnesses its famous wind. It does so by generating significant amounts of energy from wind turbines but also through some interesting wind-inspired public art (fig. 7.4), including a Wind Sculpture Walk, highlighting the work of artists, such as Phil Dadson's Akau Tangi (box 7.1).

The city's biodiversity plan also gives prominent mention to the concept of biophilic cities and to the city's participation in the Biophilic Cities Network. Strongly supported by Mayor

**Box 7.1. Wellington's Wind Sculpture**

"Akau Tangi consists of 10 stripe painted poles, each supporting a kinetic conical element that varies with wind direction and spins on its axis according to wind speed, producing dynamo-operated LED lighting that brightens or dulls according to wind speed. Aeolian flute and whistle tones are produced from each of the 10 sculptures by wind-driven flutes at the cowl end of each form."

Source: The Arts Foundation.
http://www.thearts.co.nz/news/akau-tangi
-wind-sculpture-installed.

Wade-Brown and the city's staff, the biophilic cities moniker and framework truly suit Wellington. In 2013 I had the chance to ask Wade-Brown whether Wellington was a biophilic city, and, not surprisingly, her answer was an emphatic yes: "Wellington is absolutely a biophilic city! That's why I live here; that's why I stayed here. The connection with the coast, the ability to wander in the forests, it's the birds . . . whether it's kākā or penguins, you can see them on a daily basis. You don't have to say 'right, I'm leaving the city, going to a nature reserve 100 kilometers away.'"

"City–nature are like this," said Wade-Brown, linking the fingers of her two hands together, showing visually the integration of these realms. Nature is all around in Wellington, it is true, and residents value this in deep and important ways. The profound connections Wellingtonians have to the natural world can also be seen in the references to nature and animals in the architecture and urban design throughout the city. Examples include the fern-shaped bollards throughout the downtown, trash cans etched with tree shapes, and the city's new central library, which integrates a series of pillars in the shape of native palm trees. It is not clear what exactly explains this seemingly pervasive and deep nature sensibility. One explanation may have to do with the presence and continuing importance of Maori culture, for which interconnections with the natural world are central. But undoubtedly it is a creative mix of popular support for an outdoor lifestyle, strong political leadership, and the underlying ecology, history, and culture of this special city.

# 8

# Birmingham, United Kingdom:
## *Health, Nature, and Urban Economy*

Cities today face a myriad of issues, including very poor air quality, the need to adapt to climate change, a variety of diet-related health problems, rising obesity, and a lack of physical activity. These are complex and challenging issues. One potential solution is to develop more integrative, holistic models that can tie these problems together and provide integrative, catalytic solutions.

Insights for beginning this process can be found across the Atlantic, in the United Kingdom. The former industrial city of Birmingham, is now on the cusp of developing strategies that will explicitly connect health, nature, and economy. Birmingham has declared its intentions to be a green and sustainable city and has taken a number of impressive steps to underscore this commitment. For example, it has set one of the most ambitious greenhouse gas emission targets anywhere in the country, or the world for that matter.

But what is especially promising from the perspective of fostering a biophilic city is Birmingham's early efforts to tie together so many different strands of a green city agenda, especially through the lens of health. Nick Grayson, who heads the city's program in Climate Change and Sustainability, has been involved in an ambitious effort to map many of the dangers and health relationships in the city—for instance, mapping where future urban temperatures will be the highest and where air quality is the worst. Reforms to the United Kingdom's vaunted healthcare system are shifting responsibilities to the local level, suggesting that cities will have more opportunities (and perhaps more incentives) to understand how their programs and actions can affect health.

### Biophilic and Healthy

These various health issues, and thinking about how to adapt to long-term climate change, is where the Birmingham approach veers into the innovative. The city is making new connections between health and nature, and exploring new ways to forge co-investments in these things and in developing economic flows that can acknowledge and reward the ways in which urban conservation and nature improve residents' health. Much of this new philosophy can be seen in the city's new Green Living Spaces Plan (City of Birmingham, 2013).

The Plan lays out a set of principles and vision for greening the city in the future, building on and extending programs and partnerships already underway. Not always thought of as a natureful city, the existing nature is impressive. Forest canopy coverage is around 23% (fig 8.1), and there are some 8,000 allotment gardens in the city, located in 115 growing sites. Visiting the center, one sees flowers and floral displays everywhere it seems, and for several years the city has even organized the Birmingham Floral Trail, a several mile walking route connecting floral displays. A spectacular green wall, at the city's New Town rail station, has been part of the trail, and indicative of the city's shift towards natureful design (fig 8.2).

A key element in this planning vision of the city as a green and healthy place are the 400 kilometers (250 mi.) of mostly aboveground small waterways. While lacking a major river, Birmingham has an impressive blue network that reaches every part of the city. Urban rivers and streams lay an important foundation for outdoor living and physical activity in cities. Nick Grayson explained to me his notion that opening up access to this network could create the basis for a citywide grid of walking trails and pathways.

The network of small streams through the city, and the occasional flooding that occurs, represent, not problems so much as an opportunities. The city can't engineer its way out of these flood problems, nor should it. His recommendation is to "turn that on its head and work with a grain of nature . . . and you'd say actually that's literally a blueprint to make Birmingham the first walkable city." Unlike in many American cities these streams need not be daylit; they're already at the surface. "But they are hidden and they're unsafe," according to Grayson. The streams are a tremendous urban asset, but one that needs tending, care, and visibility, and it should become a priority to put them to work on behalf of residents.

Many of the medical maladies find their ultimate root cause in chronic stress, and here there is much potential to utilize the environment and nature to make people much healthier than they currently are. Grayson points out that chronic stress has been medically proven to be the cause of our health problems—cancer, depression, dementia, and cardiovascular problems, to name a few. The conditions of the physical environments

**Figure 8.1.** The trees and skyline of the city of Birmingham, UK. Birmingham has declared its intention to become the first biophilic city in the United Kingdom. Credit: Photo compliments of the Birmingham City Council.

in which residents are living greatly influence this chronic stress by creating conditions that foster it or, alternatively, that help to diminish or control it. Nature and greenery are key stress-reducing elements in cities. And Birmingham's extensive network of blue and green assets can be a partial but powerful antidote to these stresses.

The city is developing creative new planning tools to advance this more integrated

**Figure 8.2.** A green wall at the New Street (Rail) Station, Birmingham, UK. Credit: Photo by Tim Beatley.

health–nature–economy framework. One important step will be the designation of so-called Natural Health Improvement Zones, which represent places in the city where health conditions and depravations are overlapping and the most severe. Here investments, both public and private, will be focused and coordinated. In the areas identified as having the greatest need, new greening efforts (trees, green roofs and walls, interventions to enhance mobility and walking) will be concentrated to maximize the health benefits to residents. Here efforts will be made to "intensively green these areas," and "seek to alter or enhance local walking and cycling choices" (City of Birmingham, 2013, p. 16).

### Toward Natural Capital Cities

Birmingham is also impressively moving forward with the assumption that its environment is its essential natural capital from which economy and health must flow, and has declared its intent to be the United Kingdom's, or perhaps the world's, first natural capital city.

Even though the plan is in its early stages, Birmingham already has insights about how to protect and leverage this natural capital. Despite the reputation as a gray industrial locale, Birmingham harbors quite a bit of biodiversity, more impressively so given the highly urbanized context. Nature here includes the only urban National Nature Reserve, the 1000-hectare (2500-acre) Sutton Park. A new comprehensive survey of the flora of the Black Country (the larger urban conurbation that includes the four boroughs to the west of the city) shows remarkable nature. And the process by which the survey occurred—through use of an army of volunteers physically walking the 750 1-kilometer (0.6 mi.) squares—delivers important benefits for health and well-being as well. This work will likely continue to help in reimagining the urban areas as a connected urban ecosystem. Birmingham is now one of only 12 Nature Improvement Areas (what were originally called ecological restoration zones), resulting from a national competition and administered by the Department of Environment, Food and Rural Affairs. Among the 12 areas, Birmingham is the only entirely urban site. As a result some national government funds have been leveraged (about six times over) to provide funds, 43 million pounds in total, over 3 years.

How to estimate and concretize the economic values associated with nature remains a significant challenge, but the connection between health and nature is one place where there are possibilities. Grayson envisions a future in which the health-enhancing value of those streams might then flow back to the city in the form of funds (from forgone medical expenses as more residents walk and spend time in nature), in turn allowing the city to better manage and maintain the streams and trails. He sees a day when the distance that people walk or jog along these stream trails is automatically recorded and sent to their doctor, providing the basis for calculating at least a portion of the health benefits of the city's nature.

And there are other potential new income sources. It turns out that much of the flooding problem along these streams is a function of clogging from downed trees and delayed forest maintenance. Harvesting and extracting some of this wood serves to reduce flood costs, and, through sustainable harvesting, some of this wood could be used as a biomass energy source, producing a further income stream and helping to lower the city's carbon footprint. And there are also green jobs and employment that could result.

As Grayson notes, this more integrative health–nature–economy agenda is also about linking-up and leveraging funds and programs that already exist in these individual areas. This is a model of joint investment in key assets in the city, such as streams and trees, that will deliver multiple and ongoing benefits.

The city is also imagining a new natural capital metric for reviewing and evaluating development projects in the future—one that would broaden the consideration of the scope and stream of potential benefits and expand the range of stakeholders who might benefit (or lose), especially when projects are assessed over a much longer time

**Figure 8.3.** Ancient oak trees provide a visual contrast against the sky in Sutton Park, Birmingham, UK. Sutton is, at 2500 acres (1000 hectares) in size, one of the largest urban parks in Europe, and home to a diversity of flora and fauna, including a herd of rare Exmoor ponies. Credit: Photo by Tim Beatley.

**Box 8.1. Sutton Park: Wild in the City**

Sutton Park is described on the City of Birmingham's web page (http://www.birming-ham.gov.uk/suttonpark) as "delivering a sense of wilderness within an urban environment." Sutton Park, in its size and natural qualities, certainly conveys a wildness, but it is also a landscape that reflects thousands of years of human alteration and habitation. The park was originally a royal forest, then later a deer park. It is an early example of a natural area set aside for the enjoyment of the public, and King Henry VIII deeded the park to the village of Sutton Coldfield in 1528 (now within the City of Birmingham). There is much ancient history present here, including prehistoric "burnt mounds" and a section of a major Roman road (ca. AD 80) running through the park.

It is a National Nature Reserve and Site of Special Scientific Significance, and has been designated as a Scheduled Ancient Monument (something the park shares with Stonehenge).

At around 2500 acres (1000 hectares) in size, Sutton is said to be the largest urban park in Europe. Located only 6 miles (9.6 km) north of Birmingham's city center, it is very close to where many urban residents live. It is a remarkable landscape—a mix of ancient oak woodlands, heathlands, wetlands, and ponds—it provides opportunities both for remote contemplation and for more active recreational activities. The heathlands are quite impressive, a remnant of what much of the British midlands looked like. It has been a working landscape and for many years supported cattle and sheep. In more recent years Exmoor ponies (a shy and rare breed) have been introduced, in part to keep nonnative trees and plants in check.

The park is home to diverse and abundant wildlife. There are foxes, hedgehogs, common lizards, 12 species of dragonflies, and of course many species of birds (e.g., redstarts, warblers, and woodpeckers), for which the park serves as a significant breeding area. Several species of orchids grow in the marshy areas of the park. There are 29 species of butterflies, including the notable holly blue butterfly (*Celastrina argiolus*), associated with the holly forest understory and chosen as the emblem of Friends of Sutton Park Association, the active stewards of the park since 1950.

The park is heavily used and highly prized, and it sees more than 2 million visitors each year. From dog-walking and strolling, to fishing, to rowing, a number of different activities are accommodated within the boundaries of the park. On the day I spent rambling and exploring in Sutton most others I encountered were doing the same. It is a park that permits one to escape the sights and sounds of the city, and other people if one chooses, and while there are pathways and preestablished walks, it is a park that accommodates launching off in any direction that looks intriguing. Getting lost was a worry (for me), but losing track of time (and becoming lost in time) were more likely outcomes.

*—Tim Beatley*

frame (Grayson mentions 50 years). With a natural capital frame, Grayson envisions new stakeholders that might wish to co-invest in future developments. "The Water Company might get a benefit [from a proposed project] in 30 or 40 years' time because it's pre-programed that it will meet its demand . . . and won't overshoot [the supply of water]."

## The First Biophilic City in the United Kingdom

Birmingham is in many ways already a very natureful city. It can boast one of the largest urban parks in Europe, Sutton Park (box 8.1). Sutton is at once an ancient and a modern park, and a place of remarkable beauty and respite and wildness (fig. 8.3). It is beloved and an important part of the city's natural capital.

In the spring of 2014, Birmingham took important steps toward becoming the UK's first biophilic city. The Birmingham Council adopted an official resolution and declared its intent to extend and expand its green vision, to explicitly aspire to bio-philic urbanism. And it announced these goals at a major national conference taking place in Birmingham—the annual meeting of the Institute of Chartered Foresters. What ways the city will become more "biophilic" remain to be seen, but clearly they will involve creative integration and merging of natural capitalism ideas, and a strong focus on health and equity.

And it will undoubtedly continue through a strong spirit of collaboration and partnerships. The presence of strong universities will be an important factor mov-ing forward. The University of Birmingham is an important local asset, and is, for instance, engaged in world class research of forest ecology (e.g. Rob MacKenzie's work and newly established forest research center) and urban ecology (e.g. James Hales' and his colleagues' work around bats and light; University of Birmingham, 2015). These are important areas of research and scholarship, with implications beyond Bir-mingham, but which find local application and which can serve to guide and inspire future urban policy and planning in Birmingham. Birmingham City University rep-resents yet another set of resources, with students studying for fields from landscape architecture to film (and recently a group of film students making a documentary film about Birmingham as a biophilic city!).

Birmingham is an emerging example and leading case of a city that recognizes at once the importance of preserving and growing its natural capital, and the many ecosystem services and values delivered by it, and the emotional and health values that everyday proximity to nature provide. As Nick Grayson is now proclaiming in his presentations about his city, it is Birmingham "a natural city" but also "a biophilic city."

# 9

# Portland, Oregon:
## *Green Streets in a River City*
### Julia Triman

The city of Portland, Oregon, is situated in the US Pacific Northwest at the confluence of the Willamette and Columbia Rivers. The city is known for its close proximity to an abundance of beautiful natural scenery, including the Columbia Gorge, Mount Hood, the high desert, and the Oregon Coast. Portland also has an impressive amount of nature within city limits, and many people and organizations there are dedicated to stewarding this nature. Like many US cities, Portland also has a significant amount of impervious surface in the form of pavement, buildings, and other hardscaping. Throughout the city's history, many efforts have been taken, with more under way, to find places for vegetation and wildlife, even in the densest areas, fostering biophilic urbanism at multiple scales across the city.

## Green Streets

Due to geographic and climatic conditions, for much of the year Portland's roofs, streets, and people are covered in everything from a fine mist to a steady downpour of rain. These consistently moist conditions make Portland the lush, green, beautiful city that it is, but also present ongoing challenges for managing rainwater. The city's Bureau of Environmental Services and other divisions have accepted this challenge in the form of their forward-thinking and exemplary Green Streets Initiative. In the 1990s, in response to state pressure to better manage stormwater and pollutant runoff into streams and rivers of the region, the City of Portland developed a stormwater management plan to change the way water flowed and was captured throughout the city. In the early 2000s, a Sustainable Stormwater

Management Program was formed within the Bureau of Environmental Services, and among several planned interventions was the construction of a series of "green streets" throughout the city (see box 9.1 for more about the green streets program). These green streets include landscaped curb extensions (fig. 9.1), bioswales, planter strips, pervious pavement, and street trees, all of which collect and retain rainwater and in many cases add bits of green space and wildlife habitat to otherwise hard-scaped environments. Many of these interventions, in addition to retaining water and fostering a greener environment, also provide ways for people to interact with and enjoy the water—the sound of it trickling and the sight of lush vegetation popping up on the side of the street. Reserving streetside space for vegetation also provides a buffer between pedestrians and autos, and adds visual and multi-sensory interest for those driving, cycling, and riding transit through the city.

### Riverine Biophilia

While the Willamette River, which runs through and connects the heart of Portland's downtown, has been a vital part of the city's life since its founding, human activities in the city and along the river have not always promoted water health and quality. In the early 1990s, around the same time that the Green Streets Initiative began, the city developed a "River Renaissance" vision and strategy, and human impact on and care for the river has been changing dramatically since then. As part of early efforts, the city produced a Willamette River Atlas to document and publicize existing land and water uses in an effort to aid in the "restoration of the Willamette River's health for the benefit of fish, wildlife, and people" (City of Portland, Oregon, 2001). Over the years, work has been ongoing, both to remediate adverse impacts on the rivers and to reconnect people with the water flowing through the city. A large part of these efforts has been Portland's

**Figure 9.1.** One of the more than 1400 green streets in Portland, Oregon. These bioswales collect stormwater and also provide an important measure of nature in this compact, walkable city. Credit: Photo by Tim Beatley.

## Box 9.1. Green Streets

Managing stormwater is a challenging task for most urban landscapes across the world. Among the many sustainable strategies being used to manage stormwater, the tactic of green streets is one of the most compelling. The City of Portland, Oregon, has one of the most successful green streets programs in the United States. Green streets not only assist with stormwater management but also bring nature back into cities.

According to the City of Portland, a green street can be defined as a "street that uses vegetated facilities to manage stormwater runoff at its source" (City of Portland, n.d.). Green streets initiatives have many positive effects on communities, ranging from improving water quality and reducing flows to beautifying urban settings with native plants.

With 3 feet of rainfall each year and approximately 70 square miles of impervious surfaces from rooftops and pavement, it is easy to understand why Portland must prioritize stormwater management. A traditional hard infrastructure system left the city facing sewer overflows, flooding, and water pollution, leading to a Clean Water Act lawsuit.

With the lawsuit requiring a series of mandates, Portland could have spent $150 million in increasing pipe networks or consider other ways to absorb and filter excess stormwater. To grapple with these issues, Portland created a two-pronged approach in 2007 that included a traditional pipe system but also incorporated green infrastructure. Green streets have been used as part of this green infrastructure approach and include a range of strategies, from simple street planters and green strips to more ambitious retention ponds and parks.

Portland's green streets initiative includes four different strategies. The first is modifying an existing planting strip to allow stormwater in and to add plantings that absorb and filter water. The second is to create curb extensions where plantings replace street parking. This helps to shorten pedestrian crossings while also increasing permeable surfaces. Street planters are another way of greening streets when surface planting is not feasible. These planters usually consist of concrete boxes along parking spaces that divide the street parking from the sidewalks. Finally, identifying unused urban spaces that can be transformed into parklike settings is another example of a Portland green street strategy.

Design is not the only tactic that Portland city officials have used to attain stormwater management goals. The city has developed many policy tools to support and extend the green streets efforts, including a watershed management plan, stormwater management manual, green street policy, city building eco-roof policy, and a Green Street Inventory sheet.

In addition to the many environmental and social benefits, Portland's experiment with green streets saved the city an estimated $60 million dollars in pipe replacement costs. Green streets have been a win–win for Portland, Oregon, and for many communities around the world.                                         —*Carla Jones*

commitment to converting existing impervious spaces in the city to green infrastructure projects (such as green streets). According to Matt Burlin, the City of Portland's Willamette Watershed Environmental Program Coordinator, adoption of green infrastructure strategies in many cases started with very small scale pilot projects, which were monitored and evaluated for performance over time. A larger, coordinated effort, the city's Tabor to the River program, emerged out of both previous small-scale green infrastructure efforts and a larger mission to update and rehabilitate the city's stormwater management infrastructure, starting with the Brooklyn Creek Basin on the east side of the city, spanning from Mount Tabor to the east to the banks of the Willamette to the west. The Tabor to the River program features repairs and replacement of stormwater sewer pipe, along with as many as 600 sustainable stormwater facilities and planting several thousand new street trees in the area. In addition to infrastructural improvements, the program intends to increase native wildlife habitat, raise awareness among Portland residents about the importance of watershed health, and improve resident and neighborhood connections to the Willamette.

Another tangible way Portlanders are connecting with the river is through The Big Float, an annual event begun in 2011 by the nonprofit organization Human Access Project. Each July, Portlanders float across the Willamette River in inner tubes and on other flotation devices (fig. 9.2). While one of the key ingredients of The Big Float is fun, the event is also intended to encourage people to come into closer contact with the waters of the Willamette, promoting the biophilic value and importance of preserving the river and continuing to develop recreational opportunities in the riverine heart of the city (TheBigFloat.com).

In event invitations, organizers explain that the reason for The Big Float is "to give our river a hug"—and Portlanders certainly do! Each year since the event started, more and more people participate—in 2014, more than 1500 people floated across the river, and over 2500 were expected for the 2016 event. Floaters congregate on the west side of the river, march in a "paddler's parade" to the put-in point, then float downstream for a beach party celebrating a successful float and continued improvements to the Willamette's water quality and accessibility. Such an event is a great example of grassroots efforts to connect with and improve the "blue" nature within the city, encouraging people of all ages to have memorable experiences on the water, sparking curiosity about and care for a previously underacknowledged urban nature resource.

The Big Float is not the only opportunity to get on the water in Portland; there is activity along the Columbia River as well, including the annual Columbia Slough Regatta, and other paddling events offered by the Columbia Slough Watershed Council. The Council also runs the Slough School, with education programs both in

**Figure 9.2.** The Big Float in Portland is a massive watery party, where every manner of watergoing vessel can be seen. Credit: Photo by Matt Burlin.

the classroom and on the water for students in kindergarten through college, as well as the Tadpole Tales program for children ages 3 to 5 with their parents, encouraging Portland's youngest citizens to develop early and lasting connections with the aquatic nature in their own backyards (Columbia Slough Watershed Council 2016).

## Portland Parks

Portland has an impressive parks history, dating back to the city's founding in the mid-1850s. At the turn of the twentieth century, the Parks Board commissioned a study by the Olmsted brothers' landscape firm, which recommended, among other things, a series of waterfront plazas along the banks of the Willamette. Throughout the early to mid-1900s, city leaders chose to build flood control walls along the river banks and erected a freeway (Harbor Drive) along the west banks in the 1940s. It wasn't until Governor Tom McCall initiated a study in 1968 to explore creating a waterfront park along the west banks of the Willamette that the Olmsted brothers' original recommendations were realized (City of Portland, Oregon, Parks and Recreation 2016a). As a result of Governor McCall's efforts, the City of Portland demolished Harbor Drive, during a time period when many other cities were constructing highways separating downtowns from their waterfronts, and constructed new public space along the river that would become known as Tom McCall Waterfront Park. Today the park is a success story of reconnecting Portlanders to the river and includes over 35 acres of public space along the riverbanks. The park has a number of water features, a plaza of cherry blossoms, and a great lawn popular with picnickers and concertgoers during sunny summer months. In recent years, the east banks of the Willamette have become more accessible as well, through the construction of the Eastbank Esplanade. The Esplanade, a floating walkway that gently undulates as you walk along it, giving the feeling that you are walking both along and "with" the water, extends from the Hawthorne Bridge to the south to the Steel Bridge, with a connection under the Steel Bridge to Tom McCall Waterfront Park. In addition to being a spectacular way to walk or jog right along the river, the Esplanade is also a demonstration project for improved habitat areas for fish and wildlife (City of Portland, Oregon, Parks and Recreation 2016b). Lucky passers-by may encounter wildlife such as beavers, herons, and salmon, depending on the time of day and season.

Portland boasts one of the highest per capita park space ratios in the United States, with over 14,000 acres of parks. Ranked high among US cities for providing parks and access to parks, Portland's parks range from tiny to massive and are known for being innovative in terms of design, as well as being loved by residents and visitors. One of the newest parks in Portland's system is Tanner Springs Park, a nearly 1-acre constructed wetland at the north end of the Pearl District that evokes the natural history and ecological processes of the neighborhood (fig. 9.3). The park's name pays homage to Tanner Creek, which once flowed through the area and is now enclosed in underground pipes. One of a series of parks and public spaces conceived during the planning process for transforming the predominantly industrial area into a new mixed-use neighborhood, Tanner Springs was designed by the firm Atelier Dreiseitl, with collaboration and input from over 300 local residents. Although small, Tanner Springs Park allows neighbors in surrounding midrise residential buildings the opportunity for respite and connection with plantings and water features that evoke the feeling of what the land might have been like long before urban development was initiated.

A bit farther west, in May 2012, citizens and experts conducted the first-ever bioblitz of Portland's Forest Park, the largest forested park entirely within a city's limits in the United States. Teams found salamanders, arthropods, owls, and more—a total of nearly 250 species in 24 hours ("Oregon Field Guide: Forest Park BioBlitz" 2012). Forest Park, over 5000 acres of protected forestland and recreation area within Portland's city limits, is one of the city's best-loved natural jewels and provides many opportunities for residents and visitors to connect with nature, whether on a bioblitz, hiking or bicycling on the 30-mile Wildwood Trail, or simply taking in nature sounds and spectacular views. In contrast to Tanner Springs and other local neighborhood parks, Forest Park is a park at the scale of the city, a place where one can encounter wild nature and find peace and solitude in a forested setting. While many people drive to access Forest Park, it is also possible to reach the park via city bus, or, for the adventurous, by a steep hike through winding hilly

**Figure 9.3.** Tanner Springs Park, a small but intensively used park, is found in the Pearl District of Portland. Credit: Photo by Ramboll Studio Dreiseitl.

neighborhood streets. In addition to exploring the park on your own, there are a myriad of events throughout the year, including the All Trails Challenge, in which participants commit with a team or on their own to complete the length of trails in Forest Park within 6 months. Other events include Discovery Hikes with different themes throughout the year, and the Forest Park Marathon, held every August as a fundraiser for the Forest Park Conservancy (Forest Park Conservancy 2016). Forest Park also has its own iPhone application, "Forest Park PDX for iPhone," which provides detailed navigation and trail maps, as well as information about the park's history and ecology. Parks are not the only places Portlanders seek and appreciate urban wildlife—urban birders can be found throughout the city, and young and old gather to witness spectacular urban bird moments, such as Vaux's swifts roosting at Chapman Elementary School (box 9.2; fig. 9.4).

### The Intertwine Alliance

In addition to being home to an impressive array of parks and natural areas, the people of Portland also take great pride in these places and have considerable organizational efforts in place to advocate for the importance of nature at the city and regional level. One prominent example is the Intertwine Alliance, a regional nonprofit organization

**Box 9.2. Vaux's Swifts**

Every September, Portlanders gather for Swift Watch, a truly spectacular experience at Chapman Elementary School in northwest Portland. During their fall migration, the captivating Vaux's swifts use the school's chimney as a place for their evening roost. Similar to the spectacle of Mexican free-tailed bats emerging from under the Congress Avenue bridge in Austin, Texas, the birds, as they are preparing to migrate south, fly by the hundreds into the chimney in the early evenings.

The Audubon Society of Portland has been tracking a specific population of the species that has been returning to Chapman Elementary since the 1980s. The school is one of the largest known roosting sites for the species (Audubon Society of Portland 2015). On some evenings, over 2000 people gather on the lawn and in a nearby park to watch and listen to the birds make their grand entrance into the chimney. The crowd can be heard exclaiming "oohs" and "aahs" of delight at the speed and intensity of the giant flock of birds. Often, representatives from the Portland Audubon Society will be on hand to deliver information and answer questions about the Vaux's swifts. That so many people gather to observe and delight in the wonder of these birds is indicative of a special kind of care and interest in urban wildlife, one not unusual to find in Portland.

—*Julia Triman*

formed in 2011 to formalize a coalition of private firms, public agencies, and nonprofits working to advance the position of nature and natural areas in the greater Portland region through acquisition of funding and leveraging investments, and finding ways to "more fully engage residents with the outdoors and nature" (TheIntertwine. org/about). Members of the Intertwine Alliance recently collaborated to produce two significant documents: "The Regional Conservation Strategy" and "The Biodiversity Guide," intended to steer future conservation efforts as well as increase public understanding and appreciation for the region's native plants and wildlife.

The Intertwine Alliance worked for 2 years to develop "The Regional Conservation Strategy," a freely available document that the authors describe as an "owner's manual" to address the many challenges facing nature and natural systems in the Greater Portland area, while at the same time finding new and innovative ways to inspire residents to find connections with and care about nearby nature and nature in the greater region. The Regional Conservation Strategy builds on a long tradition of conservation planning in the Portland region, but it is also distinct from previous plans and comparable plans for other regions for its consideration of nature and conservation practices in the urban setting. Strategies are tailored to fit individual

**Figure 9.4.** Vaux's swifts arrive in dramatic fashion at Chapman Elementary School in Portland, Oregon. Credit: Photo by Matt Burlin.

landscape types, including natural areas, working lands, and developed areas. Conservation recommendations are guided by a conservation mapping method that prioritizes land of highest ecological value, which can be understood at a variety of scales, including regional, local, and neighborhood scales.

Initially formed with 28 nonprofit groups, the Intertwine Alliance is now an active coalition with over 100 partner organizations, with a set of interrelated initiatives under way. The Intertwine Alliance uses a "collective impact" approach, seeking common ground among diverse organizations and investment in initiatives such as active transportation, conservation, equity, and health and nature. The Intertwine is both a place and an organizational and advocacy strategy, and Alliance members actively share events and opportunities to advance the interests of nature and connect people with nature in the region.

## Nature in Neighborhoods

Impressive efforts are being made at the local level as well. Portland's regional government, Metro, sponsors a grant program called Nature in Neighborhoods, which disperses annual grants to individuals, community groups, nonprofits, and government agency applicants wishing to improve natural features in their community (Metro 2016). Grants are awarded in three categories: Restoration, Conservation Education, and Capital Grants. Examples of grant recipients include a coalition of community partners who transformed a vacant lot into Nadaka Nature Park just outside city limits in Gresham; OakQuest, a collaborative community mapping project to document and promote conservation of Oregon white oak ecosystems in the Portland region; and the One North Community Courtyard, a restoration project at the Catlin Gabel School creating a natural area with an easement for public access.

Metro gives priority to neighborhood grant requests that will bring nature to underserved areas, and those with multiple and diverse community partners. The grants are awarded on a yearly cycle, and were initially seeded by a 2006 natural areas bond measure. Grants may range from less than $25,000 to as much as $1 million; a total of $4.5 million was awarded for the 2014 grant cycle, partly in thanks to a 2013 voter-supported Natural Areas Levy, which also allowed for the establishment of Conservation Education grants (Metro 2014). Seeding money to local groups not only provides the immediate benefits of neighborhood improvements but also draws partners and organizations together in unique ways, creating mini-coalitions for improving human–nature connections throughout the city and the region.

## Conclusion

The city of Portland is home to incredible natural beauty and ecological complexity, and also to many residents and organizations committed to protecting, enhancing, and finding ways to enjoy the nature around them. Citizens and community leaders have found ways to draw upon the unique conditions of the city and the region: the wet climate, the river flowing through the city, and a strong sense of place that the various types of nature throughout the city—from Mount Tabor to the winding trails in Forest Park to the vegetation taking root along the city's green streets—elicit among residents and visitors. Portland is known as a place people want to "keep weird," and events like The Big Float simultaneously draw upon this reputation and spirit while bringing attention to the riverine nature at the heart of the city.

Ideally, other cities looking to emulate Portland's biophilic efforts might draw upon unique climatic conditions, the "personality" of the city and its people, and local ecological history (as at Tanner Springs Park). All of these things together set Portland apart as a place with a variety of efforts at multiple scales that continues to build upon a strong foundation of biophilic urbanism. From the waters of the Willamette and Columbia Rivers to the dense vegetation in Forest Park, to the hundreds of green streets throughout the city, Portland continues to build upon its rich natural history and look for ways to increase the balance between future development and a nature-rich city and populace.

# 10

# San Francisco, California:
## *Biophilic City by the Bay*

San Francisco has often been understood as the gold standard when it comes to sustainable cities. It has an impressive waste recycling rate (currently exceeding 80 percent in its landfill diversion rate) and has set the ambitious goal of reaching zero waste. It has a long history of supporting solar and renewable energy and has formally adopted the precautionary principle, using it to do such things as shift away from the use of pesticides and herbicides for vegetation management in its parks and natural areas. It has also has been participating in our Biophilic Cities Project as a partner city for several years.

San Francisco has abundant nature and is taking many steps to steward, protect, and restore this nature. It has been innovating in urban ecology and urban nature in many ways, from innovative micro-parks ("parklets") to temporary use agreements, to shifting its development codes to make it possible (and legal) to undertake many important forms of biophilic design and planning (e.g., installation of sidewalk gardens, commercial urban farming). More recently it has adopted innovative standards for bird-safe buildings and, in many ways, is taking steps to make room for butterflies and other species.

### A City Prized for Its Parks and Nature

The city's park system has also been highly praised, with especially notable elements including Golden Gate Park, the Presidio, and Mount Sutro. The Trust for Public Land, in their annual City Parks Report, is often complimentary to San Francisco compared with many other cities. In their 2014 report, San Francisco achieves the first rank among the nation's 50 largest cities in terms of percent of the population within walkable distance of parks (deemed to be a half mile). The report estimates this number at an impressive 98.2 percent! (Trust for Public Land 2014, 12).

But when it comes to other aspects of nature, such as tree canopy coverage and smaller green spaces, the picture of the city is less impressive. San Francisco is a largely developed city, with few opportunities to establish large new parks or green areas, and with significant space limitations for planting new trees and greenery.

An important part of San Francisco's biophilic innovations are the creative new ways that very small parks and green spaces have been created, notably the installation of new sidewalk gardens, and the idea of parklets, small parks and gathering spaces created from two or more on-street parking spaces (fig. 10.1).

Is it possible for a city to grow and develop densely, to provide all the qualities we recommend for conditions of sustainable urbanism, but at the same time foster, protect, and restore nature and biodiversity? San Francisco demonstrates that it is indeed possible to have nature and density, and it offers some creative ideas for doing so.

### Growing Food in the City

San Francisco has a long and proud history as a city that has grown food, a place where victory gardens were planted in front of City Hall during World War II, for instance, and in more recent years where new and creative places to insert gardens and grow food have been explored. And San Francisco has been a leader in code reform to make it permissible and legal to grow and sell food commercially in many more places in the city.

Some of the city's innovations involve imaginative arrangements for temporary use, like the one established for Hayes Valley Farm in 1989. One of the inherent risks of living in the Bay Area, and in California more generally, is earthquakes. There have been many, and small ones occur with considerable frequency. Occasionally larger events create unusual opportunities to rethink community and place. The Loma Prieta earthquake in 1989 did just that. One opportunity presented by this disaster involved the Central Freeway, where an on and off ramp collapsed in the central neighborhood of Hayes Valley. A decision supported by the neighborhood was to convert this land (2.2 acres in size), into something that would contribute to the neighborhood. Eventually the land was transferred from CalTrans (the state's department of transportation) to the city, with the idea that it would be made available for private development. But a unique Interim Use Agreement was struck allowing for the operation of an urban farm, what became

**Figure 10.1.** San Francisco is a relatively built-up city but is still finding ways to convert small spaces to parks and nature. Its green urban innovations include parklets, street parks, and opportunities for neighborhoods to install sidewalk landscaping. This image shows the city's first residential parklet, and its designer Jane Martin. Credit: Photo by Tim Beatley.

the Hayes Valley Farm. It operated for about 3 years, with an extensive network of dedicated volunteers, until, consistent with the temporary use agreement, it was discontinued, and land was transferred to private developers. Its existence, however, continues to foster biophilic initiatives throughout the city.

I had the chance to visit the Hayes Valley Farm several times. In a short period it became a significant center for the urban farming community in the city. There were workshops, and an on-site community seed bank was created. It was a place where gardening enthusiasts and permaculturists would meet and compare notes. As the farm closed, many of the plants and fruit trees on the farm were moved to other sites.

While there was a certain understandable sadness when the farm use ended, it is also true that the farm served as the catalyst for many other projects throughout the city and also served to cultivate a new view of urban farming, including modifications to the city's zoning code to make it legal to sell food grown on one's land in the city and also to facilitate the processing of food.

The so-called legacy projects catalyzed by the Hayes Valley Farm include one started and now run by the local beekeeping organization Bee-Cause. Called the Bee Farm, it also runs a 2-year Beekeeping Apprenticeship Program, "designed to train new beekeepers who will manage SF Bee-Cause honey bee colonies, on a volunteer basis, at one of our San Francisco beekeeping sites" (San Francisco Permaculture Guild n.d.).

Another project that has benefited from the Hayes Valley example is the Please Touch Garden on Grove Street (fig. 10.2). A collaboration of the Lighthouse for the Blind and Visibility Impaired, and the Arts Intersection, it is described as an example of "the greening of a public eyesore into a multi-use community space that would be accessible to all, regardless of disability" (see http://pleasetouch-garden.org/story.html). It is another temporary use, combining arts and urban agriculture. It is intended, among other things, to be a demonstration site for new urban agricultural ideas and technologies, such as Habitile, a kind of stackable vertical wall made from recycled foam and styrofoam, the creation of local designer Aurora Mahassine.

## Trees and Trails in the Dense Coastal City

San Francisco is not a city with abundant trees and forests, and the estimated tree canopy coverage is a relatively low 12 to 13 percent. But the city, which historically and geologically is largely made up of coastal dunes, has never had much of a forest, and the trees that do exist, largely eucalyptus, are not native to the region. That said, there is a goal to plant more trees, and several organizations and agencies have played a key role.

Foremost is the nonprofit Friends of the Urban Forest (FUF). They are able to plant about 1200 trees a year and have served as both an active volunteer-based tree-planting organization and a major advocate for urban trees in San Francisco. FUF does many different things and runs a number of different tree-related programs in the city. These include an innovative youth program, for example. There is an open-source Tree Map, and a tree carbon calculator.

In recent years maintaining and caring for the city's trees has been a controversial topic, with the city's department of public works seeking to shift care of street trees to private homeowners. And city funds for maintenance and care of the city's trees have been in decline. It is fair to say that the City by the Bay has had a conflicted relationship with trees, and this will likely continue in the future. Nevertheless, organizations like FUF continue to do good work and to make at least some progress at growing and expanding the urban tree stock.

**Figure 10.2.** The Please Touch Garden on Grove Street in San Francisco. Credit: Photo by Tim Beatley.

The city's controversy surrounding its trees may be changing, however; 2014 saw the preparation of an Urban Forest Plan, a collaboration between the City Planning Department and FUF. The first phase of work has been focused on street trees.

Another dimension to the nature story in San Francisco is the impressive work developing a regional and local trail system. Dating back to the late 1980s is the San Francisco Bay Trail, a bold vision of a 500-mile-long continuous trail that would encircle the San Francisco Bay. It would provide unusual visual access to the Bay shoreline and serve to connect more than 130 parks. Much of it—some 340 miles— has already been completed, and eventually it will cross 47 municipalities and 9 counties. It is an impressive biophilic vision and an impressive accomplishment in that so much of it has already been completed.

One segment of the Bay Area Trail that runs through the city will correspond to what is referred to as the Blue Greenway. The Blue Greenway consists of the 13-mile corridor running along the city's eastern waterfront. The idea is, in part, to use the greenway as a catalyst for cleaning up contaminated sites and for bolstering the working waterfront in these areas.

**Wild Nature in the City by the Bay**

There is an immense amount of nature in San Francisco, perhaps more than most would think. The list includes larger mammals (e.g., coyotes and gray foxes), diverse plant life (e.g., the Franciscan manzanita), and remarkable birds (e.g., the Anna's hummingbird). The larger context of the Bay Area provides even more remarkable nature. There are healthy populations of mountain lions, and efforts like the Bay Area Puma Project work to track and understand them and to educate about them (see the Pioneer Profile of Zara McDonald, founder of the project, in chap. 13, box 13.1). The aquatic and marine setting of the city mean that chances are one will encounter a marine organism—like the now-famous sea lions of Pier 39 (there is now a sea lion cam for watching them at home or from the office: http://www.pier39.com/home /the-sea-lion-story/sea-lion-webcam-2/). Not far offshore there is a remarkable watery migration route followed by 15,000 gray whales, who sometimes venture into the Bay: it is the longest migration—10,000 miles—made by a mammal. The local non-profit Nature in the City has produced an impressive map of the city's nature (see http://sfrecpark.org/wp-content/uploads/nature_in_city_map.pdf), though it succumbs to our usual terrestrial biases.

There are some emerging good examples of efforts at protecting and restoring wild nature in dense urban environments. A combination of the efforts of bottom-up community groups, and top-down city programs and policies, the city is pioneering a new urban ecology that understands the city as a place of nature and urbanites as stewards and cultivators of that nature, seeing the sidewalks, the backyards, the many interstices and other leftover spaces in the city as opportunities for bringing back native wildness.

The City has designated a certain considerable acreage as Natural Areas, together making up nearly a third of the area of the city's parks (about 1100 acres). These are areas maintained by the city's Department of Recreation and Parks Department, though with significant help from volunteers from other local organizations, such as the Presidio Trust. The restoration of these areas has been guided by a Significant Natural Resource Areas Management Plan, originally adopted in 1995.

The Open Space Element of the City's general plan defines and lays out criteria for the designation of these areas. A Significant Natural Resource Area is defined as "(1) relatively undisturbed remnants of San Francisco's original landscape that either support diverse and significant indigenous plant and wildlife habitats or contain rare geologic formations or riparian zones; (2) sites that contain rare, threatened, or endangered species or areas likely to support these species; and (3) areas that are adjacent to other protected natural resource areas." (San Francisco Recreation and Parks

Department 2016). A management plan is to be prepared for each of these natural areas that will identify the needed restoration and ecological management steps.

An interesting case of a wild area in the city can be seen in Mount Sutro (fig. 10.3), one of the highest points in the city (900 ft.) and one of the largest parcels of land in the city. Named after Adolph Sutro, a nineteenth-century landowner, the land sits adjacent to the University of California–San Francisco (UCSF) Medical Center. Its unique micro-climate (e.g., fog during summer months) has meant the development of some unique native assemblages.

With the encouragement of UCSF a volunteer group was formed in 2006 to help with habitat restoration and trail development. Sutro Stewards has emerged as one of the largest and most active groups of volunteers in the city. Already significant restoration of native plants and trees has occurred, and they operate a nursery that specializes in growing these now rare species.

One of the key issues here surrounds how to manage the nonnative trees present on site—the blue-gum eucalyptus, Monterey pine, and Monterey cypress—and this has been a point of considerable controversy for some citizens who live in the surrounding neighborhoods who have come to love and enjoy these trees. The city has decided to move ahead with replacing some of the 18,000 nonnative trees with native trees and plants (Harless 2013).

**Figure 10.3.** Mount Sutro provides a dramatic view of the city. Credit: Photo by Tim Beatley.

### Making Room for Butterflies

One of San Francisco's key claims to innovation in biophilic planning is finding creative ways to fit more nature into an already heavily built and developed setting. This has occurred through a number of interesting new mechanisms, including new permits that allow for the installation of so-called parklets and sidewalk gardens (more about these later).

One innovative program, called Street Parks, has sought to make hundreds of small parcels of land, owned by the city's Department of Public Works, available for neighborhoods to reclaim and repurpose as parks and community spaces. Groups must apply to take over a parcel and must prepare a plan for what they intend to do with the land, what they intend to plant, and generally how the land will be used. The designs generated by community applicants are quite detailed and in many cases reflect considerable design sophistication. The San Francisco Parks Alliance, a nongovernmental organization, provides training programs and helps the groups to organize the work they would like to undertake. There are already 120 parcels that have been designated as Street Parks.

One group participating in the Street Parks program is Nature in the City, founded in 2005, just before the city hosted World Environment Day. Peter Brastow founded the group and now serves as the city's biodiversity coordinator. I had the chance to visit with him at the site of the street park his group is working to restore. It is a small piece of sloping land, a place that might be overlooked even by residents of the neighborhood, but that has in the last few months been transformed into a verdant swath of native greenery. Nature in the City has taken on seven parcels, that, together with existing larger parks, will form a habitat corridor for butterflies. Providing habitat for the coastal green hairstreak (*Callophrys dumetorum*), a local endangered butterfly, is a major goal (box 10.1). Getting neighbors to plant host species, such as coast buckweed and deerweed, as well as nectar plants, in their yards and spaces around their homes, is a longer-term goal.

The mission of Nature in the City, Brastow tells me, is to "preserve and restore all the natural lands and wild habitat left in the city and the northern tip of the peninsula, and to connect nature and people where we live through getting to know native plants and animals in their neighborhoods and throughout the city." It is a tall order, but essential in an increasingly urbanized world where contact with nature seems difficult and a low priority. Connecting with the less exotic nature, the more everyday nature, in and around where people live is essential. Brastow says, "We're really trying to transform our culture to be more in tune with the natural environment and it's as important to do it here as in Brazil and Borneo and Burundi and everywhere else."

**Box 10.1. Tigers on Market, San Francisco**

In addition to Nature in the City's efforts to create habitat for the locally endangered green hairstreak butterfly, other species are getting a boost as well. The latest chapter in San Francisco has been an effort to study and raise awareness about the western tiger swallowtail butterflies that inhabit Market Street, the main commercial and pedestrian corridor in the city's downtown. Artists and lepidopterists Amber Hasselbring and Liam O'Brien have taken to the field to study these butterflies and have found a remarkably re-silient urban population. The butterflies live in and patrol the canopy of European London plane trees, an urban environment that largely mimics the stream or river corridor that would be their natural home.

A "convergence of happenstance," is how Hasselbring and O'Brien explain it to me. "It's sort of using Market Street as if it were the Colorado River cutting through the Grand Canyon," O'Brien says. This realization has led the two to argue that the important habitat provided by the trees should be taken into account when the street is redesigned (one op-tion being considered would eliminate many of the trees, though this now seems unlikely thanks to their advocacy).

"We have an opportunity to connect so many people in a dense downtown to a moment in nature, and that's really the thrilling thing," O'Brien says.

How the renovation of the street can accommodate and further enhance the habitat needs of the butterflies remains to be seen, but Hasselbring and O'Brien are working on this through their project Tigers on Market (ideas range from butterfly kiosks to installing Swal-lowtail Swales with new nectar sources such as flowers).                    —*Tim Beatley*

To the east of the butterfly corridor is an even more interesting concept for the city: a combination of parks and green spaces that Nature in the City is calling the Twin Peaks Bioregional Park. The first of its kind in the city, it would seek to tie together several of the largest parks in the hilly center of San Francisco: Mount Sutro, Twin Peaks, Glen Canyon Park, and Laguna Honda Hospital and Park. The bioregion could provide the basis for coordinated management of these lands, both for but-terflies and for people, and raise awareness of the need for butterfly habitat as well. Part of this bold vision is imagining a connected trail system that would allow one to hike from Crissy Field in the north (an old army airfield converted to wetlands and meadows), through the center of this dense city (right through the Bioregional Park), ending up at Candlestick Point on the Bay.

Nature in the City works on behalf of butterflies in other ways, notably through a new initiative Tigers on Market, an effort to understand and support Market Street (the main commercial boulevard in the city) as a habitat zone for Western Tiger Swallowtails (see box 10.1). Nature in the City does other important work. It has published a natural heritage map of the city, now in its second printing, and thousands have been distributed to residents. Every city should have such a map. Brastow describes the map as an important tool: "We have these wonderful places right here in the city, and [the map] gives them a way to figure out how to get to them." The organization also produces a native butterfly guide and organizes popular nature hikes in the city (about a dozen of these urban treks were offered last year, and all were packed).

### ¡Vamos a la Playa!

My favorite aspect of the street parks program is the requirement that each street park must assign ongoing management to one or more community stewards, volunteers who live in the neighborhood. Stewards must agree to shepherd the parcel for a minimum of 4 years; no small commitment, of course, but that is part of the point. The stewards come from many walks of life. Brastow tells me of one of the more enthusiastic steward is a retired fireman, who is propagating native plants at his home for planting in the butterfly corridor.

Another interesting example San Francisco is is the new La Playa Park, in the Sunset district of the city. La Playa Park is an impressive demonstration of what is actually possible in a very small and oddly shaped urban space. It is a slender, narrow site, 550 feet long, but only 16 feet wide (fig. 10.4). A small amount of funding for this impressive urban microspace was provided through a Community Challenge Grant, through the mayor's office, but for the most part this is a low-cost project. It is a labor of love and already seems a beloved neighborhood site, a pearl, the more so for all the effort and ingenuity that have gone into its creation.

It is essentially a median strip, quite narrow in spots, that is actively and vigorously being turned into a linear green oasis and park, part native plants sanctuary, part community gathering space, and including of all things a bocci ball field. The merging of these different uses arose from the fact that two different applicants sought to use the space. Brianna Shaeffer, one of the stewards and initiators of this park, showed me around, sharing her enthusiasm for what she and her group of neighborhood volunteers have been able to do in transforming this site. They have joined with the Surfrider Foundation to install a demonstration bioswale and permeable landscape where a variety of edibles are growing, including blackberries, strawberries, blueberries, and even a patch of artichokes.

**Figure 10.4.** La Playa Park is an example of a median strip converted to a small neighborhood park and green space, through the City's Street Parks program. Credit: Photo by Tim Beatley.

There is an emphasis on California natives, plants that are drought tolerant and important pollinators. There is a surprisingly roomy gathering space, made from flagstones, edged by drystack stone walls, with distinctive half-moon tables jutting out from old wooden barrels that have now become planters. Many recycled materials are used in the park, including former granite curbs supplied by the Department of Public Works that, with the help of a volunteer stone mason, have been converted into benches. There are five different stewards for this park, each taking charge of a section or part of the park, in addition to the many neighborhood volunteers who have given time and energy to the park.

What the cumulative, long-term impact will be from the conversion of these small leftover spaces to parks and nature is hard to predict. Will they have a significant impact on the hydrology and urban ecology of the city? This needs studying in the future, but early observations seem to indicate they will not be insignificant. Already native plants and natural habitats in places like the butterfly corridor are flourishing (and in fact last year the very first green hairstreak butterflies were seen). And Street Parks lays a helpful foundation for grander visions of restoring nature in the heart of this dense city, as seen in bold proposals for the Twin Peaks bioregion. The social benefits are also not to be understated or underestimated; each of these parcels has served as a catalyst, a physically tangible focal point, for community engagement and volunteering, thereby providing opportunities for residents to gather, socialize, and imagine meaningful positive change in their neighborhoods.

### New Kinds of Parks in the City

San Francisco has found new and creative ways to imagine new small parks and natural areas crafted out of hardscapes and pavement, in the process empowering neighborhoods and community groups to take charge. In the Mission District there is another impressive story, this one involving repurposing the overly large, wide sidewalks, and reimagining them as spaces and places for gardens. Architect Jane Martin, who has founded the nonprofit Plant*SF, has been a leader here. She designed and built (with her neighbors' help) the first sidewalk gardens (this story is told more fully in Beatley 2011). Obtaining official permission from the City was expensive and time consuming, but thanks to Martin's advocacy the city created a special one-page permit just for such projects. Martin estimates that, since 2006, there have been around 2000 Sidewalk Landscaping Permits issued by the city. So, a sidewalk gardening movement has been ignited, and the evidence can be seen on many streets in the Mission District. The interventions are often not very large, but they are lovely and add small but important moments of experiencing greenery and nature among the traffic and buildings.

The creation of *very* small urban parks, referred to as parklets in San Francisco, is something for which the city has garnered international attention and praise. The basic idea is that of converting two to three on-street car parking spaces to a small public park. This idea is being applied in many other cities around the world.

The parklet movement is an extension of the very temporary (single-day) Park(ing) Day, when the first parklet was created in 2010. Now there are 26 permanent completed parklets scattered around the city, and another 42 in progress. Several of the more impressive ones can be found along Valencia Street, in the Mission District. One example is a parklet created from two spaces, with bike parking in the middle, which is an outside extension of a restaurant/café.

This street is also home to the very first parklet associated with a residential unit, designed by Jane Martin. It creates a new public space in the neighborhood and also adds an important new element of green. Martin has designed a pair of elevated planting boxes that intentionally provides a degree of vertical mass approximating that of an automobile. The plantings are visually interesting, with the most dramatic feature being a one-of-a-kind wire dinosaur with plants growing out of it, affectionately called Trixi (a nod to the deeper geological past of the location).

There has been at least one study by the Great Streets Project to evaluate the effects of establishing parklets, but the long-term impact of parklets remains to be seen. The Great Streets Project collected observational data from three parklet sites, comparing pedestrian traffic before and after the parklets were created. The study found that pedestrian foot traffic increased in one of the three locations, and the number of people engaged in stationary activities increased substantially at all three parklets. As the study concludes: "The most tangible benefit of parklets this study identified is the creation of new public spaces for anyone to sit, relax, and enjoy the city. . . . The influence of this increase in activity on people's perception of the area varied with other neighborhood conditions. Although the benefit to businesses is most clearly felt by the sponsoring business, no negative impacts on nearby businesses were identified" (San Francisco Great Streets Project 2011, 1).

It may be too early to judge the long-term impact of the parklets idea, but these findings are encouraging. Taking a tiny bit of space in the city and offering new opportunities to sit and gather could have huge impacts if this happens on many streets throughout the city of San Francisco.

### Striving to Be a Bird-Friendly City

San Francisco sits right on the Pacific Flyway, and some 250 species of birds pass through and stop near the city during migration. In 2011, the city adopted Standards for Bird-Safe Buildings. The standards address two categories of hazards: (1) location-related hazards, and (2) building feature–related hazards. Under the city's standards special bird-friendly treatments are required for new buildings or major additions "located inside of, or within a clear flight path of less than 300 feet from an Urban Bird Refuge" (green spaces or open water of 2 acres or more). More specifically, treatments are required with the so-called bird collision zone of buildings—the first 60 feet of the building from ground level, which has proven to be the zone where most bird fatalities occur. Here facades require bird-safe window glazing treatments (no more than 10 percent untreated glass is allowed), minimal and shielded lighting, and the avoidance of horizontal wind turbines and vertical axis turbines that are not solid in appearance. "Bird-safe glazing treatments" are further specified in the standards to include "fritting, netting, permanent stencils, frosted glass, exterior screens, physical grids placed on the exterior of glazing or UV patterns visible to birds" (City and County of San Francisco, Planning Department 2011, 32).

In addition there are also standards stipulated for feature-related hazards, which include free-standing clear glass walls, skywalks, greenhouses on rooftops, and balconies that have unbroken glazed segments 24 square feet and larger in size (City and County of San Francisco Planning Department 2011, 30). The standards require treatment of the entire building features, for instance the installation of fritted glass on a skywalk between two buildings. The standards do include special exceptions for historic properties and buildings in residential zones.

It is interesting that the standards also seek to reconcile bird safety with other city goals, such as the promotion of renewable energy. The city has in recent years encouraged the installation of small micro–wind turbines, and these can sometime be fatal to birds. Consequently the standards call for wind turbines that "present a solid appearance," and thus are more visible to birds.

In addition to the mandatory treatment requirements, the standards also incorporate Recommended Actions and Bird-Safe Stewardship. These include a variety of suggestions and additional suggested treatments, such as sensitive placement of exterior greenery and vegetation, and tenant education efforts. The standards include a detailed Bird-Safe Building Checklist, which building owners are encouraged to apply.

Lights Out for Birds—San Francisco has been operating since 2008, a joint effort between the City, Golden Gate Audubon, and Pacific Gas and Electric. Participation in the lights-out campaign during periods of peak migration is recommended in the Bird-Site Standards, but not required, as is participation in some form of collision-monitoring effort.

In 2014, the city developed a new program encouraging individuals to become Certified Bird-Friendly Monitors, and buildings to become Certified Bird-Friendly. The former requires individuals to participate in weekly monitoring activities. The latter allows for the certification of buildings within designated green zones in the city, and those meeting the 2011 standards automatically qualify.

## Conclusions

San Francisco has been a world leader in environmental sustainability and has developed a well-deserved reputation as a green and sustainable city. But it is a city with significant and impressive biophilic credentials; a city that has pioneered a number of new and creative approaches for inserting nature—from parklets to sidewalk gardens to urban agriculture—many being embraced and replicated in other cities around the United States and the world. Especially to its credit, the city has been willing to create new permitting structures to make it easier to undertake some of these new urban greening interventions (such as the sidewalk landscaping permit), and to make room for temporary and more experimental urban greening projects. It is a city, moreover, where a significant number of citizens are actively engaged in the enjoyment of nature and restoration of habitat as members of groups like the Sutro Stewards or Friends of the Urban Forest.

San Francisco continues to lead the nation in setting and achieveing many sustainability goals and targets, from high recycling rates (and the vision of a zero-waste city) to shifting to renewable energy. The city has adopted an ordinance in 2016 for instance, that requires the installation of solar panels on new buildings (Sabatini 2016). Many of these bold steps will help nature. Dramatically lowering the city's greenhouse gas emissions reflects a global biophilic city commitment. San Francisco's early ban on plastic shopping bags, as another example, reflects a concern about impacts on marine organisms.

The city's new Transbay Transit Center is yet another example of merging biophilic and sustainability goals. Currently under construction, this facility will provide a point of connection and intersection between 11 different forms of public transit (e.g., BART, Amtrak, Muni, buses) and will include a number of green and sustainable features. Most impressively its rooftop will add to the park space and nature in the city. The rooftop park will be 5.4 acres in size and some 1400 feet long, providing both new space for public events and more quiet green areas, with 10 different points of entry (TransbayTransit Center n.d.). The Transbay Transit Center itself is a further reflection of the city's efforts to find new spaces for greenery and nature, sometimes in unlikely places.

There is much more to discuss about this city that limited space prevents. There is the impressive work of the San Francisco Unified School District in incorporating schoolyard gardens and outside learning, and the work of the nonprofit Corps for Education Outside, the nation's first "science-and-sustainability service corps" (see https://www.educationoutside.org) Or the biophilic work of work of some of the city's exemplary

---

**Box 10.2. Biophilic Mobility**

Joe Kott, a local transportation consultant, spoke with me about some of the ways that some local decisions have sought to take advantage of the city's spectacular natural scenery.

Knott notes that, in designing the San Francisco Muni light rail, "specifically the route that serves the N and T lines along the Embarcadero near the Bay waterfront," riders' views were taken into account. "Muni got an exemption to the Buy America regulations from the Federal Transit Administration to purchase light rail passenger cars from the Italian manufacturer Anseldo Breda (http://www.ansaldobredainc.com/) that had larger than standard windows so as to maximize views of the Bay and other San Francisco sights for light rail passengers. The land-use component of Embarcadero redesign from partial elevated freeway to multimodal boulevard included open gaps from the street to the Bay, mainly in the form of Bayfront public parks. These provide great views of the Bay for light rail passengers on Muni!"

Source: Personal communication with Joe Kott, transportation consultant, 2014. —Tim Beatley

museums and civic organizations (e.g., the California Academy of Sciences, in a very biophilic building, and the Exploratorium at Pier 15, among others). Or the efforts that have been made to ensure visual access to the natural beauty of this coastal city, including from the windows of light rail cars (box 10.2). San Francisco is far from a perfect story, and I have been critical at times that it hasn't embraced as fully as it could the larger marine setting within which it sits. But its biophilic credentials grow each year, and its commitments to, at once, local and planetary environment, are commendable and inspiring.

# 11

# Oslo, Norway:
## *A City of Fjords and Forests*

On almost every physical measure—protected nature, tree canopy coverage, access to parks, and ability to walk and hike in the city—residents of Oslo have access to an extraordinarily high degree of nature.

Oslo is a city of 454 square kilometers (175 sq. mi.) with a population of about 570,000 (part of a larger metropolitan area of around 1.2 million residents). Oslo's planning motto in recent years has been "the blue and the green and the city in between," which captures nicely the basic physical context of this city. Located on the Oslo Fjord, the city is flanked to the north and east by large uninterrupted blocks of forests.

Affectionately referred to as the *marka* (Norwegian for forest), they possess a value and societal importance almost mythical and certainly sacred. And the size and extent of forest near the city is considerable—in fact, two-thirds of the area within the municipal boundary the city is in protected forest (fig. 11.1). There is a marka line, beyond which the extension of urban development is to be prohibited, and while there have been efforts at swapping or trading land, this boundary appears largely immovable (legally but also politically). These forests are a remarkable resource and amenity for residents, and in many ways they shape the quality and texture of life in Oslo.

It is hard to overstate the importance of forests to residents of Oslo, and to the biophilic qualities of this city. Nature is not just nearby and seen from windows but is actively visited and enjoyed. The marka holds a special cultural and social importance, and is a place visited frequently by residents of Oslo. By one statistic, 81 percent of the city's population had visited the forests around the city during the previous year.

**Figure 11.1.** Two-thirds of the city of Oslo is contained in protected forests. These forests are popular to visit and an important aspect of the history and culture of the city. Credit: Photo by Tim Beatley.

Access to these large forests, in combination with smaller greenspaces in the city, means that residents of Oslo are never far from some nature. More than 94 percent of the city's residents live within 300 meters (328 yd.) of a green area, and the amount of green spaces and parks per capita is very high at 47 square meters (56 sq. yd.). In Oslo there is abundant nature, and most residents are not very far from a park or green space.

This city's nature works for residents because they can reach it easily and quickly, thanks to investments in public transit, particularly a fantastic metro system. Development density is low around many of the stations, boding well for accommodating future population growth around transit nodes (they're expecting an increase of 200,000 in the city by 2030).

One day on a visit to Oslo, I traveled by metro from the center of the city to the forest edge, a trip that took only 15 minutes and delivered me to the boundary of a massive forest reserve. The Sognsvann metro station is just a few meters from Lake Sognsvann, with a busy trail circling it, and, on this day, lots of families were walking and picnicking along the shore. Similarly, there are other metro stations (and tram stops) that provide unusually good access for residents wishing to reach these large areas of nature.

And this ease of mobility extends even into the small islands of the fjord, with regular ferry service for the cost of a bus or metro ticket. In early summer I witnessed these ferries filled with groups of small children on school trips to beautiful spaces around these islands—remote nature so close to the center of the city. It has been said on several occasions with pride that schools in Oslo (and throughout Norway) place a priority on getting their pupils outside and directly experiencing these natural resources.

There are plenty of cars and car traffic in Oslo, but the city deserves to be given considerable credit for attempts to constrain them. Oslo was one of the very first cities to put in place a ring toll that charges cars that travel into the city. Much of the revenue generated from this ring toll goes to support public transit.

## Compact and Green

The city's longstanding commitment to compact urban form is impressive and has done much both to promote more walkable, sustainable urban conditions and to create conditions in which a large portion of the city has close proximity to the forest edge. The city has seen success in its efforts to densify. Between 2000 and 2009 alone, the city's density, as a result of these planning policies, has increased by about 11 percent, a quite considerable increase in a relatively short period of time.

Compactness in turn reduces the amount of land needed to accommodate urban growth and in many ways makes possible the conservation of large blocks of forests at the city's edge. Again, two-thirds of the municipality's land area, a little over 300 square kilometers (116 sq. mi.), is either in forest or in lake, and so an immense amount of nature is owned and managed directly by the City of Oslo. Within the urbanized areas, about 20 percent is considered green and open land, so there is a fairly sharp contrast between the urbanized city and the large forests that surround the city to the north and east. And beyond these municipal forests lie even larger expanses of nature.

The city's large area of forests provides diverse and abundant recreational opportunities. There are some 70 bathing lakes, some 100 rivers and lakes suitable for fishing, and 460 kilometers (286 mi.) of cross-country ski trails. This is made possible in large part because of the impressive spatial planning principles, according to which the city is essentially surrounded or encircled by large extensive blocks of forest. And the delineation of the forest boundary line or border (so-called *markagrensa*) is a significant step, indicating that those areas beyond the line (beyond the urbanized city) are to be protected and not developed. Oslo's current Municipal Master Plan is one of strengthening its compact urban form, hand in hand with strong protections for the city's forests and green areas; "The boundary between the forest and building zone will be maintained and fjord, green spaces and rivers and streams will be protected" (Oslo City Council, 2008, p. 48).

### Green Aspirations: Lessons from the Akerselva

Oslo has prepared an impressive green plan, or Green Structure Plan (*Grøntplan for Oslo*), which carefully and methodically takes stock of these green qualities and also lays out an ambitious future vision for further restoring and growing nature in the city. The plan sets goals and a series of strategies for achieving those goals. As already mentioned, the first strategy is to develop a "continuous green network of public green areas," where residents can walk or ride their bike from one to another of these parks and green areas (Oslo Kommune, 2007). The green plan argues for the importance of not a single kind of park, but for three sizes of parks, small, medium, and large, each providing access to different types of experiences and functions, and identifies spatial and access deficiencies in different parts of the city. And while the results are generally good, there are suggestions for ways that access to all three forms and sizes of parks can be assured. The city's green plan calls for 69 new parks in places that help correct for deficiencies in access.

Most boldly the plan envisions daylighting and restoring the eight main rivers that flow through the city on their way to the fjord. The city's Green Structure Plan lays out the vision of bringing all of these rivers back to the surface and restoring them to mostly natural conditions. It is a bold vision, and one on which the city has already made significant progress. An impressive green ribbon that runs through the heart of the city, the Akerselva (*elva* meaning river in Norwegian) was in medieval times the main source of water, then later where much of the city's industry was located. Today the Akerselva is the most spectacular example to date of a nearly complete river restoration, with waterfalls and bicycling and walking trails and abundant riparian nature close to dense housing (fig. 11.2). The river is at times quiet and calm, but in many places it is fast moving and loud, and there are some unexpected and dramatic waterfalls.

The trail and pathway system along the river is in many places on both sides of the river, and the river is itself quite wide in parts, with small islands in the center. The pathways consist of a hard surface that is elegantly trimmed with a line of stone. There are a number of footbridges along the route providing opportunities to cross over and experience the river from the other side. While the river is crossed at a

**Figure 11.2.** The restored Akerselva River in Oslo, Norway. One of the many natural elements found in this biophilic city are its rivers, and the plan has been developed to restore them and bring them back to the surface, connecting the city's large forests to the fjord. A former site of water-powered industry, today the paths and spaces along the Akerselva provide dramatic views of water. Credit: Photo by Tim Beatley.

number of points by roads, there are pedestrian underpasses that ensure continuity of the path system. There is a remarkable amount of development and housing along the river, and large apartment blocks, with ready pedestrian access to the river, which is one of the main reasons this green element works. Rather than being remote, it is highly accessible to lots of residents, with the result being lots of walkers, joggers, and bicyclists, and a feeling of safety, even during the evening hours. There are new cultural amenities here along the river as well—new clubs, theaters, artists' studios—that help to further enhance its popularity and attractiveness, and that further generate foot traffic and visitation.

Another design lesson can be seen in the creative ways in which parks and open spaces are woven into the river corridor, places that on a sunny Sunday were full of people picnicking. Others were dog-walking and several were flyfishing. There are lots of built-in benches and small spaces to sit and watch the river or read a book. The sounds of the river can be heard many meters away and are actually deafening near some of the falls. The grasses along the banks sloping down to the river have in many places been cut along the edges leaving, on the day of my June visit, spectacular floral displays of yellows and greens. There is a municipal cutting policy evident here that mows only the perimeters, enough to show that the spaces are being taken care of, and the beautiful fields of flowers are intentionally left to grow. In strolling around I encountered on several occasions people who had clearly been collecting bunches of flowers to take home or bring with them to whatever social engagement they were on their way to. More recently the city has embarked on a major effort to similarly restore the Alna River, and has already restored impressive sections of several of its other rivers.

**An Urban Trail to Get You There**

Another important aspect of the nature story in Oslo is its impressive citywide network of trails. This network adds to the considerable ability of residents to reach the Akerselva and many of the other green areas. The Oslo environment provides an unusually high degree of connectivity for residents, and many ways to get around without an automobile. The trail system is quite impressive. The extent of existing and planned trails is some 365 kilometers (226 mi.), and, judged on a per capita basis, it is one of the most extensive urban trail efforts anywhere (fig. 11.3). These are largely natural trails conveniently marked like highways (I like the sense of parity here) by a combination of number and letter ("follow the A2," for instance) that

**Figure 11.3.** The city of Oslo has one of the most extensive networks of trails of any city in the world. They provide immense opportunities for residents, like this trail bike rider, both to get around the city and to experience much of the abundant nature nearby. Credit: Photo by Tim Beatley.

residents can take to many natural areas in the city. There are beautiful trail maps available to guide you into the different sections of the city.

One of the most spectacular sections of trail—a real surprise for me—was along the A4, which I accessed from the east (connecting with the A12). This section of trail, from Husebyskogen south to the Radium-hospitalet, takes you along the Maer-radalsbekken River. The sheer wildness of this stretch of river was a pleasant surprise. One wants to linger here, listening to the sound of the fast water, and watching a steady stream of hikers and mountain bikers pass by. The ability to get residents out of their autos, and walking and bicycling, is a major challenge for any biophilic city in the industrialized North, and here Oslo excels as well. Car dependence is the norm and typically has the effect of sealing us off from the natural world and from each other. Oslo has many cars but also has taken a number of steps to moderate their impacts, and the numbers suggest good results in creating conditions for a walking city. One reported statistic is that some 85 percent of the city's children get to school either by walking, bicycling, or public transit. Compared to typical American cities, then, there is relatively little use of cars to shuttle kids to and from school, perhaps setting them down a life path of walking or bicycling, and offering at least some of the conditions of a more biophilic urban childhood.

## Strengthening Connections to Waterfront and Sea

It is impressive to see the new thinking in Oslo about how and in what ways the city's waterfront growth might take advantage of the unique and special water setting. Indeed urban designers and planners in that city are speaking of Oslo as the "Fjord City," and imagining how future building will connect with and respect this special aquatic environment. A Fjord City Plan, laying out principles and visions for the future of the waterfront there, has been prepared, with some interesting concepts.

Oslo's more recent history of planning and development has clearly sought to reinforce connections to the water. Perhaps, most impressively, Oslo has begun a long-term process of transforming its waterfront, putting major roadways in tunnels and creating amazing new connections with the fjord. The Fjord City Plan lays out this vision: a new fjord city park, new "activation" of the water areas (i.e., creating spaces for boating and swimming), a harborwide promenade, limits to the height of new buildings in the city to ensure visual connections with the water, among others. And much of this is already happening. A series of dense vertical buildings, with visually interesting designs (referred to locally as the "barcode buildings") and spectacular views of the waterfront, stand immediately adjacent.

All of the new waterfront development will be connected by a harbor promenade, which will also allow pedestrians and urban hikers to connect with the city's more natural trails on either end. Some of this waterfront transformation has been under way for a number of years, and not that long ago there were multiple lanes of traffic separating the city's town hall from the water. Today a large plaza links the central city—*sentrum*—with the fjord and provides residents and visitors the chance to connect with this amazing water environment.

The recent and dramatic design of the Oslo Opera House exemplifies some of the possibility here. A design by the architectural firm Snøhetta was chosen in a design competition, with a primary design element being enhancement of connections with the harbor and inner fjord. The building's dramatic, almost 4-acre (1.6-hectare) granite roof slopes into the fjord water, creating a large and unique urban plaza, and allowing visitors to virtually touch and dip into the surrounding aquatic world.

And there is a larger marine realm close to the city. There are some 40 islands in the Oslo fjord, and they are mostly accessible to the public. Oslo provides exceptional public access to its coastal and shoreline environments, and it doesn't have the high degree of privatization and cordoning off from public use that commonly occurs in many other parts of the world. This ease of mobility extends even into the small islands of the fjord, with regular easy ferry service for only the cost of a regular bus or metro ticket. Oslo has already had considerable success and some international acclaim for its waterfront development. The district of Aker Brygge, with its mix of offices, shops, and relatively dense housing and very compact and walkable design, puts many residents in close proximity to the water and has created a destination for visitors as well. This complex, built during the later 1980s and early 1990s, is highly regarded by urbanists. Aker Brygge has a number of other biophilic aspects, in addition to the important one of creating the context and conditions to entice residents to be outside and to walk and stroll. Much of the public art that one sees here reflects biophilic shapes and forms (such as the prominent seashells sculpture).

It is clear that this is a marine city, and it's not just because of the cruise ships and other harbor traffic. The images of marine life and mythology seem to permeate the city and appear in interesting ways. I ended up one day on a street where a striking feature was a sea horse vertically fixed like a beacon to the entrance—it turned out to be an important 1941 building (Radhusgatten 25), designed by notable architects Andreas Bjercke and Georg Eliassen. The most dramatic adornment was a beautiful vertical fish sculpture. And this is not an unusual sight walking around Oslo; mermaids and fish and water scenes appear on buildings old and new. The fish on the Bjerke and Eliassen building was indeed a delight. This seems not the result of any official policy. These shapes and images and natural forms do enhance the biophilic experience of this already very green city. The City's new green plan seeks to further strengthen the city and region's green infrastructure, especially the eight major rivers running through the city. As already mentioned, the plan sets out the bold goal indeed of bringing all of these rivers fully back to the surface and restoring them as green and ecological features in the city. These rivers would restore the historical ecological connections between the marka, or forests, to the north and east, with the fjord waters, as well as connecting a network of smaller green spaces and parks in the city.

## Other Biophilic Dimensions to Life in Oslo

While the city has set aside a large forest it is also taking steps to manage it in responsible, sustainable ways. The city manages this land under ISO 14,001, and specifically employs a "Living Forest" management standard and certification standard that seek to protect ecological functions while allowing some amount of sustainable harvest. The Norwegian Living Forest management certification system sets out a series of standards, including requirements for leaving uncut a certain number of trees (an average of 5 to 10 living trees per hectare), for buffer zones in riparian habitats, and restrictions on altering dead wood and damaging terrain. This is further evidence of the long-term stewardship values of the city.

Biophilia is multisensory, of course, and as much a function of the sounds, smells, tastes, and bodily sensations one feels in living environments. We often privilege the visual, and sometimes forget how essential these other senses are to our connections to place and our environment, and how the senses work together to deliver the sensations and experiences that make up the ordinary nature around us. It is often the totality of these sensory inputs that determines our experience of place—the breeze on our skin, the sounds, the smells, the tastes of the food we eat—along with the sights.

Oslo is addressing sound in several ways, primarily through efforts to control noise. The Oslo Noise Action Plan attempts to at least partially take this on through the designation of quiet areas in the city—some 14 of these places, where noise levels are below 50 dB which the plan describes as: "Areas which can offer recreation, outdoor experiences, and/or cultural activities in surroundings sheltered from or distant from dominant noise sources" (Oslo City, n.d., p.38). The city's river corridors would constitute about half of these (linear) quiet zones. About a quarter of the city's population suffers from an excess of noise (over 55 dB during the day), not an insignificant amount, and mostly connected to roads and auto traffic. The more the city is able to discourage driving and to put in place other steps to control car noise (design using quieter road surfaces, discouraging studded tires in winter, for instance), the greater will be the possibilities that residents will connect with the more biophilic sounds all around them but presently difficult to hear.

That is a good step (and partly responds to an EU directive), but more could always be done to better understand and nurture the positive soundscape, natural and human made; not just by avoiding the negative or noxious but by actively rekindling a sense of the sounds in the city and region, that evoke deep recollections and memories, immensely enjoyed by those who hear them.

Quiet areas may be parks but could extend to other places in the city and offer the possibility that by reducing the impact of car noise, more biophilic and therapeutic sounds might become more audible to residents. There are, moreover, a number of points in the city where distinctive natural sounds can be heard, including the sound of fast water and the roar of waterfalls along the Akerselva, suggesting, again, other soundscape benefits of fully restoring the city's eight rivers on their way to the fjord.

### Future Directions in Biophilic Oslo

Overall, Oslo is already a very biophilic city, there can be no doubt. It can be especially proud of its work to protect forests and to provide an unparalleled degree of access and proximity to wild nature—especially forests and shorelines and water. It already lives up to its motto, "the blue and the green and the city in between" and has set some extremely ambitious goals for the future, especially daylighting and restoring the remaining seven rivers flowing aboveground (at the moment in pipes underground) through the city. This is visionary, bold, and transformative and has the potential to do more than any other strategy to enhance the quality of life and to help further grow and nurture a biophilic population. It will also be an exemplar for other cities to follow.

There are still many ways in which this green city could be more biophilic and could further strengthen its biophilic qualities. Partly the challenge will be to enhance and restore the natural qualities in the densest and oldest parts of the city. This will require a variety of creative biophilic design techniques and ideas not yet in wide use (e.g., vertical gardens and green walls). Urban trees, rooftop gardens, bird- and wildlife-friendly building designs are just a few of the many things the city could do in these more intensive urban zones. Reimaging the urbanized city as a bountiful city, and looking for every opportunity to insert and integrate food production, is another avenue to explore. The possibilities could include planting fruit trees in public spaces, encouraging balcony gardens, and converting small urban spaces, where possible, to community gardens.

In recent months Oslo has made the global environmental news by starting a pollination highway for bees through the city—the *Pollinatorpassasjen* in Norwegian. The idea is to encourage "feeding stations" for bees every 800 feet or so through the city by providing vegetation where bees and other pollinators could stop. It is a private endeavor, spearheaded by the nonprofit ByBi ("bee town") (Hickman 2015). There is an online map showing these stations and offering some guidance about where new urban plantings are needed (http://www.pollinatorpassasjen.no/intro).

Oslo has much to teach other cities. Most important is the lesson that it is possible (indeed essential) to work on the basic elements of sustainable urban form (good transit, increasing densities around transit stations) at the same time that investments are made in restoring and growing the wilder and more natural forms of infrastructure in a city. Wildness in the city is not only possible in Oslo, but a defining quality of urban life there.

# 12

# Vitoria-Gasteiz, Spain:
## *Nature in the Compact City*
### Carla Jones

## A Natureful City

The European Green Capital of 2012, Vitoria-Gasteiz, Spain, is a beautiful, natureful city. Vitoria-Gasteiz is the capital of the autonomous community of the Basque Country in northern Spain and dates back to 1181. It is a relatively compact, concentrically developed city with 28,000 hectares and has a population of approximately 240,000 people. It is also one of a few European cities boasting the largest proportion of green areas per inhabitant, roughly 25 square meters (30 sq. yd.) per capita (2012-Vitoria, Gasteiz 2012). Because of this compactness and the region's geography, residents feel connected to the countryside and the mountain ranges that provide their water.

## Biophilic Successes

The city of Vitoria-Gasteiz began moving toward a biophilic future in the 1980s when the city was facing extreme population increases, began sprawling, and was dealing with stormwater management challenges. The efforts began when Mayor Jose Angel Cuerda created the Environmental Studies Center (CEA) to conduct research and provide education on environmental issues in the region (Orive and Dios Lema 2012).

Since the 1980s, much has progressed in Vitoria-Gasteiz, from the expansive parks system to outer and inner greenbelts, the city is connecting residents with nature every day. It isn't difficult to connect residents with nature because walking is a favorite pastime of most Vitoria-Gasteiz citizens. With one of the highest biodiversity

**Figure 12.1.** The new green concept for Vitoria-Gasteiz, capital of Spain's Basque Country, building on its famous green ring that circles the city, includes developing an interior green ring, bringing nature into the heart of the city. Credit: municipality of Victoria-Gateiz.

indices of the region, it is important that the city protect this precious resource and amenity. In fact, one-third of Spain's endangered vertebrate species are found in the municipality (Orive and Dios Lema 2012).

### Biophilic Challenges

Many of Vitoria-Gasteiz's successes have come because of the city's unique geography and past challenges. Many of these initiatives, including the extensive greenbelt system, began as strategies to mitigate and clean up excess stormwater. Many streams had been contaminated by sewage systems. In the 1990s, one of Vitoria-Gasteiz's prominent water features, the River Zadorra, was channelized, and stormwater issues were exacerbated. The River Zadorra has since been restored and is included as a vital corridor in the European Ecological Network Natura 2000 as a site of community importance. Vitoria-Gasteiz has faced many development pressures over the years. It has been able to maintain so much nature in the city because of the strong connection between residents and the natural world. This fervent citizen activism is a unique feature of Vitoria-Gasteiz and has helped preserve and enhance urban nature (Orive and Dios Lema 2012).

## Urban Green Infrastructure

Urban green infrastructure has been a priority for Vitoria-Gasteiz. There are multiple goals in mind: improving air quality, reducing the heat island effect, reducing atmospheric contamination, increasing biodiversity, promoting agriculture, and improving the mental and physical health of residents. Vitoria's green infrastructure plan's goal is to make the city as permeable as possible. There are multiple greenbelts that have developed around the city, including the Interior Green Belt, Peri-Urban Green Belt, Agricultural Belt, and Upland Ring (Orive and Dios Lema 2012). The plan links all greenbelts through radial axes that act as ecological corridors (fig. 12.1).

## Greenbelts

The greenbelt system in Vitoria-Gasteiz is impressive and has garnered international attention; in 2000, the United Nations rated it as one of the 100 best projects worldwide. Rightfully so, as it has brought awareness of biodiversity to citizens. Greenbelts are not a new concept to cities. The idea was first proposed by Ebenezer Howard in the late 1800s, but the way cities are using greenbelts has changed significantly. Vitoria-Gasteiz has an impressive network of greenbelts that extend 35 kilometers (22 mi.), with plans to cover a surface of 1000 square kilometers (386 sq. mi.). The city has restored the peri-urban fringe and created this publicly owned amenity for the community.

### *The External Green Belt*

The outer greenbelt efforts began in the 1990s as the areas around the city were in a state of disrepair and abandonment (Orive and Dios Lema 2012). There were opportunities for natural areas to be restored to their original ecological value and for other degraded areas, such as landfills, to be reimagined. How could the city address these degraded areas and also increase the quality of these undervalued ecological places in the city? The city decided to connect the entire periphery of the city with a large-scale project known as the External Green Belt.

The External Green Belt was approved in 2003 and consists of five large suburban parks (Salburua, Zabalgana, Armentia, Olarizu, and Rio Zadorra) with recreational areas surrounding the city center.

In 2012, the city initiated a project entitled Roots of Tomorrow, which aims to plant 250,000 trees and shrubs over a 3-year period. By the end of 2014, 129,133 trees and shrubs have been planted. The project was made possible through partnerships with 13 companies that are now part of the Green Belt Protector program. This project contributed to the nomination of Vitoria-Gasteiz for the Dubai International Award for Best Practices to Improve the Living Environment (Luis Lobo, e-mail, December 15, 2014).

Through this comprehensive process, there are now 650 hectares (1606 acres) of External Green Belt (Luis Lobo, e-mail, December 15, 2014). While there are still parts of the External Green Belt to regenerate, the External Green Belt is an incredible resource for the city; it has increased biodiversity, improved stormwater management, helped to promote environmental education, and controlled future growth (box 12.1).

### The Interior Green Belt

The outer greenbelt system was so successful that Mayor Javier Morato ran on the platform of expanding the greenbelt to the city interior (box 12.2). The Interior Green Belt is forming from the development of a green grid in the city center (Luis Lobo, e-mail, December 15, 2014). The Interior Green Belt is in the pilot stage, with the first project set for one of the main roads in the city, Gasteiz Avenue. This is a very visible, highly trafficked area that includes many of the city's largest cultural centers. This pilot project takes away space given to automobiles and prioritizes spaces for natural areas that will improve biodiversity and assist in stormwater management. The next phase of the project remodels another significant street and is currently in draft design.

### Parks System

A popular pastime for citizens of Vitoria-Gasteiz is walking through the parks and green pathways throughout the city. Fifty percent of all journeys in the city are on foot. Vitoria-Gasteiz has been working diligently to ensure that every resident has a park within 300 meters (328 yd.) of where they live and has planted 130,000 trees in city streets. Each park is

**Box 12.1. Salburua Wetlands**

One of the most successful stories from the External Green Belt is the restoration of the Salburua Wetlands. The Salburua Wetlands are part of the extensive greenbelt and parks system and serve as an important place for biodiversity, especially for birds. The area, once used for agriculture, was restored to its natural state in 1998 by diverting the Zadorra River to protect the city from flooding. This in turn has provided a series of benefits, including the reentry of local endangered species and wildlife. This amazing resource is a mere 15-minute bicycle ride from the center of the city.

—Carla Jones

**Box 12.2. International Workshop on the Interior Green Belt**

In the summer of 2012, the city welcomed students from countries around the world to participate in a progressive workshop to brainstorm and create innovative ideas for the four corridors of the proposed inner greenbelt. The students examined the current proposed corridors for opportunities and developed various design schemes to increase the green aspects of the city. According to Holly Hendrix, a workshop participant from the University of Virginia, whose team focused on the eastern part of the corridor, "the eastern axis offers an opportunity to express the regional hydrology, connecting to the drainage of water off the mountains in the south and the watercourses that flow through the city, ending at the Zadorra River in the north. This topographic condition makes this axis of the anillo an excellent place to integrate stormwater management infrastructure, such as bioswales and retention areas, as part of public space. An agricultural identity has also been proposed for this axis, linking the interior urban gardens to the farming practices on the city's periphery. The eastern axis is being seen as a dual corridor with an urban edge that reaches through the proposed anillo and a parallel pedestrian and cycling corridor that will follow traces of a historic rail line and provide a quieter, meandering journey along the axis." The final proposals were thought provoking and included ideas such as elevated parks and watchtowers for residents to feel connected with other parts of the city.

—*Carla Jones*

connected via a series of urban pathways. These pathways prioritize walking and cycling, which help residents experience the natural features around them.

Public gardens make up 33 percent of the urban area in Vitoria-Gasteiz. There are currently three public community market gardens dispersed throughout the city. These public community market gardens each have a different focus and provide opportunities for elderly and other specialized groups to utilize them. The gardens to the north of the city are called the Market Gardens of Urarte. The gardens to the south of the city are among the oldest, called the Market Gardens of Olarizu. Most recently developed were the community market gardens in the Zabalgana neighborhood, located in the western part of the city.

### Connecting Residents with Nature

A source of pride for Vitoria-Gasteiz's citizens is the Center for Environmental Studies (CEA). Mayor Jose Angel Cuerda created the CEA in the 1980s. The goal of the CEA is to conduct research and to educate citizens about the environmental issues in the region. It began as part of the greenbelt implementation project and was, in part, initiated by the Department of Economic Development. There were many people who were underemployed or unemployed, so the Department of Economic Development gained approval and support from the mayor to create the autonomous organization, known as the CEA. It is a part of the city, but also independent. This has worked in their favor as the independence that they have had has given them the opportunity to be advocates for and protectors of the environment. The CEA helps provide the city with a basic level of ecoliteracy by hosting exhibitions (nine in 2013 that had over 12,500 attendees), celebrations of major events (Biological Agriculture Trade Fair and World Bird Day), and educational conferences and workshops (topics ranging from apiculture to nature photography). There are events for every age group and demographic in the city and beyond.

There are other projects that also provide residents with an opportunity to engage with nature in a different way. The Olarizu Botanical Garden was recently finished and is meant to represent different European forests. It began as a garden, mostly for older adults. They had free use of the land allotments but had to undergo training before using them. The garden is open to the public, but the older population manages it. It is a very healthy landscape where the managers decide what to plant, and they have extended the programming to include those with disabilities.

The Olarizu Botanical Garden also boasts an impressive seed bank that since 2010 has conserved 19 threatened species, which accounts for 45 percent of the municipality's threatened flora. In 2011, this project helped rediscover and restore the third known population of northern bedstraw (*Galium boreale*), which has been reported as missing for 28 years. It has also participated in the OpenREDBAG Project through contributing to the creation of a data portal of phytogenetic resources.

This is a big project that has the potential to have big impacts. It is very interactive and has been incredibly successful. There are multiple educational materials that help patrons interpret the wealth of nature around them. These materials are also available online. The project received investment from the Basque government.

In addition, there is a strong network of citizens that formed the Environment Sector Council, which was established in 2000 and comprises approximately 40 groups. There is a plethora of citizen scientists in Vitoria-Gasteiz who are active in the Participation Program in Citizen Science. Thus far, four Citizen Conservation Projects have launched in collaboration with the Green Belt and Biodiversity Unit and the Department of Environment and Public Space. Approximately 50 residents have participated in these projects, including the Urban Bird Conservation Project, the Odonata Conservation Project, the Orchid Conservation Project in the Green

Belt, and the Orchid Conservation Project in the City of Vitoria-Gasteiz. Of the participants, over 85 percent participate regularly in the program. The biggest proportion of work with these projects has consisted of collecting baseline data to compare future efforts to. For example, the Orchid Conservation Project in the Green Belt has identified 43 different taxons of orchids, 36 species and subspecies, and 7 hybrids. This means that the greenbelt alone holds 69 percent of the orchid species in Vitoria-Gasteiz (Luis Lobo, e-mail, December 15, 2014).

## Local Strategy for Biodiversity Conservation

The city feels that urgent measures are necessary to promote the rich biodiversity in the region. In order to act appropriately, the city included biodiversity in its Action Plan of Agenda 21 2010–2014. The plan goes beyond biodiversity conservation and states its objective as "halting the loss of biodiversity and achieving a favorable conservation state of habitats and species of the municipality within ten years, promoting the recognition of their values and functions for society" (Luis Lobo, e-mail, December 15, 2014).

The strategy document outlines different sites that have been analyzed for their biodiversity weaknesses and proposes actions to meet this objective at each site. The strategy also proposes a way of evaluating the strategy's effects on the local ecology. The strategy was approved on February 13, 2015.

There have been specific efforts to prevent the European mink (*Mustela lutreola*), the most endangered Mustelidae in Europe, from facing extinction. The Lutreola Life Project was initiated to save this species from extinction by eradicating its biggest predator, the American mink (*Neovision vison*) and increasing the current population of the European mink by releasing individuals that have been raised. A major component of this project is to educate the public about the dangers the European mink faces, through public outreach and awareness events.

## Conclusion

Vitoria-Gasteiz is a commendable example of how a city can plan for nature and foster the connections between residents and urban nature. With over 8 percent of land protected for its ecological value and an active populace that advocates for its ecological resources, it isn't surprising that this city offers many lessons for compact cities across the globe. Consistent planning, followed by assessment and evaluation, is critical to strengthening the relationship between humans and urban nature. Capitalizing on the culture of the populace and creating programs and places that celebrate that place have been big biophilic successes for Vitoria-Gasteiz.

# PART 3:

# A Global Survey of Innovative Practice and Projects

What follows is a set of short case studies that succinctly describe innovative biophilic projects and planning efforts around the US and the world. These are highlights of notable efforts, intended to inform and inspire, rather than offer a comprehensive look at all biophilic projects. Projects have been selected to provide geographic diversity and to demonstrate the many different ways biophilic design and planning principles can find application in cities.

There are many more creative and innovative projects under way or completed that aren't mentioned in this section—space prevents their inclusion. Undoubtedly, there are many projects and initiatives that we are unaware of, and it is our hope that readers will help us to learn about and include additional cases in future editions of this handbook and on the Biophilic Cities Network website.

# I. Biophilic Plans and Codes

## Green Roof Bylaws, Toronto, Ontario, Canada
### *A Shift Toward Mandatory Green Roofs*
*Carla Jones*

The City of Toronto is considered one of the leaders in green roof policies. In 2009, Toronto became the first city in the world to enact a green roof bylaw. The City of Toronto Act (COTA) gave the City Council authority to pass a bylaw requiring and governing the construction of green roofs.

The bylaw applies to new commercial, institutional, and many residential developments. Up to 50 percent of the roof may be required to be green for multiunit, residential dwellings over six stories, schools, nonprofit housing, and commercial and industrial buildings. According to Shayna Stott, Environmental Planner for the City of Toronto, the eco-roof incentive grants program gives financial incentives to those that are not mandated under the bylaw, such as owners of existing buildings, through its Eco-Roof Incentive Program. These programs together help the city meet the goals of its Climate Change Action Plan.

There are four main components of Toronto's Green Roof Strategy:
- Installation of green roofs on city buildings
- Pilot incentive program to encourage green roof construction
- Use of the development approval process to encourage green roofs
- Publicity and education

Green roofs have many environmental benefits, such as absorbing excess stormwater, increasing energy efficiency, filtering air, and beautifying our cities. One of the most interesting characteristics of green roofs is that they have the potential to increase biodiversity. One of the City of Toronto's goals with this green roof bylaw is to foster connections between natural habitats across the city.

Stott believes that Toronto's Green Roof ByLaw has been successful thus far because the standards are very tangible and can be designed to fit any need. When asked about her advice for other cities interested in enacting such a bylaw, Stott recommends starting off with solid research to clarify the real costs and benefits. This is critical to understanding where exceptions to the policy might be necessary. She also recommends starting off with a voluntary approach. Lastly, she suggests that the locality must allocate enough resources to educate the public.

## Greenest City Action Plan, Vancouver, British Columbia, Canada
### Aspiring to be the "Greenest City in the World"
#### Tim Beatley

Vancouver is a city known for its green credentials and progressive planning, a city that has sought to grow compactly and vertically, all in the midst of a spectacular natural landscape of mountains and water. The latest chapter in Vancouver's efforts are its bold intentions and declaration that it intends to be the "Greenest City in the World," by 2020. An initiative begun by Mayor Gregor Robertson, this vision is being implemented through the Greenest City Action Plan. The Action Plan sets ambitious targets, establishes baselines, and identifies specific actions for 10 areas, including climate change, waste, transportation, and food.

Action Goal 6 addresses "Access to Nature," and specifically sets the following targets: (1) "All Vancouver residents live within a five-minute walk of a park, greenway, or other green space by 2020," and (2) "Plant 150,000 new trees by 2020" (City of Vancouver, 2010).

To support the vision a Greenest City Fund was created in April 2012, with funds provided by both the City of Vancouver and the Vancouver Foundation. A 4-year funding initiative (just ending) allocated some $500,000 in the first year, supporting some 150 different projects, many with a youth orientation. Much of the funding has gone to support a variety of neighborhood-based greening projects (City of Vancouver, 2012).

Vancouver has also led the way in efforts to coexist with coyotes, spearheaded by the Stanley Park Ecology Society. These efforts have included education and advice to

Biodegradable cards dropped in the Georgia Strait, in an effort to involve citizens in understanding how quickly an oil spill would spread. Photo Credit: Georgia Strait Alliance.

residents about interactions with coyotes (e.g., hazing, ways to keep pets safe). One of the key methods for effective coexistence is to ensure that coyotes continue to be fearful of humans, and making noise is one way to do this. Toward this end, there are even online instructions for making your own "coyote shaker" by placing pennies in a soda can (Stanley Park Ecology Society n.d.[a]). There are a number of other elements in the coexistence program, including educating school kids (and they have prepared a teacher packet about coexistence) community coyote walks and workshops, and coyote sightings map (e.g., see Stanley Park Ecology Society n.d.[b]).

There are NGOs doing equally impressive work to raise awareness and connect residents to the nature around them. Vancouver is a port city and sits on the Strait of Georgia, part of the larger Salish Sea connecting the city with the Pacific Ocean. Remarkable marine life can be seen in and around Vancouver, including the iconic orca. The Georgia Strait Alliance, an NGO based in Vancouver (with the orca as its symbol) has undertaken a variety of marine conservation and education initiatives, including a Waterfronts Initiative that is helping to explore new ideas for design of the city's waterfront, a clean marina program, and events like the annual Water's

Edge Day, which entices residents to visit some of the marine nature close by. One of the most creative initiatives has involved organizing dropping drift cards (see photo), and enlisting the public in retrieving them and registering online where they have been found—an effort both to learn how quickly oil spills might contaminate the Strait, and to raise public awareness about this environmental threat.

# II. Citizen Science and Community Engagement

## Camping in Urban Parks, New York City, New York
### *Sleeping Under an Urban Sky*
*Briana Bergstrom*

New York City, with its soaring skyscrapers and bustling street life, wouldn't strike most as the ideal setting for wildlife viewing, night hiking, and sleeping under the stars. But New York City, the densest city in the United States, is also home to over 29,000 acres of parkland, including 51 nature preserves, 600 miles of shoreline, and a vast network of hiking trails covering all five boroughs. And in fact, what might surprise most is that overnight camping, or perhaps more appropriately, urban camping, is in fact possible without ever needing to leave city limits.

The Urban Park Rangers, a faction within the New York City Department of Parks and Recreation (NYC Parks), have been providing this opportunity and connecting thousands of New Yorkers with the great outdoors for over 30 years (Urban Park Rangers n.d.). With initiatives ranging from environmental education to outdoor recreation to wildlife management and conservation, the Urban Park Rangers introduce, reacquaint, and deeply engage New Yorkers of all ages with the city's abundant ecosystem and natural amenities throughout the year.

The Urban Park Rangers' Weekend Adventures Program, one of NYC Parks' several regularly offered programs, encourages New Yorkers to interact with the natural wonders that exist in the city's backyard through weekend outdoor recreation activities. Almost every weekend of the year the program offers opportunities such as hiking, canoeing, fishing, biking, archery, wildlife viewing, wilderness survival, nature art and photography, astronomy, and conservation and restoration.

Some of the most popular Weekend Adventures activities are the family camping trips, which begin in late spring and run throughout the summer every year. Available on a lottery system, these trips provide families, many of which are first-time campers, the opportunity to pitch a tent and connect with the natural world in city parks throughout all five boroughs. Families are offered this opportunity free of charge and are even provided supplies for the trip, a perk of the program that enables many families to participate who would otherwise find the cost and travel requirements of overnight camping too burdensome.

The trips, which are led by Urban Park Rangers staff, commonly include a cookout, night hikes, wildlife viewing, and roasting marshmallows around a campfire. Families are offered the opportunity not only to relax in a natural setting but also to learn about the diverse ecosystem in which they live. Children learn how to pitch a tent while adults soak in the relaxing sounds of the cicadas and wind through the trees. By introducing families to urban camping, the Urban Park Rangers hope to foster relationships between New Yorkers and the natural world that surrounds them, promoting environmental stewardship over time. For many, these trips provide the first introduction to outdoor recreation and environmental education and, perhaps more importantly, the notion that an escape into nature is not far from home no matter where that might be.

## Urban Slender Loris Project, Bangalore, India
### *Working on Behalf of the Slender Loris in the Garden City of India*
Tim Beatley

Bangalore, India, has historically been known as that country's "garden city," a green oasis of trees and orchards, and two prominent botanical gardens. The city has grown rapidly in recent decades—now with a population of some 10 million—and much of that greenery is being lost. Nevertheless, there are new efforts to engage the public around the needs of urban wildlife. One recent initiative is the Urban Slender Loris Project (USLP). The slender loris (*Loris tardigradus*) is a small, large-eyed primate indigenous to Sri Lanka and southern India. This nocturnal creature lives in treetops and depends on a continuous belt of trees for its mobility. While it faces many different threats (illegal poaching, pet trade), its numbers have dropped mostly because of habitat loss. Most alarming has been the loss over several decades of thousands of trees in Bangalore, a function especially of road-building projects. The city has also witnessed the loss of the extensive orchards at the city's periphery, which have provided important wildlife corridors (Soumya 2015).

The USLP is led by Kaberi Kar Gupta, a wildlife biologist with the Wildlife Institute of India (see www.urbanslenderlorisproject.org). Some 150 citizen volunteers have been involved in the project so far, conducting nighttime survey walks and, in the early phases of the project, working mostly on developing a database of information about the slender loris population.

# III. Biophilic Architecture and Design

## A. Bird-Friendly Urban Design

### Aqua Tower, Chicago, Illinois
#### *A Vertical Wave Reaches for the Heights in Chicago*
*Tim Beatley*

This striking 82-story tower graces the skyline of downtown Chicago, just north of Millennium Park. Designed by architect Jeanne Gang (and Studio Gang), the building includes a mix of uses—the lower levels of the structure are a hotel, but there are also condominiums and rental apartments in the building as well. It includes a number of green features, such as a large podium park on its third level, the use of bamboo, and low-flow plumbing fixtures.

Most distinctive, though, is the look of the building's wavy exterior. Frequently described as undulating and rippling, it is the wave- or waterlike form of its exterior that is most distinctive and pleasurable to the eye.

It is indeed a very visually striking building—a biophilic facade. As Suzanne Stephens of GreenSource writes, "The sinuously curved concrete decks on each floor assume different configurations where balconies extend anywhere from 2 to 12 feet" (Stephens n.d.). These balconies seem to ripple across the vertical plane, and it is a striking view looking up at this structure against a blue sky. Christopher Hawthorne, the architectural critic for the *Los Angeles Times*, refers to the building's "liquid personality. . . . The effect is particularly dramatic if you stand at the base of the tower and look up. From that angle the facade resembles the rolling surface of the ocean" (Hawthorne 2010).

One of the most impressive aspects of the building is the importance given to birds, and the efforts to design a tower that minimizes fatal bird strikes (of which there are close to a billion each year in the United States, according to one study).

149

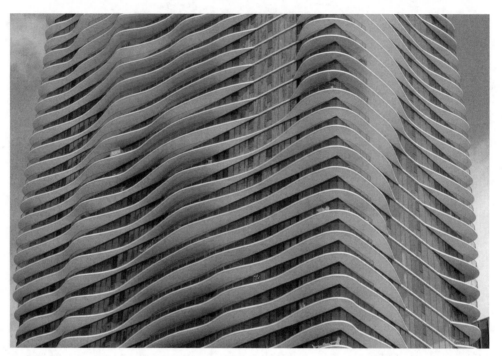

The Aqua Tower, in Chicago, is a distinctive biophilic design, and a bird-friendly building. Photo Credit: Tim Beatley.

Much of the glass used is fritted ("dot-etched"), and the balconies and wavy exterior help to make the building's edge more visible to birds. For this, the building was awarded a "Proggy" award (standing for "progress") from People for the Ethical Treatment of Animals (PETA). In the letter from PETA's president (Ingrid Newkirk) that accompanied the award, Newkirk speaks of the importance of design that considers other forms of life: "The American architect Louis Sullivan coined the phrase 'form follows function.' In the Aqua Tower, form follows compassion" (Magellan Development Group 2010).

Jeanne Gang is inspired and motivated by a concern with nature. In a recent interview with BirdNote she talks about the importance of reducing the impact of buildings on birds. "As an architect, I didn't want to be one of the biggest killers of birds." The experience of designing this bird-friendly tower, which was completed in 2009, seems to have strengthened Gang's commitment to birds. "My love of birds has just flourished since then" (BirdNote 2013).

# B. Biophilic Factories, Business Parks

## Hero MotoCorp Garden Factory and Global Parts Center, Neemrana, India
### *A Factory Growing Vegetables and Motorcycles*
*Julia Triman*

Renowned international architecture firm William McDonough + Partners collaborated with Hero MotoCorp to create a forward-thinking and biophilic manufacturing facility and parts center for motorcycles in Neemrana, India, in the arid state of Rajasthan. The factory is just over 100 kilometers (62 mi.) southwest of New Delhi. It is the company's fourth factory, but the first to adopt a garden concept. The architects describe the factory as "a garden of health and productivity," featuring significant sustainable building features, such as solar panels, rainwater harvesting, and an energy-efficient design. Vegetation is also incorporated into the building design and practice in a variety of ways (Hero MotoCorp n.d.).

The factory boasts rooftop greenhouses, indoor vertical gardens, and an extensive exterior planting plan featuring drought-resistant native plants to suit the surrounding landscape and lack of nearby available water. The designers and business owners also prioritized creating a healthy and restorative experience for factory workers: natural daylight is incorporated throughout the building design, creating a connection between inside and outside and also counterbalancing traditional images of factories as dark, windowless places full of smoke and noise. The greenhouses incorporated into the building design are intended to support food production for the factory café; the company's promotional video for the project describes this as "motorcycles being grown in the same lands as vegetables," and there is some indication that, if food production takes off in the greenhouses, it also might be made available to the local community (Hero MotoCorp Garden Factory n.d.).

While the Garden Factory's goals and design intentions are laudable (one reporter cites it as a revolution for the industrial workplace to one that is "beneficial, healthy, and even life-affirming"), time will tell if this project succeeds and becomes a model for other industrial development, and which of the biophilic interventions are best received by factory workers who inhabit the space day to day (Bahl 2014).

# Park 20|20, Amsterdam, Netherlands
## *A Different Kind of Business Park*
Tim Beatley

There is a unique business park under development just outside Amsterdam in the Netherlands. Called Park 20|20, it has been designed and organized around the principles of "Cradle to Cradle (C2C)," the powerful design paradigm advocated by American architect Bill McDonough and German chemist Michael Braungart, and expounded most fully in their groundbreaking book of the same title.

Owen Zachariasse, the sustainability officer for the park, gave me a tour of the site. Built in phases, the entire park is expected to be completed by 2018. The project covers an impressive area of about 18 hectares (44 acres).

The Cradle to Cradle design philosophy imagines a world where things are made either from biological nutrients that can biodegrade and be returned as earth and soil, or technical nutrients that can be recovered and endlessly reused. The project reflects these design principles in every aspect, from the selection of the materials used in the buildings, to the site's restorative landscaping, to the ecologically integrated energy, water, and other infrastructural systems of the park. Much of the energy needed is produced onsite, with building-integrated photovoltaics already a major design element in early buildings, such as the Inspiratiehuis.

The park includes a system that filters and reuses all of its gray water. Many of the buildings will contain vegetated rooftops, and there are plans to grow food on rooftop greenhouses as well. The site already contains several greenhouses, one of which is already growing food for the park's first restaurant. As Zachariasse explains, currently ground-level greenhouses will likely rise as new buildings rise and will be moved to the rooftop. There are technical and biological "pavilions," intended to showcase products and technologies and to educate about the C2C approach. All construction will be encouraged to utilize materials that have received C2C certification, such as the Accoya wood on the exterior of the Inspiratiehius, a natural material treated with a natural vinegar (rather than a toxic chemical).

The working environment in Park 20|20 is yet another innovation. The buildings are designed to emphasize smaller, temporary meeting and work spaces, rather than dedicated, permanent offices for workers. Zachariasse describes it in Dutch as *Het Nieuw Werken*, or the new way of working. This leads to a more efficient use of space, which results in less space being needed and a smaller, less costly structure. Also, the buildings (all designed by McDonough + Partners) are designed for adaptive reuse later, or disassembly if necessary.

It is billed as the first example of C2C design at an integrated district scale in the Netherlands, but probably also in the world. This is a holistic model of design and planning. Nature is not an afterthought, but a core design element. Incorporating nature is a key goal in Park 20|20, and when completed the landscape will enhance and restore native biodiversity and create the conditions for a more positive connection between workers and occupants with abundant nature around.

There are plans to enhance habitat for many local species, including birds, butterflies, and bees. There are also plans to establish native fresh water mussels in the main canal in the park and to install bat nests in the trees. There is a softscape walking boulevard that includes trees and benches to sit on. The landscape plan calls for different planting zones and landscape qualities (and small natural spaces that are surprises, that you just stumble upon as you walk through the park). There is a "meadow" on the front side of the Fox Vacations building that was in full bloom when I visited (and it did not look planted, but it was). Water features prominently in the park design, already with a functioning waterfall and central ponds that collect, filter, and recirculate water in the park. The water network includes interesting small water runnels that have been created in the brick stairs and walking surfaces of the public areas, where water will be flowing at certain times. The nature elements in Park 20|20 are part of a comprehensive vision of sustainability, and there are many other features here that make a difference.

A major goal is to overcome some of the usual inside–outside barriers to experiencing nature. Zachariasse says the goal of every building design in the park is to bring the inside out and the outside in (or in Dutch *binnen–buiten/buiten–binnen*). The Inspiratiehuis is a good example of this, with a dramatic green wall that extends through much of the interior of the building and out into the exterior front of the structure. There is a "wow" factor to this feature. The interior wall has been extremely well received, as well as the large windows and abundant natural light (all the buildings will be designed with large atria).

These green design elements and connections to nature are not just add-ons, but are understood as essential to creating improved work environments where workers are more productive, benefiting to the profit margins of the companies choosing to locate in this unique park. As Zachariasse argues, "We believe that the quality of the work environment directly affects the quality of the work itself." In the shifting paradigm of work, it is an emphasis on quality of these work spaces, and nature is a key aspect. The downsized structures, which shared work spaces allow, reduce the per meter cost, in turn allowing the Park to invest more funds in the green features and nature restoration.

Zachariasse stated, "So we increased the quality per square meter with direct attention to human-centered design that works towards increasing productivity of the employees." The human payroll is a major part of the expense of these businesses, he reminds me, and creating more pleasant, inspiring, and nature-connected work settings will do much to ensure those human investments deliver.

There are larger ethical reasons why we are duty-bound to restore the biodiversity and nature we so often destroy with development, but there are also helpful economic arguments that can be employed. These economic arguments often carry the day with business and corporate stakeholders, who may more effectively drive the changes we want to see in the direction of greater biophilic design and planning. In the Cradle to Cradle view of the world, business is understood to be the "engine of change," and there is a lot of evidence that this is the case at Park 20|20.

## C. Green Rooftops and Walls

### Green Roofs, Chicago, Illinois
#### Green, Green, Green Everywhere in the City of Chicago
Carla Jones

Simply planting trees in the Windy City helped Richard M. Daley, former mayor of Chicago, Illinois, begin his green legacy. During his time as mayor, he oversaw the planting of more than 600,000 trees (Kamin 2011). He had the goal of making Chicago the greenest city in America and aggressively pursued programs that worked toward that aspiration. The City went above and beyond tree plantings. One of Chicago's most successful efforts has been to encourage green roof construction in the city.

Chicago is home to more square feet of green roof than any other city in the United States (Chicago Green Roofs 2016). With a total of over 350 green roofs that equate to 5 million square feet, the city is becoming greener at a variety of heights (Chicago Green Roofs 2016). Much of the growing number of green roofs in Chicago can be attributed to the city's green roof incentive programs, including the Green Roof Improvement Fund and the Green Roof Grant Program. The Green Roof Improvement Fund provides a 50 percent grant match for the cost of placing a green roof on an existing building located in the Central Loop Tax Increment Financing (TIF) district (Seggelke 2008). The program will provide grants up to $100,000 per project (Seggelke 2008). The Green Roof Grant Program provides assistance to small commercial and residential projects in the amount of $5,000. These small incentive programs have proven successful at increasing the square footage of green roofs in the city.

## Azoteas Verdes, Mexico City, Mexico
### *Green Roofs for Hospitals and Schools*
*Julia Triman*

Mexico's capital city, in the heart of the Valley of Mexico, is the largest city in Latin America and home to over 20 million people. Despite a reputation for violent crime, socioeconomic segregation, and crowding, Mexico City has made major strides in a variety of ways over the past few decades to become a greener and more livable city. Former Mayor Marcelo Ebrard adopted Plan Verde ("Green Plan") intending to reduce carbon emissions across all sectors of the city (Villagran 2012). Several initiatives, including city tax incentives for green rooftops, and installation of green walls to help remediate poor air quality and add beauty to the urban landscape, are significantly increasing the presence of nature and greenery in Mexico City.

Mexico city's goal, which started with the adoption of Plan Verde in 2007, is to install 30,000 square meters (35,880 sq. yd.) of green roofs annually. The Azoteas Verdes program was launched in 2010 to provide greenery and absorb sunlight on Mexico City's typically flat roofs. The program targets primarily hospitals and schools, but is also encouraging adoption of green roofing techniques in the private sector, for both commercial and residential properties. Government tax incentives for installing green rooftops include up to a 10 percent discount on property tax in residential buildings for greenery covering at least one-third of the surface area of roofs in Mexico City (Agencia de Gestión 2014). While Mexico City's green roof goals are ambitious, thousands of square meters have already been planted on roofs across the city, including at Old City Hall, Belisario Dominguez Hospital, and Felipe

Carillo Puerto primary school, which alone boasts 50,000 square meters (59,800 sq. yd.). One unique example in Mexico City is Coca-Cola Company's conversion of a former helipad into a small interactive green roof space. Local design firms Rojkind Arquitectos and AGENT collaborated to create a new work space beneath the former helipad, topped with a xeriscaped green roof with curved wooden walkways and spectacular city views.

## GreenSkins, Fremantle, Perth, Western Australia
### *Piloting Green Walls and Studying Their Effects*
*Jana Soderlund*

In 2011 a local council in Perth, Western Australia required the construction of a green wall as a condition of development for a builder of a block of housing units. The council saw a green wall as a beneficial and attractive addition that would mitigate the loss of the view for the current tenants of the existing units. The developer took the council to court over this condition, won the court case, and had the condition removed. His defense was the lack of precedence and local knowledge in Perth with this scale of green wall construction in local climatic conditions. This led to recognition of the need to trial green wall plants and systems in the climatic conditions of Perth and the suburb of Fremantle so precedents might be available to future developers. Globally there are many examples of successful green walls but few in climatic conditions similar to those in Fremantle, where there are long, hot summers, high evaporation rates, and salty sea breezes. Curtin University Sustainability Policy Institute along with the City of Fremantle established a partnership to trial green walls in Fremantle. In early April 2013, two trial green walls were installed in Fremantle after three months of growing off site. Two sites and two different green wall systems were chosen. Challenging sites, both socially and climatically, were intentionally chosen. Site A is a north-facing wall in a little-used mall with significant antisocial behavior. The area is a sun trap in summer with a high level of radiant heat from the paving and surrounding walls. Site B is a west-facing streetscape wall, again with antisocial behavior. It is more exposed to the late afternoon westerly sun and strong sea breezes.

The test walls were planted with a combination of local plant species and exotics, chosen for their resilience in hot, dry conditions. Both sites are irrigated with a monitored watering system.

Temperature and humidity sensors have been installed and are providing continuous data over the year-long trial period. They are located behind the wall, in the plant canopy, and 15 centimeters (6 in.) out from the canopy. Sensors are also installed on a blank control wall and behind a wooden panel to gauge any difference the plants have on the parameters being measured. Water meters at site A are measuring water in and water out so evapotranspiration rates can be extrapolated. Plant growth rates are regularly visually assessed to determine which species are thriving. Thermal imagery will also provide visual data on which plant species are providing greater cooling capacity.

Assessment of the social response to the green wall is an important component of the trials, with pedestrian counts and behavioral mapping undertaken before the installation of the walls. These are being replicated at different periods throughout the year-long trial. Intercept surveys were conducted at both sites. On-site signage offers information on the project as well as a QR (Quick Response) code link to the website and online survey.

Responses to the green walls have been very positive. Nearly 50 people attended

One of the pilot green walls in the Green Skins initiative in Fremantle, Western Australia. Photo Credit: Jana Soderlund.

the early Friday morning opening in April, exceeding expectations, with continuing media coverage in local papers, radio interviews, blogs, and websites.

The number of online survey responses is steadily growing and providing some interesting results. When asked for one word to sum up thoughts around the green walls, words such as *brilliant, positive, breathtaking, inspiring, alive, unique,* and *beautiful* are being used.

Questions to gauge peoples' response to nature in general are revealing a strong appreciation of beauty. The highest response of 84 percent strongly agreeing is to the statement "I enjoy the beauty of nature." This is higher than the 79 percent strongly agree response to "Being in nature is a great stress reducer for me" and the 55 percent strongly agree response to "I need time in nature to be happy".

Peoples' perception of the functional attributes of green walls also reflect appreciation of beauty, with 86 percent strongly agreeing to the statement "Green walls can help make a city more attractive and liveable." By comparison, "Green walls could help reduce heat reflected off streets and buildings" had 62 percent strongly agree and "Green walls can help preserve nature" had 57 percent strongly agree. A resounding 95 percent stated that the City of Fremantle should make provision in their budget for more green walls.

The green walls were intentionally installed in our mild autumn, and the plants all thrived except for one species, which had to be replaced after 5 weeks. They have survived the winter storms and are currently enduring hot summer conditions. There has been much appreciation and interest and no vandalism. Some of the species have just failed after 7 weeks of summer sun, no rain, and high evaporation. These are being replaced. The other species are green and lush, providing a workable pallet of suitable species to choose from for future green walls in our city.

Further information and the survey can be found at http://sustainability.curtin.edu.au/projects/.

# One Central Park, Sydney, Australia
## *The Tallest Green Wall in the World*
### *Hilary Dita Beard*

At the intersection of city, nature, and art is One Central Park, a new residential project by architect Ateliers Jean Novel in collaboration with French botanist Patrick Blanc. Located in Sydney, Australia, One Central Park includes the tallest vertical gardens in the world; at 150 meters (approximately 500 ft.) tall, the construction includes 21 garden panels with 370 species of Australian flowers and plants that change seasonally. With 5,000 shrubs and 11,000 perennial plants, vegetation covers much of the facade of two high-rise residential towers (Arch Daily, 2015). In one of Sydney's inner western suburbs, the project resides in a lush and spacious 6,400-square-meter (approximately 1.5-acre) park (Mordas-Schenkein 2014).

Blanc describes the effect of One Central Park as being "like a natural cliff, as though [one has] cut a giant slice out of the Blue Mountains and put it in the middle of the city" (Vertical Garden Patrick Blanc n.d.). The park and building complex that constitute the "urban village" house the "residential towers, retail shops and collaborative spaces for artists and architects." The park will host music and arts festivals as well.

In an arduous process of research and plant selection, Blanc chose local species best suited to the climate and seasons. Facing strong wind, intense heat, dehydration, elevation, and humidity, and differing levels of sun exposure, the native plants were also then tested for hardiness. The research required multiple trips around the region to see different plant life in natural habitats as well as laboratory stress testing. Blanc's design process meticulously considers a variety of functional factors. He reduces maintenance and energy cost with biodiversity. A high level of biodiversity both decreases nutrient and water consumption and prevents insect damage and disease. This eliminates the need for pesticides or chemicals.

To construct his vertical garden, Blanc uses a growing medium of felt made from recycled clothes, which he uses to cover building faces that he intends to plant. It is purposefully nonbiodegradable and will not have to be replaced. Overall, the vertical gardens will require maintenance only three times a year. Additionally, the biodiversity creates a tapestry of different plants, resulting in a beautiful and dynamic visual texture.

The green walls increase energy efficiency, serving as natural insulation for the building, as well as an air filtration system that transforms pollutants into useful plant fertilizers. Providing jobs and utilizing local plant species, economic stimulus and educational opportunities coincide, providing a connection between city dwellers and the natural flora of their habitat.

Every aspect of the project serves multiple purposes: aesthetic, academic, social, and environmental. Designing and building One Central Park has contributed valuable new knowledge and research to the growing collaborative fields of urban landscape architecture and architecture. Additionally, One Central Park will provide residents with an unprecedented experience of natural living in an urban environment. Building urban green walls and integrating large-scale living structures is a challenge, but one that many consider the future of urban architecture.

# D. Green Terraces and Towers/Vertical Nature

## Stacking Green, Ho Chi Minh City, Vietnam
### *A Biophilic House Made from Planters*
Carla Jones

Window planters occupy almost every window and balcony along the streets of Ho Chi Minh City, Vietnam. These pockets of nature create beautifully green streets and serve as inspiration to architects Vo Trong Nghia, Daisuke Sanuki, and Shunri Nishizawa. How could this adoration for planters translate into housing design? This is how the Stacking Green House concept was created.

The three-story home fits snuggly in the typical "tube plot," which is 4 meters (13 ft.) wide by 20 meters (66 ft.) deep (Architectural Review 2011). The

The Stacking Green House, in Ho Chi Minh City, Vietnam, was designed by Vo Trong Nghia. Photo Credit: Vo Trong Nghia Architects.

planters serve as more than just inspiration; each layer is made from concrete planters that vary in height to accommodate various plant types. The plants are watered by a simple irrigation system attached to a rainwater collection system. The facades protect the occupants from the elements and also reduce energy expenditure. The design emphasizes tradition, environmental awareness, and connections with the natural world.

## Jardines Verticales, Mexico City, Mexico
### *Vertical Gardens to Clean the City's Air*
*Julia Triman*

Since the 1980s, Mexico City's government has implemented a series of policy changes to address extremely poor urban air quality, including significant advances in urban transportation choices, such as reducing car travel and increasing the use of alternative modes, such as bus rapid transit and bicycling (Cave 2012). Another important strategy for addressing air pollution that the government, individuals, and organizations are adopting is the installation of a series of "Jardines Verticales," or vertical gardens. These gardens do serve a functional purpose, but they are also intended as works of art. They are tangible ways to reenvision Mexico City's image and atmosphere—visible emblems of the greater citywide efforts to improve air quality and environmental conditions. While not all the projects survive, sometimes the health of the plants—or lack thereof—can send just as strong a message of the city's health to residents and visitors. In 2012, the nonprofit organization VERDMX installed a series of green walls throughout the city, one of which was prominently featured over the motorway on busy Chapultepec Avenue (Inhabitat n.d.). The plants in the temporary installation ultimately did not fare well, a reminder to those driving by that, while serious strides were being made, air quality was still extremely poor, and changes at individual and policy levels were still needed to improve the city's environment.

## 300 Lafayette Street, SOHO, New York City
### *Lush Green Terraces Provide Prospect and Refuge*
*Tim Beatley*

This new, seven-story, 83,000 square foot office and retail building is planned for the site of a former gas station in the SOHO neighborhood of New York City. It is a project of Cook+Fox architects, who have emerged as leading proponents of biophilic design. And this design puts biophilia at the center. The most unusual aspect of this building will be its green and vegetated balconies, some 11,500 square feet of planted boxes in total. The result will be a "cloak of lush balconies" (Curbed 2013). As project architect Brandon Specketer tells me, a more appropriate way to describe these balconies is "deep integrated terraces," in that they are more than small linear spaces, but rather wrap-around terraces that extend into the interior floor spaces and provide opportunities for sitting, strolling, and, of course, planting extensive vegetation (Brandon Specketer interview, June 5, 2015). There is specific reference in the project material and presentations to the biophilic design principles of prospect and

300 Lafayette Street is a project that will include lush green terraces, utilizing native species of plants that were present on Manhattan Island when Henry Hudson arrived in 1609. Photo Credit: Cook Fox Architects.

refuge, both achievable here given the site and building configuration and the design of the terraces.

The architects were inspired by the work of Eric Sanderson, an ecologist with the Wildlife Conservation Society and the author of the groundbreaking book *Mannahatta*, a creative effort to understand what the ecology of Manhattan Island was like in 1609. In understanding the possibilities of nature of these terraces there was an explicit goal to imagine how, through this building, native vegetation—both in extent and species—might replicate or replace what existed on this site in 1609, when Henry Hudson arrived. To this end, the terraces and rooftops are being designed to accommodate a vegetated area equal at least to what was there originally. The architects have been calling this a green area ratio (GAR)—analogous to a more traditional floor area ratio. The building will then become one of the first examples in New York of a structure that achieves a GAR of 1: compensating for what nature was taken at ground level to build on the site. With the help of Eric Sanderson, a list of native plants has been developed from which the terraces will be planted. Native species of tall grasses and bushes will likely make up much of the terraced plantings. The view from inside the building will be as important as from outside. The transparency of the building will allow workers to see and enjoy the nature-filled terraces from their workspaces. The building will also include lots of daylight, with floor-to-ceiling glass throughout.

# Via Verde, Bronx, New York City
### *Density + Nature Are Possible Together in the Bronx*
#### Tim Beatley

Is it possible to build densely in cities but also ensure access to nature? A terrific new development in the South Bronx, in New York City, is showing the way.

There was a time not long ago when the Bronx was literally burning (a result of widespread abandonment and disinvestment). It was a place where, in the 1970s and 1980s, high foreclosure rates and tax delinquencies left the city owning much of the land. Much has changed since then, and increasingly the Bronx is a testing ground for ideas that merge poverty reduction and affordability, with what is green and sustainable.

Via Verde (Spanish simply for the "green way") is one such inspiring example, a very unique affordable housing project. It all began about 5 years ago with a

Via Verde, an affordable housing project in the Bronx, New York, shows how it is possible to have urban density and nature together. Photo Credit: Tim Beatley.

city-sponsored design competition, with the winning design codeveloped by Phipps Houses and Jonathan Rose Companies.

A key aspect of Via Verde is that it doesn't look at all like an affordable housing project. There is use of a varied set of materials, including prefabricated panels of cement board, metal, and wood laminate. It is a visually interesting exterior. And the large windows and distinctive sun shades are also contrary to the usual look of housing for low- and moderate-income families.

Situated on a relatively skinny lot, running from north to south, the design response is creative indeed—222 units in total, stepping up from three-story townhouses on the south end to a 20-story residential tower on the north, and maximizing sunlight as a result.

When fully occupied, more than 400 residents will live in Via Verde, and they will have an unusual green living environment. Perhaps most distinctive about this project is its multilayered green rooftops. Beginning in a grassy ground-level courtyard, residents can ascend, first to an evergreen forest on the third floor, then an orchard of dwarf apple and pear trees on the fourth floor, then on to extensive raised-bed vegetable gardens on the fifth floor. Higher floors have more traditional sedum-covered extensive green roofs. What results is an impressive set of connected rooftop community spaces, for gardening but also just for walking and strolling, providing attractive areas for residents to be and spend time.

A common question is whether the structural loads required by the trees and green elements posed a major problem. The answer is, surprisingly, no—the building's block and plank construction had only to be modified marginally: replacing 10-inch planks with 12-inch planks to accommodate the extra loads.

And will these green features also help to build community? Yes, it is hoped, and there has already been some planning about how the roof spaces will figure into the life of the neighborhood. There is a plan to organize a community event to cut down one of the evergreens as the collective Christmas tree, and to plant a new replacement tree, for example.

Growing a culture of gardeners and orchardists will be a challenge moving forward, and Via Verde has enlisted the nonprofit GrowNYC to initially plant and care for the gardens and trees for the first 2 years. They will be engaging residents and holding gardening workshops with the goal of turning over the gardens and fruit trees to the loving care of residents at the end of this period.

For Jonathan Rose, President of the Jonathan Rose Companies, Via Verde represents the new ways in which we need to design and work in the city, and especially the importance of integrating nature and density in cities. People in cities need that nature, Rose believes: "I think it's because of the biophilic nature of people. We're just seeing a hunger for it."

But is it enough nature? Rose admits that the rooftops—gardens, fruit trees, sedum—are a kind of constructed nature. "Buildings in themselves are not the solution to nature in the city. Nature in the city has to be nature," Rose argues. He points to large green systems in which buildings (and cities) are embedded, and suggests that efforts to restore and clean up rivers like the South Bronx as equally important. New York has been engaging in many of these larger greening strategies, such as creating new waterfront parks and planting a million new trees in the city.

There are also many features in Via Verde aimed at enhancing the health of residents. The relatively narrow building allows for fresh air and cross ventilation, and, with ceiling fans, there is no need for summer air conditioning. The stairwells were intentionally designed to be on the outside, and brightly painted, to encourage their use (and discourage use of the elevators). And there is some not-so-subtle messaging to residents, such as the placard in the lobby imploring residents to "take the stairs—burn calories, not electricity." There are stores and shopping nearby, as well as an onsite medical clinic and space for a community-based pharmacy.

From the beginning the project was conceived as a partnership with the city, and it has been shepherded along by city agencies (an important lesson). Via Verde was "deeply supported by all the city agencies who collaborated together with us," Rose notes. This has been a helpful arrangement when special waivers and approvals have been required. There is no parking provided by the project, for example, something that required a special mayoral override (and makes a lot of sense given the nearby access to very good transit).

There are other sustainability features as well. Much of the south facade is covered in angled photovoltaic panels, producing enough power for all of the common lighting. A large cistern collects stormwater that falls in the courtyard and on the roofs and it is used for watering the gardens and trees. The apartments have low-flow water fixtures and Energy Star appliances and bamboo countertops.

It may be years before the health and other benefits of Via Verde can be demonstrated. There is in fact a research project under way that will compare how healthy the lives and lifestyles of residents of Via Verde are compared with others who were unable to secure a unit there. And if the attractiveness of the project is to be judged by the interest of those who wish to live there, it is already a huge success.

Early in the history of this project there were beautiful renderings of what the connected green roofs and gardens would look like—Jonathan Rose likes to say that the actual photos of these roof spaces are better than the renderings! After visiting the real thing, I think Rose is right.

## Bosco Verticale, Milan, Italy
### *The Vertical Forest*
*Tim Beatley*

This residential project in the center of Milan gives an impressive new meaning to vertical greening. Built-in planting boxes on balconies provide spaces for planting trees that extend skyward 19 and 27 stories, respectively, in this pair of residential towers. In total some 800 trees have been planted, some as tall as 9 meters (30 ft.), and thousands of plants and shrubs as well. It has been dubbed a "vertical forest" and is the brainchild of Italian architect Stefano Boeri. Completed in 2014, the project includes some 40,000 square meters (approximately 430,000 sq. ft.) of residential space. The project is the recipient of the 2014 International High Rise Award.

Most impressive is the research and testing that went into choosing the trees to be planted, which vary in species by floor and side of the building. Fruit trees were placed on the south side, while deciduous trees were sited on the north end to ensure maximum solar gain in winter. Decisions about which trees to plant were made floor-by-floor, taking into account specific site and micro-climatic conditions. A drip irrigation system provides water to the trees. Tree species, and the structures designed to hold them in place, were even tested in a Florida wind tunnel. Caring for the trees is the responsibility of a single management company, and flat owners pay a fee that covers the cost.

Much emphasis in the planting scheme has been placed on the enhancement of biodiversity. In the end some 94 different species of trees have been included, providing habitat for an estimated 1600 species of birds and butterflies (Woodman 2015). In architect Stefano Boeri's words, the project represents a "model of vertical densification of nature within the city . . . that contributes to the regeneration of the environment and urban biodiversity without expanding the territory of the city" (Boeri 2015).

# E. Healing Spaces/Health and Nature

## Spaulding Rehabilitation Hospital, Boston, Massachusetts
### Healing Harbor Views
Tim Beatley

The newly opened 132-bed Spaulding Rehabilitation Hospital, located on a former brownfield site in the Charlestown Navy Yard, incorporates a number of innovative features. Designed by Perkins and Will, its most important feature is its harbor front location, which is something the 262,000-square-foot hospital takes full advantage of. The structure does this by abundant windows, which are lower in patient rooms so the harbor views can be enjoyed by those in wheelchairs. The views from patient rooms are breathtaking and in this way enlist the water as a major aid in the healing process!

Three-quarters of the space of the building's first floor is set aside for community use, and the building includes design features that work to minimize exposure to sea level rise and flooding. These include placing major heating and cooling equipment on the roof and elevating the structure an additional foot. Three-foot landscape berms have also been placed around the building. There are also operable windows that can be opened by building occupants in the event of electrical failure, make the structure livable following a storm event (also creating a "safe haven" for the surrounding community; Guenther and Vittori 2013). There are "therapeutic terraces" on several levels and a green roof that retains stormwater (Perkins and Will 2013).

The building importantly sits on the city's harbor trail network, HarborWalk, and also provides physical access to the water, which can be used for a variety of water-related therapies, including windsurfing and kayaking (its Adaptive Sports program; Spaulding Rehabilitation Hospital 2013). There is physical therapy equipment provided along this harbor trail.

## Credit Valley Hospital: Carlo Fidani Peel Regional Cancer Center, Mississauga, Ontario, Canada
### *Forest in a Hospital*
#### Tim Beatley

There are few places where the power of biophilic design is more needed than in hospitals and spaces where patients and families struggle with illness. The design of the Carlo Fidani Peel Regional Cancer Center, at the Credit Valley Hospital, in Ontario, offers a creative and hopeful example of how the design of these interior spaces can make a difference. Architect Tye Farrow imagined a different kind of space for this 320,000-square-foot facility, one that would bring an element of nature inside and instill in patients a sense of confidence about the treatment they would receive. Farrow spoke with cancer patients about the building's design and found that they wanted something that would

The atrium lobby of the Credit Valley Hospital is designed as a sheltering tree. Photo Credit: Tye Farrow Architects.

embody hope, and "something that is alive" (Farrow 2007/2008). The main atrium of this center delivers on this request and has been designed to feel like a forest. There are four large "tree" columns, made of laminated Douglas-fir, that sweep skyward, with smaller limbs branching out from the main trunk. The look is visually dramatic and very much the feeling of being in the midst of large, sheltering trees.

In architect Farrow's words: "Powerful arching forms soar skyward, suggesting a human-scale cathedral in the midst of a bustling hospital. Patients, staff and visitors gather in this sheltered sanctuary to share news and talk through emotional issues" (Farrow 2007/2008, 55–56).

There are other biophilic features as well. In addition to the main atrium there are three smaller "skylight lanterns" that bring daylight into the interior spaces of the structure. Extensive daylight throughout the facility is a main feature. There is also an exterior survivors garden.

The design of these massive wooden members was complicated and innovative. Early on these developed as an internal bracing system that would avoid the use of outside metal plates, and a special misting system was developed as an alternative to the usual chemical-based fire suppression. The creative building design not only resulted in creating a sheltering, living environment but saved money as well (as compared with the more conventional steel construction methods).

## Healey Family Student Center, Georgetown University, Washington, DC,

### *A Biophilic Student Center Seeks Connections to the Potomac River*

*Tim Beatley*

The new 44,000-square-foot Healey Family Center, on the campus of Georgetown University, in Washington, DC, was designed by ikon.5 architects and opened in fall 2014. It has already become a popular place to study and socialize on campus.

The building incorporates a number of biophilic features. Most dramatic are the interior green walls, which adorn and naturalize the structure's great room. These green walls are expansive, extending from floor to ceiling, reaching at the top large skylights. The building includes a large fireplace and is awash with natural light. There is an emphasis on the use of biophilic materials, wood and stone especially.

There are large windows throughout, and the building provides an excellent connection with the surrounding outside world. Use of artificial light is kept to a

The new Healey Family Student Center at Georgetown University includes a number of green elements, including several interior green walls. Photo Credit: Tim Beatley.

minimum. There is an outside terrace, including fire pits and movable chairs and tables. The building is oriented to the south, providing visual connections to the Potomac River. The view of the river from the outside terrace is expansive and panoramic (and gives a feeling of being very close to the river, even though there is a road and other development directly in the path).

The structure's open nature makes it possible to see through the structure from one end to the other, as windows and natural light abound. Even the fireplaces are designed to provide visual connections to the other side. The facility includes study spaces of various kinds, conference rooms, dance studios, and music practice spaces, as well as a pub run by Bon Appetit, a company that emphasizes the sourcing of local food.

On a recent visit to the center I found the great room's couches and chairs, and the meeting spaces, all fully occupied. Students naturally orient facing out the great windows to the south, or around and along the living walls. And on nice days, students can sit outside looking out over the trees and the Potomac River not far away.

# F. Multisensory Biophilic Design

## Phipps Conservatory and Botanical Gardens, Pittsburgh, Pennsylvania
### Bringing the Sounds of Nature Inside Living Buildings
#### Tim Beatley

Located in Pittsburgh, the Phipps Conservatory and Botanical Gardens was founded in 1893. An important institution in the region, in recent years it has been a major leader in advancing sustainability and green building. Several of its recent building additions have pushed the green building envelope, including a new welcome center and green café. Most important has been the example of the new Center for Sustainable Landscapes (CSL), which includes a number of biophilic design elements. This structure is Leadership in Energy and Environmental Design (LEED) certified Platinum (the highest level) and also meets the standards of the Living Building Challenge (zero net energy and zero net water, among others). Its landscapes have been certified under the Sustainable SITES Initiative, and the building includes an extensive green roof. The CSL reflects an integrated approach to water and wastewater (including constructed wetlands for treating wastewater; onsite stormwater retention, including rain gardens; underwater water storage; and the use of porous pavements). There are, it seems, few ecological ideas or technologies not in use in the CSL.

The structure is also a pilot WELL–certified Building (Platinum), which is a designation for buildings that prioritize human health and well-being (Phipps Conservancy n.d.). There is also a model sustainable classroom onsite, the SEED (Sustainable Education Every Day) Classroom ("Classroom of the Future"). It is a modular structure built by EcoCraft Homes, intended to "model how classrooms of the future can be built to maximize student wellness and potential" (Phipps Conservatory n.d.).

Natural sounds have recently been incorporated into the facility through the work of sound artist Abby Aresty. Aresty has recorded sounds throughout the Pittsburgh area and brought them back to the Conservatory, where they are broadcast through 12 speakers in the CSL's main atrium. The sounds heard change over the course of the year (with the seasons), and in response to changing weather (e.g., precipitation, wind), guided by a computer program. This "sound collage" intends to educate, but also adds an important biophilic quality to an otherwise quiet interior space (a desire of Conservancy director Richard Placentini to overcome some of the

The Center for Sustainable Landscapes at the Phipps Conservancy, in Pittsburgh, is a certified Living Building. Photo Credit: Tim Beatley.

"blockade of nature" resulting from the otherwise commendable use of triple-paned windows that work against hearing the outside world (Karlovitis 2014).

The sound installation has now become part of the Conservancy's permanent display called the BETA ("Biophilia Enhanced Through Art") Project. BETA is a permanent exhibition of biophilic art throughout the facility and includes everything from wood tables to glass blown lizards to watercolors of flowering trees. There are steel sculptures and fossil replicas embedded in surfaces intended for touching, and there are even Paolo Soleri "windbells" to introduce earthly vibrations.

# IV. Restoring and Reintroducing Nature into the City

## A. Rivers and Riparian Nature; Blue Urbanism

### Revitalizing the Los Angeles River, Los Angeles, California
#### From Concrete Drain to "Green Ribbon"
##### Briana Bergstrom

After centuries of degradation resulting from industrialization, pollution, and general neglect, urban rivers around the globe are being reclaimed by the cities they traverse. The Los Angeles River is one such waterway being revitalized and reimagined as an urban amenity. As several public and private projects come to fruition, many Angelenos are hopeful that the city will reengage with their river, restore its ecosystem, and celebrate it as a valued natural asset and cherished public space.

Over the course of the city's development, the LA River and its floodplains have become highly urbanized—transformed from a once healthy meandering river to the engineered flood-control channel that exists today. After a devastating flood in 1938, the Army Corps of Engineers channelized three-quarters of the river, demoting it to an enormous concrete drain. The now barely recognizable river is designed to transport stormwater from the streets of Los Angeles to the Pacific Ocean in record speed, and does so quite successfully. But by channelizing the river, blanketing floodplains with impervious surfaces, and developing on riparian habitat, the city has starved itself of the precious water, ecosystem services, and recreational opportunities the river could provide. Sadly, over time, the LA River has become little more than another piece of the city's vast gray infrastructure.

Luckily, the tides in Los Angeles have changed. Now over 30 federal, state, and local agencies in addition to countless private sector and nonprofit groups are working to change the fate of the once sorely undervalued waterway. The Los Angeles River Revitalization Master Plan, which represents the collaborative efforts of these groups, includes plans for habitat restoration, improved open space and recreation, the reinvigoration of riverfront commerce, and significant economic development for the neighborhoods along its banks. Those behind the plan envision a "green ribbon" of public space complete with parks, bikeways, dining facilities, and gathering spaces that will attract residents and tourists alike and serve as a source of civic pride.

One specific project in the Army Corps of Engineers' plan, known as Alternative 20, will resurrect 6 miles of the river, replacing concrete with wetlands and planted terraces. These new green edges will merge into the ribbon of parks that will be built on vacant lots being acquired by the city. This effort will stitch together public spaces along the river's 51-mile expanse, creating a continuous greenway. Cleaner water will provide improved recreational space for kayakers and healthier habitat for the hundreds of species that call the river home. A new pedestrian and bicycle bridge named the La Kretz Crossing will improve access from existing river trails in the neighborhood of Atwater Village to hiking and equestrian trails in Griffith Park to the west, helping to weave the river into the city's existing fabric of green infrastructure.

The success of the river revitalization will be compounded by the many initiatives throughout Los Angeles focused on converting unused lots and underused street space into parklets and green alleys that will employ stormwater management tactics, such as permeable pavements, drought-resistant plantings, rain gardens, and bioswales. These efforts will not only help clean the water entering the river but will also slow the movement of water to the ocean and provide much needed green spaces throughout the city.

As these projects continue to materialize over the coming years, the Los Angeles River will slowly transform into a green corridor stretching from the San Fernando Valley to the Pacific Ocean, creating a grand public open space that will connect communities, restore natural habitat, and serve some of the city's more park-deprived neighborhoods. The river revitalization plans also have the potential to help the city improve overall environmental health, add open space for recreation, more efficiently manage stormwater, improve public health, foster economic development, and enhance quality of life for all. While the river will never be restored to its original meandering glory, with the help of Los Angeles's efforts, the LA River has the chance at a new beginning and an opportunity to become the next great urban green space.

# James River Riverfront Plan, Richmond, Virginia
## *A Wild River Runs Through It*
### Tim Beatley

Few cities have as much wild nature close to a dense urban core as Richmond, Virginia. Especially important is the James River, which makes its way through the city. The city's history is intimately connected to the river. Its location is on the fall line, and its early industry and economic and political life are closely linked to the James. In recent years the city and its citizenry have renewed their appreciation for the river, recognizing its importance and centrality to the experience of living in the city, and actively planning new strategies and projects to further connect to the James. A downtown plan prepared in 2009 refers prominently to the James as the city's "great, wet Central Park" (City of Richmond 2009). In 2012 an ambitious Riverfront Plan was adopted, declaring the river to be "a singular resource that should be publicly accessible and protected for future generations" (City of Richmond 2012, 6). Prepared by a team headed by Hargreaves Associates, the plan identifies a variety of projects and improvements that would make the river even more accessible and an even more central part of life in the city.

There is much intrinsic wildness to Richmond already, and any visit to the city's Riverfront Park system will generate awe at the extent of nature and the proximity to downtown. Recently, the author took a group of urban planning students on a field trip to the river. There was a running joke on that trip: what other capital city can boast nesting bald eagles, class 5 river rapids, and a great blue heron rookery a stone's throw away from downtown?—Nathan Burrell, who heads the James River Park, came up with the comparison—"Juneau, Alaska, maybe!" The rest of the day we talked about the "Juneau of the South and East." The extent of wild nature in Richmond is indeed quite remarkable, a function of the siting of this city on the banks of the James, in a spot on the fall line, where navigable waters end, accounting for the turbulent nature of the water and the surf.

The wildness of the James River is a unique mix of the human and human made and the natural. One of the jewels in the river park system is Belle Isle, a 54-acre island that divides the path of the river in two. Today a visit to Belle Isle is mostly a natural experience, but the island has a long history of human and industrial use, with remnants of this former past evident. It was the site of a prison during the Civil War, the location of a metal works and a quarry, and the site of an old hydroelectric facility that powered the city's street lamps. Much of the latter still exists and is a popular destination for those who want to climb old ladders and walk along concrete foundations.

The Pipeline Trail is a dramatic pathway along the James River in Richmond, Virginia. Photo Credit: Tim Beatley.

Access to Belle Isle is provided in dramatic fashion through a hanging footbridge, attached to the underside of the Lee Bridge, which traverses the river. The bridge undulates and moves, and it provides unusual views of the river as one crosses. There is a walking trail that circles the island, and numerous points where one can reach the water. On the island's north side there is an extensive set of rocks and water pools, and on any nice day families and couples can be found picnicking on the rocks and kids and dogs can be seen jumping and running and splashing among the rocks. These areas of rocky edge also provide unparalleled views of downtown Richmond.

One of the most unique features along the river and one of the more special ways to get up close to the river is on the Pipeline Walk. Literally this is a walk on top of a pipeline, a city sewage line, lying a few feet out into the river, and while reassuring handrails are there for much of the walk, at a certain point they end (it was at that point that I completely understood the sign at the beginning of the walk warning visitors not to walk when water is overflowing the top of the pipe). Nearby there are shad literally teeming, and herons are perched strategically to snatch them up. The rookery boasts some 40 blue heron nests. There was an osprey flying nearby and the constant press and roar of fast-moving river water on that day.

The City of Richmond has taken considerable steps to reconnect its citizenry to the James, and even more is envisioned in the Riverfront Plan. It calls for new pedestrian and bicycle trails (completing key missing links), new streetscape connections, new river terraces on both sides of the river, and a new pedestrian crossing (the Brown's Island Dam Walk), among others. Together these improvements should further strengthen the physical (and emotional) connections the city has to the James, and immeasurably enhance the quality of life in this biophilic city.

# Cheonggyecheon Stream Restoration Project, Seoul, South Korea

## *Knocking Down a Highway and Re-earthing a River in the Heart of the City*

*Carla Jones*

The now well-known Cheonggyecheon Stream Restoration Project in Seoul, South Korea, is a remarkable example of the power of reclaiming brownfield land for environmental, social, and economic benefits. The Cheonggyecheon Stream was buried underneath an elevated highway. In the 1990s, it became clear that there were safety issues with the integrity of the highway. The elevated section was in such disrepair that the entire highway needed to be reconstructed at a cost of approximately 93 billion won (approximately US$8.4 billion) (Jane n.d.). Plans were developed in 2001 to demolish the highway and reconstruct it.

The political debates of the 2002 mayoral election helped transform the conversation from reconstruction of the highway to the restoration of the Cheonggyecheon

The Cheonggyecheon river runs through downtown Seoul, and was once the site of an elevated highway. Photo Credit: http://flickr.com/photos/w00kie/138793454/.

Stream. There were many interests to consider, but ultimately the government decided to focus on just the publicly owned land.

In addition to stakeholder interests, there were many needs for the restored stream to serve, including historical, environmental, and social. The restoration needed to pay homage to the site's highway past, capture stormwater, and provide recreational space to citizens. The entire restoration cost 1 percent of Seoul's total budget, which was feasible to implement. The design of the linear park is a progression from more pavement to more nature. There is a museum to educate the more than 60,000 visitors per day on the importance of the stream restoration.

As if the reduction of heat island effect, improved air quality, and better flood control were not enough positive effects, the restoration has transformed a 3.6-mile corridor with no nature into a thriving place for people to connect with nature.

## St. Louis Great Rivers Greenway District's River Ring, St. Louis, Missouri
### *Connecting People and Nature across State Lines*
*Amanda Beck*

To celebrate all four beautiful seasons, the goal of the Great Rivers Greenway District is to connect people to nature all year long. The governmental organization was voted into existence by the people of St. Louis, St. Louis County, and St. Charles County in November 2000 when Proposition C, the Clean Water, Safe Parks, and Community Trails Initiative was approved (Sable-Smith 2013). The Great River Greenway gets at the core of how nature enhances everyday life while also reconnecting people with each other. Indeed, the organization established a bold vision when, in 2003, the River Ring network was launched to connect the city, St. Louis County, and St. Charles County through a series of 45 greenways spanning 600 miles of trails. The initiative is supported by the citizen-driven River Ring regional plan, and the future of the River Ring has expanded so that one day, Missouri and Illinois will be connected through the various greenways in a regional greenway district.

Residents can spend time in Forest Park exploring Picnic Island, and then take the Centennial Trail along Washington University's campus to the historic Delmar Loop district. Or locals can walk the 11-mile North Riverfront Trail, which follows the Mississippi River and ends at the historic Old Chains of Rock Bridge, which is part of the iconic Route 66 (United States National Park Service n.d.).

# El Parque del Agua Luis Buñuel, Zaragoza, Spain
## *A New Kind of Park That Makes Room for Flooding*
### Hilary Dita Beard

As part of the 2008 Zaragosa Expo, the Alday Jover architecture firm designed the Water Park Luis Buñuel in Zaragoza in a meander of the Ebro River. To integrate the city and the Ebro, the park incorporates wetlands that can safely be flooded and an intricate water-based ecosystem, while also being accessible to city residents. Using hydraulics, it incorporates a closed system for recovering water from the river, naturally purifying it for public bathing, and then organically filtering it before returning it to the river.

The park is much more than just a beautiful attraction; it provides important ecological services (Alday, Jover, and Dalnoky 2008). The park requires little maintenance, using 40,000 shrubs and 25,000 trees that form a self-sustaining ecosystem. This former agricultural land is reimagined as a public park, but the park utilizes existing tracks created by the work of farmers and gardeners through the years to minimize heavy-handed adjustment of microtopography.

The Water Park represents the crossover of river to city to public space. A main concept of the design was to integrate the natural life cycles of the river, including flooding, and make them compatible with the space. It is a space of negotiation between the city and the river, between nature and people. It includes three beaches and many public-use buildings, such as an amphitheater and event spaces.

The outcomes of the completed park so far are very positive. Only one in a series of projects reconnecting the city to nature and people to the river, and shifting the paradigm of urban design, the project is very popular with locals. It is the second most valued space in the city, and despite being on the periphery of the city, it is intensely used.

The micro-climates emerging from the growth and maturing of the wetlands and layers of varying vegetation have brought a great deal of biodiversity to the space, especially from migratory birds. An island in the park has even been set aside for a rare species discovered to be inhabiting it. This leads to a greater respect and understanding of biodiversity and native and migratory bird species, and it provides educational opportunities for park visitors (Alday, Jover, and Dalnoky 2008).

In an interview, architect Inaki Alday of Alday Jover referred frequently to "giving back to the river." From the soil, to the vegetation, the heart of this project is in the "space of negotiation" between human use and ecosystem (Inaki Alday, interview with D. Beard, January 7, 2015). This project truly represents a new paradigm for designed spaces integrating city and nature, with equal respect for both and a value system shifting away from the anthropocentric and toward the biocentric.

Two images of water park Luis Buñuel in Zaragoza, Spain, one showing the park dry (top), and following a major flooding event (bottom). Photo Credit: Alday Jover Architects.

# B. Trees and Urban Forests

## RE:LEAF/Street Tree Initiative/Mayor's Street Tree Program, London, United Kingdom
### *New Trees and Woodlands in the Neediest Places of the City*
*Mariah Gleason*

RE:LEAF is a program intended to increase London's tree cover 5 percent by 2025, amounting to one tree per Londoner. The program seeks to encourage planting and management of trees and woodlands in areas of London that most need them; enable communities and organizations to plant more trees and look after trees and woodlands within their neighborhoods; ensure the economic value and climate change adaptation benefits of trees and woodlands are realized; and secure investment for trees in London. The program works to accomplish these aims by pursuing projects that increase London's tree cover, increasing awareness of street trees, and mobilizing thousands of Londoners to care for, and plant more, trees. This program functions as a partnership between the city and multiple organizations, including the Forest Commission, Groundwork London, Trees for Cities, The Woodland Trust, The Tree Council, and many other prominent groups.

RE:LEAF makes it easy for people to get involved. The Greater London Authority (GLA) website for the project guides people to additional grant sources for street tree projects. It also advertises ways to volunteer and donate, and provides tips for planting trees in private yards and gardens (Greater London Authority [more trees], n.d., 9).

Many goals have been accomplished through RE:LEAF, including the planting of over 16,300 trees, new orchards and woodlands in four London boroughs, creation of London Tree Week (a weeklong celebration of trees and woodlands in London), and a Tree-Routes app (an iPhone/iPad app that showcases trees of interest by borough or tube line).

# Urban Forest Strategy, Melbourne, Australia
## *From Trees in the City, to a City in a Forest*
### Tim Beatley

The capital city of the state of Victoria, Melbourne, has achieved considerable acclaim for its quality of life and culture. It has been a leading Australian city in environmental and climate change areas, and in the last several years has been developing a suite of initiatives aimed at enhancing its urban forests and nature. The city has explicitly adopted a nature-immersive, biophilic vision: it aspires to be a city in a forest rather than a forest in a city (Lynch 2015). The impacts of a long drought and recent heat waves that have led to significant loss of human life (2009 event leading to 374 deaths), have been motivators. At a certain point the city stopped watering its tree stock and city landscapes, which has stressed trees and led to tree mortality. This has led to an estimate that the city, if it does not replace trees, will likely see a 40 percent loss of tree stock over the next 15 to 20 years. The city intends to move in the other direction, and specifically to double the city s tree canopy coverage from its current 20 percent to 40 percent. Addressing long-term heat in the city is a major goal and the city believes that doubling the canopy coverage would reduce average temperatures in the city by 4°C (39°F). An Urban Forest Strategy lays out the specifics, which include planting 3000 new trees in the city each year. The city also seeks to increase permeable areas in the city by converting some paved areas to parks and to green its laneways. And it is installing rain gardens and permeable paving (for instance, permeable bluestone pavers on Collins Street). It plans to maximize the impact of tree planting by planting them in streets (rather than just sidewalks). Its approach to addressing water scarcity is to move swiftly toward harvesting stormwater, which it believes could provide one-quarter of the needed water for landscaping. It is also promoting greater use of more green roofs in the city and has prepared a set of Technical Guidelines for Green Roofs.

The approach taken by the city in developing and implementing its forest strategy has been creative and has emphasized public engagement and outreach. The city has creatively used artists, and art competitions, as well as a number of public workshops and online forums. A comprehensive online map has been developed of all 77,000 trees in the city, called the Urban Forest Visual. Each tree has a distinct number and even its own e-mail address. The ability to e-mail a favorite tree is one of the most creative ideas for engaging the public, and this has been a big success. Thousands of e-mails have been sent to trees—many of them love letters. Yvonne Lynch, who heads the city's Urban Ecology and Urban Forest Team, tells the story of how one 350-year-old oak tree in Milwaukee recently e-mailed an oak tree in Melbourne! According to Lynch, "People are really captivated by this ability to connect with the trees."

The city is also working on an Urban Ecology Strategy, and in support of this has undertaken a number of equally creative steps to involve the public, including a citywide bioblitz, and the preparation of a discussion paper ("Unleashing the Power of Nature").

# C. Greenways, Greenbelts, Urban Trails

## Urban Trail Network, Anchorage, Alaska
### *Trails for a Diversity of Users from Hikers to Skiers to Dog Mushers*
#### Julia Triman

Anchorage, Alaska, is nestled in arguably one of the most beautiful and rugged places of natural scenery in the world. To complement the impressive nature around the city and throughout the state, city planners and park and trail advocates have built and continue to build a most impressive system of trails throughout the city, connecting urban residents and visitors with substantial nearby nature. Anchorage boasts over 130 miles of paved trails and 160 miles of nonpaved trails, and these are put to good use by what one *Alaska Dispatch News* reporter calls the "most diverse set of users of any trail system in any city in all of America: walkers, runners, bikers, rollerbladers, skiers, ski-jorers, snowshoers, dog mushers, birdwatchers, and horseback riders" (Goertzen 2015). This diversity of users spans times of year and weather conditions: while temperate and nearly always washed in daylight in the summer, Anchorage is also decidedly a winter city, with significant snowfall and periods of darkness throughout much of the year.

According to Vic Fisher, the city's first planning director, the reason the trail system is so successful is that early city leaders set aside land for trails at the very beginning of city planning for the municipality in the 1950s. Despite the fact that, at the time, the population was very small and there was very little development, Fisher says that people's connection to surrounding nature was strong: "You could touch the wilderness, it was right there, and people related to the value, to the beauty of the mountains and the mudflats" (Wohlforth 2015). Because of this strong connection and an engaged group of citizens, land and connections for trails were embedded in plans for the city from the very beginning, which laid the foundation for Anchorage's reputation as a "trail city" in the years to come.

One of the most notable trails in Anchorage's network is the Tony Knowles Coastal Trail, which stretches along the western edge of the city from the trailhead a few blocks north of the performing arts and convention centers past Ted Stevens International Airport (where all manner of aircraft beg for attention, including lots of tiny biplanes buzzing overhead) and connecting at the southern terminus with an extensive network of trails in Kincaid Park. Along the trail, one can experience stunning views of water; the city playing peek-a-boo in the clouds beyond; extreme changes in tides, which conceal and reveal a series of mudflats; and the occasional wildlife spotting, including one of a herd of resident local moose.

Perhaps even more impressive are the city's trail connections to the east, into Chugach State Park's nearly 500,000 acres. Several trailheads offer direct access to the park from city streets, immediately connecting residents with a substantial wilderness area within a few miles of downtown.

Despite Anchorage's substantial trail network and access to nearby nature, planners are at work to make improvements, as locals have expressed keen interest in increasing the use of trails year-round. An Anchorage Trails Plan is in the works, in consultation with dozens of local advocacy groups, from the Arctic Bicycle Club to the Chugiak Dog Mushers Association to the Knik Canoers and Kayakers, and the Anchorage Park Foundation has established an Anchorage Trails Initiative. Anchorage Park Foundation Executive Director Beth Nordlund says one goal is to better connect residents to local amenities through trails, improving awareness of local access points and creating neighborhood pride for each individual segment of the trail system (Anchorage Park Foundation n.d.).

## Chengdu's Ecological Belt and Garden City Vision, Chengdu, China
### *China's Ancient City of the Southwest Plans a System of Wetlands and Water That Encircles Its Center*
*Tim Beatley*

Chengdu, located in the southwestern mainland of China, is the capital of Sichuan Province. It is best known for its giant pandas and is sometimes referred to as the Panda Capital of the World. It is home to a panda research and breeding center (the Chengdu Research Base of Giant Panda Breeding), and large forested panda reserves that harbor many of the last remaining giant pandas in the wild. Everywhere in the city one sees the symbol and imagery of giant pandas, clearly a creature residents associate strongly with their city and are quite proud of.

This city of 15 million has a long association with water and is famous for its innovative irrigation system dating back more than 2000 years. It is a city that has aspired to be a garden city and has a history of planning that reflects a commitment to protecting natural and agricultural landscapes. The city sits on the Chengdu Plain, in between two mountain ranges to the east (Longquan) and west (Longmen), and in between has identified and protects five green wedges (the city's shorthand summary of its urban ecological network is "two mountains, five green wedges, one green ring/ecological belt"). Strong emphasis has been given to ecological landscape planning in Chengdu, to a regionwide vision of growth, and the integration of rural and urban to an unusual degree for Chinese cities. The pattern of future growth envisioned is of a regional system of cities, with much population growth happening in smaller, satellite cities, connected by greenways and transit.

One of the most impressive urban ecology projects, and a main element of the city's planning vision, is the so-called ecological belt that circles the central city and generally follows the city's elevated inner ring expressway (extending some 500 meters [550 yd.] on either side of it). It encircles the city and forms a connected network of lakes and wetlands, and it extends inwardly in places to encompass "seven wedge-shaped blocks" (Chengdu Planning and Management Bureau 2003). The ecological belt is intended to serve multiple functions: flood control/retention is a key one, but also mitigation of the urban heat island, recreation and leisure, and culture and history, and the green spaces will also provide a badly needed evacuation zone for the city. Providing sufficient areas for evacuation and sheltering in the event of an earthquake is a major concern in Chengdu because the region has experienced devastating seismic events in recent years (including a 7.9 magnitude earthquake in 2008 that killed some 87,000).

On a recent visit to the ecological belt the recreational benefits were clear, and the belt will likely serve as a sort of circular central park for the city. The predominant development pattern in this growing city is mostly in the form of 30- to 35-story high-rise buildings, and space for parks has been limited. The ecological belt serves to connect different parts of the city and offers residents throughout the central city access to nature and water. The city has also been investing in the construction of a new network of walking and bicycling paths, with the eventual target of 800 kilometers (500 mi.) of such pathways. Several of these routes have already been completed and permit residents to travel from the developed city to the surrounding rural areas.

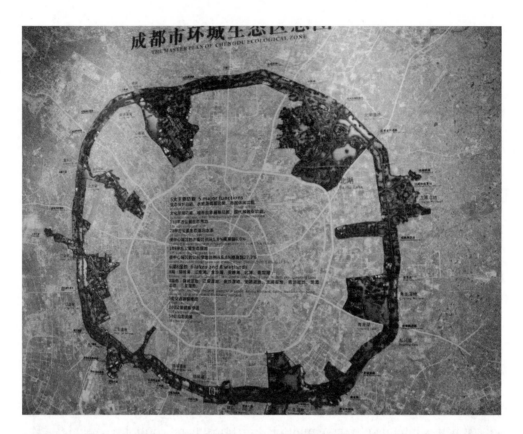

Images of the ecological belt that encircles the center of Chengdu, China. Top photo is of a map of the ecological belt prepared by Chengdu Planning Bureau. Lower image of Chengdu Skyline. Photo Credit: Tim Beatley.

# Trilha TransCarioca (TransCarioca Trail), Rio de Janeiro, Brazil
### *An Ambitious Trail That Will Tie Together People and Parks*
Tim Beatley

Rio de Janeiro is defined by its dramatic vistas and spectacular landscapes, and large forested parks, such as Tijuca National Park. One of the most ambitious urban trail projects is currently under development in Rio, and would connect Tijuca with other parks and natural areas in the city and provide an unusual way to experience this city of 6 million. The Trilha TransCarioca is a trail network that would traverse the city, allowing a resident to travel from shore to mountaintop, linking major parks and ecosystems, including Tijuca National Park. The trail will run west to east, beginning in Ponta do Picão and ending in Urca. I spoke recently with Pedro Menezes, who came up with the idea for the trail some 20 years ago and is finally seeing it come to fruition. The vision is audacious indeed—eventually it would extend 250 kilometers (155 mi.) in length, and already some 120 kilometers (75 mi.) have been built and are open to the public.

Providing movement corridors for species such as toucans is a primary goal. "We also want the trail to put the Rio population closer to its nature," Menezes tells me, "so they can cherish more, appreciate more the value of it both in terms of recreation but also in terms of ecosystem services." So far it has been largely driven by volunteer help, with some 2000 volunteers actively involved. "The enthusiasm is great," Menezes says, telling me about a recent volunteer training event where they expected 250 to sign up, but instead had more than 1,000 people attend. Such an urban trail is clearly a matter of pride for many, and will certainly become over time a highly valued aspect of the Rio urban experience.

# D. Green Alleys/Ecological Alleyways

## Green Alley Program, Austin, Texas
### *Reimagining the Spaces Behind Homes as Locations of Nature*
#### Carla Jones

The greening of alleys is becoming more and more prevalent in cities across the globe. From using existing alleys as stormwater management tools to creating new public green spaces, alleys provide a unique opportunity for nature in an unexpected place. I had the opportunity to interview Barbara Brown Wilson, cofounder of the Austin Community Design and Development Center, about a unique, 10-year collaboration between the University of Texas–Austin, the City of Austin, and many community groups to make unused alleys into livable green spaces.

The challenges with Austin's alleys have been numerous over the years. One challenge was the lack of consistent use of the alleys. These forgotten spaces soon became a liability to the city in terms of safety and stormwater overflow, which presented another issue. Lastly, Austin has been threatened by sprawl for many years because of a lack of affordable housing and land in the city. An engaged community partnership began around these issues of urban sprawl, underutilized land abutting alleys within the central city, and the need for more high-quality, affordable housing. The Alley Flat Initiative was created to address these issues. Through many community meetings, studio classes, and working with over 10 city departments, prototypes of sustainable, affordable housing were designed and built to test and promote the concept.

Public attention to the alleys expanded greatly when it became about much more than just housing. Through the Alley Flat Initiative, it became clear that these liminal spaces could be transformed into thriving community corridors for people and nature. Students in the Public Interest Design program at the University of Texas–Austin experimented with how the alleys could be used as wildlife corridors, public art exhibits, hubs for food production, and functional rain gardens. Wilson co-led the studio in which the students were able to imagine what the alleys could look like without the restrictions often placed by city departments. The community had input throughout the entire process. According to the City of Austin, the Green Alley Demonstration Project is beneficial in many ways:

- Encouraging compact neighborhoods
- Increasing the sustainability performance of public right-of-way

Images from the Green Alley initiative in Austin, Texas. Photo Credit: Barbara Brown Wilson.

- Creating a model project that demonstrates sustainability and Imagine Austin goals
- Increasing affordable housing choices with alley flats or other secondary unit infill
- Addressing gentrification issues
- Activating alleys to increase public safety
- Encouraging residents to "adopt" and care for alleys

The Alley Flat Initiative and the Green Alley Demonstration Project show that partnerships between universities and cities can strengthen projects. Wilson mentioned that these collaborations provide continuity and expansion in terms of resources and funding opportunities, as well as a third-party perspective on a civic concern. These partnerships provide a resource safety net that helps the project continue when the city, university, or community-based organizations may not have the resources to do so alone. Universities can also provide important research support that provides evidence to help secure funding and garner support in the community.

Barbara Brown Wilson says "Coalition building is incredibly critical. This project didn't really take off until we built the coalition. For the Green Alley Demonstration Project, a diverse set of interests strengthened the project. Participatory action research helped us abandon narrow interests and form the coalition around a broader collective vision."

The coalition does not end with green alleys. When asked where else you can find nature in unexpected places in Austin, Texas, Wilson mentions the greening of parking garages by integrating them into wildlife corridors. Along with Danelle Briscoe and Dean Fritz Steiner at the School of Architecture, Mark Simmons of the Lady Bird Johnson Wildflower Center, university facilities and city council members collaborated to reimagine how many public parking garages at the University of Texas and across the City could be part of a wildlife corridor. Wilson explains the compelling notion driving this team, "If we embed wildlife habitats on the sides of these garages, what impacts might it have? How might it better air quality? Improve biodiversity? What sorts of benefits might exist beyond the really deep need for people to be near nature? There are all sorts of areas that are built into our urban fabric that we don't re-imagine enough. We think of them as obdurate or 'fixed.' There really is no urban space that couldn't be transformed to be more natural to the benefit of both humans and non-human residents. Every median in the country could be a place of deep beauty and innovation."

# Green Alleys, Montreal, Quebec, Canada
## *Hidden Green Oases in Canada's Cultural Capital*
### Tim Beatley

Montreal's alleys have been lovingly greened, and the city has supported these neighborhood projects in many ways.

Josée Duplessis, who sits on the Montreal City Council and whose portfolio includes parks and green spaces, drew me sketches of her favorite green alleys—one off of St. Urbain, the other off of Rue du Square St-Louis. They are hidden gems, with doorways and openings not easy to find.

There are now more than 100 of these green alleys throughout the city (and there is even a map of them). The history of these alleys goes back to a time when they had great utility for the delivery of coal to houses. They are officially acknowledged by

Montreal, Quebec, has had one of the longest efforts to convert former alley spaces behind homes into gardens and greenery. One of these impressive green alleys is shown here. Photo Credit: Tim Beatley.

the city, and there is a process for applying for city designation (requiring approval of a certain percentage of the residents). Once officially designated, there is a Ruelle Verte sign posted prominently at the entrances to these spaces. The city provides funding for the planting and greening of the alleys through its network of so-called eco-quartiers, or eco-districts (neighborhood associations, focused on green projects and sustainability).

These green spaces are, not surprisingly, very linear spaces, with tree cookies as stepping stones or pavers embedded into the ground. Though public, most are closed on one end, and so probably not widely visited by residents outside the immediate neighborhood. The green alleys seem especially valuable to the many homes and apartment buildings that have a direct gate or entranceway to the alley. In a number of places just inside the private yard there was a vegetable garden or other tended garden space, further adding to the greenness of the alley.

The steps and actions taken to green these alleys are varied, but they often involve creative efforts to add raised beds along the edges of walls. These are constructed of a variety of materials, including stone and brick, and when planted provide a green softening of these walls. Some are bordered in plastic, others in wood or stone. In some cases there are bushes and small trees, in others, flowers and vegetables.

There are composting structures for garden and organic wastes, rainwater collection barrels, and chairs for sitting. Stand-alone pots are found, and lots of plants climbing their way up the sides of fences and walls.

Other cities have been actively promoting the greening of alleys also, although for a much shorter time. Chicago has its own highly successful Green Alley Program and has developed a Green Alley Handbook to guide interested homeowners and businesses and show what is possible in these spaces. In San Francisco, the idea of "living alleys" is picking up steam, with the first, Linden Alley, in the Hayes Valley neighborhood, showing the benefits and beauty such pedestrian and green improvements can provide. The city is now working to include the concept in area plans, and the concept of a network of living alleys is a key design feature of the Market and Octavia Area Plan.

# E. Green Infrastructure and Urban Ecological Strategies

## Costanera Norte, Buenos Aires, Argentina
### *An Ecologically Rich City*
*Amanda Beck*

Buenos Aires is an ecologically rich city located in the "megadiverse" country of Argentina, with the surrounding area composed of productive farmland and rangeland in the extensive Pampa alluvial plains. Home to nearly 2 million porteños, as Buenos Aires residents call themselves since they live in a major port city, the greater metro area is home to over 12 million people. Though the city still grapples with income segregation, and its unsettling past, Buenos Aires is working toward a future in which the city is greener and healthier for residents. Mayor Mauricio Macri announced the Plan Buenos Aires Verde in 2014, with a 20-year vision of making the city greener, cooler, and more adaptable to climate change. Initiatives will include focusing on sustainable transportation, promoting clean energy, and reducing greenhouse gas emissions; all the while increasing nature in the city by planting street trees and trees along highways, as well as encouraging developers to build green roofs in the city.

Buenos Aires has a long history of places for residents to gather, be they public plazas, parks, or the waterfront. French-Argentinian landscape architect Carlos Thays became the city's director of Parks and Walkways in 1891 and made a lasting impression on the city with beautiful tree-lined boulevards and parks. Two of Thays's largest undertakings were the expansion of the Parque Tres de Febrero, which covers nearly 1000 acres within the city, and the Jardín Botánico Carlos Thays, which Thays insisted feature many native Argentinian plants in addition to other more exotic specimens (Biografía Julio Carlos Thays n.d.). The open spaces still enjoyed today, such as the Centenario and Colón parks and the Mayo plaza, are also supplemented by a history of interaction with the bounty of the surrounding Pampa lands. For over a century, La Rural, an annual agricultural and livestock exhibition, has been bringing residents into contact with the productive pastoral lands outside the city. Visitors can interact with livestock and hear from farmers, breaking away from their normal city routine.

In cities as large as Buenos Aires, such parks or botanical gardens are the main places that locals can come into contact with nature, and the wonder these places induce can also lead to greater environmental awareness. The botanical garden at the Museo Argentino de Ciencias Naturales Bernardino Rivadavia has a special section dedicated to the vegetation of the Pampa, educating visitors about the importance of the local ecosystem's biodiversity (Faggi 2012). Without such a strong history of open spaces and green spaces it could be hard to remind residents of the benefits access to nature provides, and, luckily, porteños not only cherish their existing places to connect with the natural world, but also want to see more green in their city.

Access to nature is important in the city, and access to wilderness is equally important when living amid the organized chaos of a city, which is why Buenos Aires' Costanera Norte and Costanera Sur Ecological Reserves are such important biophilic features of the city. Costanera Norte is located behind Buenos Aires University, along the Rio de la Plata riverbank. Going south of the University, Costanera Norte also features an extreme sports park where residents can get outside to skate, longboard, bike, and try a climbing wall (Los Deportes 2013). Another place the city government created for porteños to escape the heat was what has now become Costanera Sur, which started in 1918 as a municipal riverside resort (Municipalidad de la Ciudad de Buenos Aires, n.d.)

In the 1970s, the city government attempted to reclaim land from the Rio de la Plata, but the in-fill project was abandoned by the 1980s, and nature was left to its own devices. After being abandoned, the in-fill area developed into a diverse ecosystem with two lagoons, Las Gaviotas and Los Patos, as well as countless native flora and fauna reclaiming the land, which environmental groups persuaded the city government to declare an ecological reserve in 1986. Each of these reserves provides urban wildernesses along the edge of the city, places where residents can escape the city to find nutria or American storks or search in the tall grasses for a Hilaire's toad-head turtle (Reserva Ecológica). What makes them remarkable is how they allow residents to witness the power of nature to revive an area's biodiversity by reclaiming land so wildlife might return.

## Chicago Wilderness, Chicago, Illinois
### *A Growing Coalition of Organizations Working to Restore and Celebrate the Region's Nature*
Carla Jones

Chicago Wilderness is a nationally recognized network of more than 300 organizations comprised of residents of Illinois, Wisconsin, Indiana, and Michigan. These dedicated members of Chicago Wilderness include government agencies (local, state, and federal), large conservation organizations, cultural and educational institutions, volunteer groups, municipalities, corporations, and faith-based groups who take a "regional, collaborative approach to conservation to protect and restore the nature on which we all depend" (Chicago Wilderness n.d.).

The work of Chicago Wilderness is guided by four key initiatives: Restoring Nature, Climate Action, Leave No Child Inside, and Greening Infrastructure. By restoring nature, members are improving the ecological health of natural systems by engaging residents in restoration and stewardship of natural places. Members of Chicago Wilderness take a different approach to climate action by focusing on issues of biodiversity conservation. Based on Richard Louv's theory of nature deficit disorder, Chicago Wilderness is raising awareness of children connecting with nature. Lastly, Chicago Wilderness promotes a softer, green infrastructure system that is economically beneficial and contributes to a healthy populace.

They have a commitment to using the most advanced science, collaborating to conserve, and caring for both people and nature, to benefit all the region's residents by working at the landscape scale (Chicago Wilderness n.d.). Chicago Wilderness has received national attention and many awards, including the National Planning Award and Secretary of the Interior's Partners in Conservation Award (Chicago Wilderness n.d.).

## Houston Wilderness, Houston, Texas
### *Urban Wildness From Bayous to the Gulf*
*Julia Triman*

Houston, the most populous city in Texas, is probably best known in urban planning circles as a sprawling city, and one without zoning laws. Although situated in a geographically and biologically diverse region of Southeast Texas, among forests, prairies, marshes, bays, estuaries, and other natural features, human population growth, development, and land use patterns have not always been known for putting nature first.

Like Chicago Wilderness, Houston Wilderness is a coalition of government, educational, conservation, and business organizations, as well as individuals dedicated to increasing awareness about the ecological diversity present throughout the Houston region (Houston Wilderness 2007). The *Houston Atlas of Biodiversity*, published in 2007 and modeled on a similar document produced by Chicago Wilderness, provides a richly detailed natural history of the region, followed by maps and descriptions of each of 10 ecoregions of Houston's 24-county area, among them Big Thicket, Trinity

Bottomlands, and Bayou Wilderness. The ecoregions do not stop at the shore, but also include the marine ecosystem of the Gulf of Mexico, from birdwatching opportunities on the Bolivar Flats to the hundreds of fish species found in the deep waters, to coral reefs in the Flower Garden marine sanctuary.

# Green Grid, London, United Kingdom
## *An Action-Oriented Green Infrastructure Plan*
*Mariah Gleason*

London is home to over 8.17 million citizens, making it the most populated European city. It is estimated that, by 2025, London's population will grow to 8.5 million. To ensure London improves and expands its green spaces as the city becomes more populated, the Greater London Authority (GLA), led by (now former) Mayor Boris Johnson, initiated several substantial greening programs and initiatives. The All London Green Grid (ALGG) is a policy framework and strategy for connecting London's green spaces to form an integrated network. Essentially, the ALGG functions as an action-oriented green infrastructure plan.

Under the ALGG, the city is split into 11 Green Grid Areas. Each area is under the charge of an "area group." These groups are established as collaborative partnerships to encourage work across boundaries. Each area group is responsible for identifying and reporting on projects and opportunities for green infrastructure work within their area via an Area Framework document. For each project, area groups have to identify which ALGG goals are met to ensure multifunctional green infrastructure projects are tackled. Goals include increasing access to open space, enhancing landscape character, and improving air quality and soundscapes. However, these goals are not limiting. Area groups are encouraged to expand beyond the outlined goals to pursue unique opportunities within their areas. Examples of projects include linking bicycle and pedestrian pathways, removing brick walls to renaturalize areas, and improving highway signage to lead people to parks and festivals, among others.

ALGG is primarily funded through the Big Green Fund. Launched by the mayor in July 2014, this funding campaign has dedicated £2 million (about US$3.4 million) to six major green space projects, each chosen because they collectively demonstrate social, economic and environmental benefits of investing in green infrastructure (Greater London Authority [Big Green Fund], n.d.). The Fund also supports other greening programs, such as the Mayor's Pocket Parks and Street Tree programs.

# McDowell Sonoran Preserve, Phoenix and Scottsdale, Arizona
### *Biophilia in the Desert*
#### Tim Beatley

The Phoenix metropolitan area is famous for its sprawl and is to some an icon of unsustainable urban growth and development (and the subject of a scathing book, *Bird on Fire*). Any new visitor to this metro area, however, will almost immediately notice the immense and spectacular desert backdrops there, and the region can boast some impressive exemplars when it comes to efforts at desert conservation.

In the City of Phoenix it is hard not be wowed by this city's early efforts at establishing what are today its iconic desert parks. South Mountain is a jewel in this system, now around 17,000 acres. An estimated 3 million visitors experience the park each year. On every fourth Sunday there is a Silent Sunday, when the park is closed to cars and motorized traffic and is taken over by bicyclists and hikers. There are now more than 41,000 acres of mountain parks and desert preserves in the city of Phoenix, including some 200 miles of trails. These are immense assets for residents there.

The story of preserving South Mountain is one of incredible foresight on the part of leaders there in the early part of the twentieth century. President Coolidge was convinced to sell most of the mountain to the City (for the sum of $17,000). Then 7 miles from downtown the actions were motivated out of concern for the eventual loss of or development of this important natural area. Today it is the crown in the city's park system, but the city has not rested on its laurels; it continues to add new desert parkland.

Another impressive desert conservation story continues to unfold in the nearby city of Scottsdale, where an immense desert preserve on the eastern edge of the city has been created. Conservation efforts began in earnest in 1990, with the creation of a nonprofit, McDowell Sonoran Land Trust, which later became the McDowell Sonoran Conservancy. A city-appointed board, the McDowell Sonoran Preserve Commission, which advises city councils on acquisition and other preserve matters, was created in 1993.

With these institutions we find a unique conservation and management approach, and the creation of a strong citizen-driven nonprofit in the form of the McDowell Sonoran Conservancy is especially key. This is a completely private, volunteer-based organization that started as a group advocating desert protection and has now evolved into the key organization that educates about, improves and maintains, and polices the desert preserve.

The amount of land within the preserve boundaries is quite large and has been growing with recent additions. It is now more than 30,000 acres in size and is already the largest single land preserve within the boundaries of any American city. It is an immense area of nature, and native flora and fauna, extremely close to a growing urban population. As the City's preserve director clarifies, "It is a preserve, not a park."

How to care for and manage this large area—representing about a third of the area of Scottsdale—remains a challenge, and this is where the Conservancy comes in. It has a volunteer army of 500 stewards who have gone through training and are committed to helping. Some serve as pathfinders (volunteers who greet hikers at trailheads) and nature guides, others work on trail construction and maintenance, others help patrol the trails, and still others are involved in the extensive citizen science activities focused on the preserve. The volunteers perform other essential functions, for instance, guarding the preserve on the 4th of July to prevent fire from fireworks on that festive night. Through the work of the McDowell Sonoran Field Institute, citizen scientists are collecting important data about flora and fauna, usually with the help of professional scientists. Sometimes there are even new discoveries, such as the recent discovery of new geology in the preserve—a limestone outcropping—seen in no other place in the Phoenix area.

The preserve already provides considerable public access, with 60 miles of trails in the preserve, and new trailheads, such as the Gateway, which boasts some 100,000 visits per year (an estimated 240,000 visits overall to the preserve).

The conservancy organizes many free guided tours in the preserve each year, and some of these are even holiday themed, such as the mistletoe and holly hike a few days before Christmas. Education about the desert happens in many ways, including Friday afternoon family events, and visits from local schools where the kids quickly learn to identify plants and animals and even taste a prickly pear.

Several key aspects of the Conservancy represent important inspiration for other cities. The engagement of citizens at every step and in every aspect of desert protection and management is impressive. Indeed, it has been a grassroots effort from the beginning, when the nonprofit land trust was formed. And the general public in Scottsdale has shown a willingness to tax themselves on a number of occasions, beginning with the historic vote to raise the sales tax in 1995 by 0.2 percent, to generate funds for desert acquisition. This happened again in 2004 (a 0.15 percent sales tax increase). While some funding has come from the state's Growing Smarter program, the city has raised millions to support its preserve acquisitions, and the preserve is a remarkable legacy to leave to future residents of the city and region.

The beautiful and biophilic visitors center at the McDowell Sonoran Preserve, in Scottsdale, Arizona. Photo Credit: Tim Beatley.

The civic dimensions of the Scottsdale Preserve and the unique Conservancy managing it are considerable. Each year Conservancy volunteers contribute some 40,000 hours in free labor, or something equal to more than 20 full-time city staff, according to Conservancy director Mike Nolan. These volunteers, then, represent a significant supplement to city staff in a time of budgetary limits and offer a better model of resilience in parks management than many cities that have had to cut back on parks positions. And citizen volunteers in Scottsdale have an unusually high level of emotional commitment to, and connection with, the immense natural beauty around them, something that delivers physical and mental health benefits, but also ensures the land will receive a high priority (and that support to complete the acquisition will likely remain high).

There is a great diversity of ages involved in the preserve, with the age of stewards ranging from 12 to 89. The high number of retirees in the area is one factor accounting for the presence of such an extensive group with the time and the desire to contribute. Conservancy director Mike Nolan points out the many positive benefits to volunteers, especially older residents, including physical exercise, opportunities for social interaction, and intellectual stimulation. They are "an extraordinary group of people," says Nolan. They're smart, passionate, and committed, and they often have incredible backgrounds, which they put to good use on behalf of the Conservancy.

The preserve is an impressive example of how people of all ages can become deeply engaged with the nature around them in a city. Jane Rau, who is in her 90s, and one of the founders of the preserve, lives and breathes the desert and works tirelessly to protect it, restore it, and educate others about its beauty and wonder. A passionate and highly active steward, she attributes much of her good health to this desert work, proudly declaring that she has added (per her doctor's instructions) to her bone density and is back to her high school weight.

There are other important directions here for urban nature conservation. New preserve acquisitions will allow for long-term connectivity between the desert preserve and other surrounding blocks of conservation lands, including Tonto National Forest to the east, and the Verde River beyond. And while greater Phoenix suffers from a severe heat island effect, the McDowell Preserve experiences winds and a micro-climate that allow it to stay cooler, likely to serve an important biological function as a climate refuge in the region.

# F. Innovative Parks and Nature Areas

## Pocket Parks Program, London, United Kingdom
### Expanding Contact with Nature through New Small Parks
*Mariah Gleason*

The Pocket Park Program in London, launched in 2009, works to improve public spaces through the development of small parks. The program has the following goals:

- Get more people using outdoor spaces
- Improve London's quality of life, its recreational offerings, and its public life
- Support volunteering and public participation and to equip people with skills that they can transfer to the workplace
- Help create jobs and sustain growth by increasing local pride, determination, and entrepreneurialism
- Help promote collaboration between the public bodies and local organizations that work hard to make London's public places better
- Make use of the extraordinary design and delivery skills in London

The life of this program is closely linked to Mayor Boris Johnson's political career. In his first term, 2008–2012, Johnson dedicated £850,000 (US$1,228,000) to the creation of 27 pocket parks across 17 London boroughs. Going into his second term, 2012–2016, the mayor expanded the program and made a commitment to create 100 pocket parks in London before 2015, which was accomplished. The difference in his second term was that citizens, through collaborative partnerships, community activation, and providing training and mentoring opportunities, are accomplishing projects: as of 2016, over 100 pocket parks have been created.

Organizations, including local authorities, and groups are challenged to design and submit bids for pocket park projects. Bids are then selected by the Greater London Authority (GLA) based on their ability to meet multiple criteria, including being innovative, fitting the characteristics of the area, promoting local vibrancy, investment, and economic growth, accomplishing short- and medium-term deliverables, and demonstrating local support for the project, both politically and socially. While the GLA has dedicated £650,000 (US$939,000) to the continuation of the program, through transportation funds and regeneration and environment programs, projects are required to raise 100 percent matching funds via outside funding sources. To help projects get off the ground, the GLA readily advertises outside funding opportunities that projects can apply for to raise the needed capital.

Local authorities many times act as the accountable body for the new pocket parks. However, activating local community members to design and take care of parks builds pride and cohesiveness within the community and ensures long-term maintenance and relevance of the parks. As of July 2014, 100 parks bids had been selected with offers of funding.

## Natur-Park Südgelände, Berlin, Germany
### *Former Railway Tracks Become a Place of Wild Nature*
*Julia Triman*

In Berlin, as in many European cities, after World War II there was an abundance of land no longer occupied by buildings. In many cases, vegetation sprouted where humans were no longer actively using urban land. After several decades, researchers began to investigate these new urban conditions. Herbert Sukopp's ecological investigations of vast tracts of vegetated land in Berlin were among the first studies of the kind and would later grow into the field of urban ecology. One among many locations where significant vegetation arose in formerly human-occupied space was along the railroad tracks at the Schöneberger Südgelände. Train service was discontinued to the station in 1952, and in the intervening years, a rich and complex variety of plants took root there (Kowarik and Langer 2005).

By the early 1980s, plans were afoot to reuse the site as a new train station, but local residents and leaders had other ideas in mind. Among other areas surveyed for biodiversity and species richness throughout the city, Südgelände proved a highly significant landscape ecologically, and citizens formed a nongovernmental organization to protest plans to clear the site and to advocate for its use as a park and urban nature preserve. Their efforts proved successful, and Südgelände opened as a nature park in Berlin in 2000. However, the very features that recommend the site, mature vegetation and wildlife habitat, preclude its full occupation by typical human activities. While there are sections of the park for the public to gather, access to the "wilder" parts is limited to a metal walkway, raised about 20 inches off the ground and following the path of the former train tracks. Signs along the route explain the significance of various aspects of the conservation area, and ask visitors to remain on the walkways while exploring the area.

In addition to conserving vegetation at Südgelände, several infrastructural elements remain, including the old railroad turntable, water tower, and several buildings, which have been converted for use by artists and metalworkers. Extremes of wild nature and human industry coexist peacefully at the park, offering a unique way to experience at once divergent and complementary typologies.

Natur-Park Südgelände is hardly an isolated example of citizen efforts to conserve and experience nature throughout the city of Berlin. Park am Gleisdreieck, farther north and closer to the city center, similarly occupies the triangle of a former train junction, preserving ruderal vegetation in "the grove" and also boasting a rose-scent garden and a nature discovery area for children (Grün Berlin). Südgelände and Gleisdreieck are part of Berlin's efforts to create a north–south continuum of urban green space, also proximate to the former Tempelhof airport now claimed as a vast space for community members to gather, still evolving with many different elements, including gardening, art works, and nature learning stations, among many other "pioneer projects" (Tempelhof n.d.). Berlin has a rich history of parks and nature conservation, and contemporary efforts abound to create and preserve spaces relevant to a changing and growing population.

# Gowanus Canal Sponge Park™, Brooklyn, New York City, New York

### *A Park That Cleans the Water and Remediates Contamination along a Former Industrial Waterfront*

*Briana Bergstrom*

Once part of a healthy tidal estuary, the present-day Gowanus Canal in Brooklyn, New York, has a long history of environmental neglect and abuse. In its earliest days, the Gowanus Creek, as it was originally named, and its fertile shores served as fishing and hunting grounds for Native American tribes. As Dutch settlement began in the seventeenth century, mills began to populate the shores of the creek that flowed into the New York Harbor. As the industrial revolution hit Brooklyn in the nineteenth century, Gowanus quickly became an economic hub attracting new businesses to South Brooklyn. In order to encourage growing industry, the City of Brooklyn deepened and widened the creek, completing the construction of the present-day Gowanus Canal in 1869 (Gowanus Canal History n.d.).

As a new transportation corridor, the canal attracted rapid industrialization and urbanization along its shores. With little regard for environmental responsibility, the new gas manufacturing plants, chemical factories, and shipyards that were built along the canal began to discharge industrial waste into the waterway. The discharge of toxins, such as coal tar and heavy metals, went unregulated for decades, a practice that quickly deteriorated the once-healthy ecosystem. In addition to discharges from these facilities, the canal has been polluted by years of both surface water runoff and sewer outflows coming from the city's combined sewer system, which discharges sewage into the canal during strong rain events (Gowanus Canal History n.d.).

While industrial activity in the area has decreased over the years, what remains today is one of the most polluted waterways in the country, with high levels of arsenic, lead, and volatile organics. And with oxygen levels at just 1.5 parts per million, marine life in the canal struggles to survive (Gowanus Canal History n.d.). In 2010, high contamination levels prompted the Environmental Protection Agency to list the 1.8-mile-long canal on the Superfund National Priorities List. And while water quality issues seem most problematic, the canal also suffers from limited public waterfront access and deteriorating infrastructure.

All of this is motivation behind a new innovative initiative to clean up the severely polluted waterway and transform the historic landscape into a welcoming public space. The new project, dubbed the Sponge Park™, will transform the waterfront into both a remediating and an engaging landscape conceived by an interdisciplinary team at the architecture and landscape architecture firm dlandstudio.

The working landscape will include filtration swales, stormwater cisterns, and remediation wetland basins as part of a water management system that will divert, filter, and treat surface water runoff that would otherwise further exacerbate water contamination problems (Gowanus Canal Sponge Park, n.d.). The system, which includes toxin-filtering plants and soils, promises to improve the health of the waterway over time. A new esplanade and series of waterfront recreational spaces will reacquaint residents to the waterfront and the wildlife that call it home, providing both recreational and educational opportunities for the community (dlandstudio, n.d.).

The open space system alone is projected to cost over $100 million and will be funded by city, state, and federal grants. Advocates of the new project hope that it will help heal the environmental harm done to the canal and create a healthy natural amenity for the community. While the Gowanus Canal has a long road to recovery and will likely never be restored to its preindustrial state, the Sponge Park™ design offers an opportunity to transform a neglected urban space into one that serves as both an ecological and a cultural amenity for the community along its shores.

# Qiaoyuan Park, Tianjin, China
## *A Remarkable Park That Regenerates Soil, Collects and Treats Stormwater, and Restores Biodiversity*
### Harriett Jameson

As regions in China shift from agricultural to industrial to postindustrial, and small towns beget megacities, there is tremendous cause for concern regarding the effects that this will have on local ecologies as well as the global environment. Significantly, there is also tremendous opportunity to utilize the latest sustainable methods and reintroduce nature into China's urban areas for the services it can provide for both infrastructure—in terms of management and remediation—and for human occupants—psychologically, recreationally, and aesthetically.

Qiaoyuan Park in Tianjin, China, is an exemplary case study that embodies this hope and builds upon the opportunity that nature holds for the future of urban China. The park sits on 54 acres, bounded to the west and north by a highway and an overpass, and to the south and east by densely populated residential areas. Once a shooting range, it had been transformed over time into a heavily polluted garbage dump and drainage sink for the city, with severely contaminated soils.

In 2003, the citizens of Tianjin called for the environmental improvement of the site, and the local government contacted Turenscape, headed by Kongjian Yu (landscape architect/urban designer and professor at Harvard and Peking Universities), to design a strategy for its improvement.

The resulting park is remarkable for the two purposes that it fulfills, one utilitarian and one aesthetic. First and foremost, the design attempts to repair the saline and alkaline soils and treat urban stormwater through natural processes integrating biologically diverse ecosystems and their regenerative capabilities. Its innovative strategy—called Adaptive Palettes—involved the construction of 21 ponds with varying depths, moisture, and pH levels. Integrated with the topography and carefully chosen indigenous plants, each pond produces a microhabitat—ranging from wetland to grassland—that can provide different functions for the site.

Potentially more exciting than the park's physical resilience, enabled by the design, are the social and cultural functions that it provides for the people of Tianjin. It aims to engender a love and appreciation of nature and to educate on important ecosystem services by allowing urban dwellers an intimate, bodily experience. For example, wooden platforms encourage visitors to sit right in the middle of patches of native grasses and wildflowers, among the hum of insects and birds, while a network of paths enables them to explore its messy landscape, unveiling natural processes, patterns, and species.

Qiaoyuan Park—with its bounty of untended native species and messy beauty—looks very different from the carefully mown lawns and ornamental gardens that have characteristically embodied China's park aesthetic (and US and Europe aesthetics, for that matter). In a 2010 article for *Topos* magazine, Yu wrote: "The park has unveiled a new aesthetic in China—one that adheres to environmental aesthetics and a heightened sense of ecological awareness" (Yu 2010).

Given the success of Qiaoyuan Park (over 200,000 people visited in its first 2 months), it stands to reason that it can have a tremendous impact on how residents in Tianjin view and value nature. And it can serve as an inspiration to those in other parts of the world—of the possibilities embodied in the places that we design and create to offer the public a new lens through which to view their home cities, a lens that values nature both for its performative significance and its beauty.

# G. Water Design in the Biophilic City

## Healthy Harbor Initiative, Baltimore, Maryland
### *Floating Wetlands, Oyster Gardens, and a Trash-Collecting Water Wheel*
### Tim Beatley

The inner harbor of Baltimore has become a popular tourist attraction, drawing thousands to the water's edge for recreation and entertainment. It is the site of the National Aquarium, restaurants, and a walking promenade. Even Camden Yards, the Orioles' baseball stadium, is just a few minutes away on foot. But despite these successes, the inner harbor faces serious challenges. Water quality remains poor, and the shoreline edge is largely made up of bulkheads with few opportunities to physically reach the water. Relatively few residents of Baltimore actually visit or connect, either physically or emotionally, with the water. With these challenges in mind the Baltimore Waterfront Partnership (a business improvement district, with a very unique focus on environment), spearheaded the creation of the Healthy Harbor Initiative.

This unusual solar- and water-powered water wheel collects garbage before it enters the inner harbor of Baltimore, Maryland. Photo Credit: Baltimore Healthy Harbor Initiative.

The Initiative is itself a partnership among various organizations and city agencies with an interest in the harbor. They have set the ambitious goal of achieving a fishable and swimmable harbor by 2020, and have developed a healthy harbor plan laying out steps to that end.

Already, some very impressive and creative projects have been undertaken. These include the design and installation of floating wetlands—some 56 distinct islands—with flotation provided through use of recycled plastic bottles. These floating wetlands take up excess nutrients and thus help to improve the water quality of the harbor, as well as provide habitat.

Another initiative has been the Great Baltimore Oyster Partnership. Working with the Chesapeake Bay Foundation, oyster gardens have been established at 10 sites around the harbor promenade. Here, catches containing young oysters—some 150,000 in total—sit in the water. Companies and schools adopt the cages and clean them monthly. When they are large enough, the oysters are transferred to oyster reefs in the bay. The program has been successful in educating about, and drawing attention to, the plight of the harbor (and oysters provide an important service in filtering water, yet their numbers are only about 1 percent of what they were before European settlement).

Another innovative project has been a one-of-a-kind Inner Harbor Water Wheel that uses river current and some solar power to scoop up trash and debris. The city has now entered into an agreement with a local waste-to-energy plant to burn the collected garbage to produce power.

## Buffalo Bayou, Houston, Texas
### *A Watery Network Intertwines with the City*
#### Julia Triman

The Buffalo Bayou and its tributaries have been an important water network since long before Houston's founding. Just as many cities around the world were founded along riverbanks, the Buffalo Bayou is Houston's "river," and its complex natural and cultural history has become deeply intertwined with the story of Houston itself. The 2002 Buffalo Bayou and Beyond Master Plan challenges the City of Houston to address some of the more damaging human impacts on the bayou, and to "revitalize both the Buffalo Bayou and surrounding urban setting, creating a unified Buffalo Bayou District where nature is an integral part of a new urban vitality"(Buffalo Bayou and Beyond 2002). The Plan operates at multiple scales, considering everything from the 500-acre "WaterView District," the mixed-use area where urban residents and visitors can connect with Buffalo Bayou's waters, to the overarching strategic framework of the watershed-scale 500-square-mile Buffalo Bayou Eco-Region.

Houston's Buffalo Bayou is home to a nonmigratory, year-round bat colony (under Waugh Bridge), a wetland and native Texas prairie at the Tapley Tributary, and a series of public parks, sculptures, and walking and biking trails. The Buffalo Bayou Partnership leads pontoon boat tours along the bayou, some of which highlight the Waugh Bridge Bat Colony, and some of which provide detailed information about natural and cultural history. Buffalo Bayou Park is undergoing a significant renovation, restoring natural features, improving stormwater management, and increasing recreational opportunities both in and out of the water.

In 2012, Houston voters approved a $166 million Parks Bond to create 150 miles of trails along the city's bayous, jump-starting what is now known as the city's Bayou Greenways Initiative. The Initiative intends to acquire and improve land adjacent to 10 major bayous throughout the city, establishing "an interconnected system of parks and trails linking people, places and green space, while enhancing air and water quality, reducing flooding, and stimulating economic development" (Bayou Greenways, http://www.bayougreenways.org). The trail networks are increasing recreational linkages throughout the city and beyond, providing new opportunities for Houston residents and visitors to come into contact with the aquatic and terrestrial life of the region.

## Green City, Clean Waters Program, Philadelphia, Pennsylvania
### Converting One-Third of a City's Paved Surfaces to Green Infrastructure
Tim Beatley

Despite its beginning as a "greene country towne," envisioned by William Penn's 1683 plan for the city, and boasting the largest park system in the United States, the City of Philadelphia is not especially green. Approximately 44 percent of the total city area is covered by impervious, hard surfaces, and the current tree canopy coverage rate for the city overall is only 16 percent (low compared with many other US cities). Much is in the works in Philadelphia, however, to address these deficiencies of green and to make the city profoundly more sustainable. The city's former mayor, Michael A. Nutter, was a driving force behind sustainability in the city, and declared in his 2008 inaugural address the intent to make the city the "number one green city in America."

One of the most ambitious goals set out by the city, and elaborated in much greater detail in the city's Green City, Clean Waters action plan, implemented by the Philadelphia Water Department (PWD), is the conversion of at least one-third of the city's paved and hard surfaces back into green and natural infrastructure, part of a massive revisioning of the city's stormwater collection and management system (with a goal of 60 percent of the city's land area in pervious surfaces) (City of Philadelphia 2011). It is only fitting that the American city that created the first municipal water supply system (1801), and began in the mid-1800s protecting the city's water supply through land acquisition, would now emerge as a leader in urban watershed conservation and restoration and in rethinking the nature of a highly urbanized hydrology. The city's bold one-third goal is to be achieved through de-sealing and re-greening many different kinds of spaces in the city, and the Green City, Clean Waters plan lays this out in considerable detail: schools, green streets, alleys, driveways, and parking lots, among others. The City intends to invest more than $2 billion to fund these programs over the next 25 years.

There has already been extensive tree planting throughout the city, and the unveiling of a new tree-planting initiative called TreePhilly, and the creation of several new parks in neighborhoods especially lacking in green amenities (e.g., Hawthorne Park and Julian Abele Parks, both in South Philly). The city's Department of Public Works has modified its stormwater charges to charge higher rates for more impervious sites, and has taken new steps to protect existing wetlands and create new wetlands (e.g., Saylor Grove) in the city.

The city recently celebrated the 5-year anniversary of the Green City, Clean Waters program. Much has been accomplished. There have been 1200 green infrastructure projects installed in that time, and they are displayed impressively on an online green infrastructure projects map (see http://www.philly watersheds.org/BigGreenMap). These are a mix of such things as stormwater tree trenches, planters, rain gardens, and porous paving. The City has developed many impressive guidance documents, for instance a "Green Streets Design Manual," released in 2014 (see http://www.phillywatersheds.org/what_were _doing/gsdm). There are now more than 200 green streets completed in the city. There are also a significant number of green schools and green parks, two other important programs where green stormwater projects have been implemented. The City has also created new financial incentives to support this green infrastructure push, including a Stormwater Management Incentives Program (SMIP) and a Greened Acre Retrofit Program (GARP), both of which provide grants for retrofitting nonresidential properties.

# Paley Park, Midtown, New York City, New York
## *The Power of Water in Small Urban Spaces*
### *Tim Beatley*

Paley Park (also known as Samuel Paley Plaza) is one of the first examples of a pocket park, and it is a beloved urban space. Located on East 53rd Street, in midtown Manhattan, it opened in May 1967. The space is quite small at 40 by 100 feet (one-tenth of an acre), on the site of a former nightclub, and surrounded by tall structures. Designed by landscape architect Robert L. Zion, it set in motion a reconsideration of the benefits and value provided by small parks in the city. In Zion's obituary, the *New York Times* sings the praises of the park that "delivered on its invitation to escape the hard surfaces and ceaseless motion of Midtown Manhattan," transforming "leftover space into a place of unparalleled serenity" (Muschamp 2000).

What are the elements that make this small park work? Movable chairs, the trees, potted flowers, and ivy-covered walls (what Zion referred to as "vertical lawns"), the presence of food, and the sense of feeling away, are all part of the explanation. But it is the power of the water that can't be overstated. Bill Browning, of Terrapin Bright Green, frequently cites Paley Park as an example of one of the key biophilic patterns—the presence of water. The main feature of the park is a 20-foot-high waterfall. It is quite loud, but this noise is perceived by visitors as being quite pleasant, drowning out the streets and city noises beyond.

The Project for Public Spaces has declared Paley to be one of the best parks in the world, for many of the reasons already mentioned. It is a park that entices one to enter from the street. According to the Project of Public Spaces: "Paley Park has an intimate relation with the street. Low and inviting steps and trees that canopy the sidewalk often influence passers-by to stroll through the park on impulse" (Project for Public Spaces n.d.).

# H. Wildlife Corridors and Urban Biodiversity Planning

## Urban Biodiversity, Cape Town, South Africa
### *A Natureful Capital*
Carla Jones

The legislative capital of South Africa, Cape Town, is located on the southwestern coast of the country with approximately 4 million residents in an area of 2500 square kilometers (965 sq. mi.) (Cape Town 2012). In 2013, it was the second-greenest city in Africa based on the International Green City Index (Siemens 2011). The International Green City Index examines many environmental factors for cities, including energy consumption. Cape Town has 289 square meters (346 sq. yd.) of green space per person, which is well beyond surrounding cities by about four times the index average of 74 square meters (89 sq. yd.) (Siemens 2011).

The biodiversity of Cape Town is likely its most impressive biophilic feature. One of the ways that it is able to preserve such rich biodiversity is through its eight protected and recognized UNESCO World Heritage sites (UNESCO 2015). Of those eight, three are natural areas, which contribute to the robust biodiversity of the area. The Cape Flora Region is one of the three natural UNESCO sites located near Cape Town, and consists of rich biodiversity, especially plant biodiversity. Although the land cover represents less than 0.5 percent of the area of Africa, it is home to nearly 20 percent of the continent's flora (UNESCO 2015). In fact, the flora in this area is among the most diverse and densest in the world (UNESCO 2015).

Because of this rich biodiversity, Cape Town also has the highest number of threatened species in the world (Government of Cape Town, n.d.). During the early 2000s, a planning process began to determine whether a biodiversity network was feasible. The process has been ongoing, but once implemented the biodiversity network will help inform where future development should occur and encourage conservation of Cape Town's most precious resources.

# Wildlife Passages, Edmonton, Alberta, Canada
## *Overcoming Fragmentation Planning for National Connections*
### Tim Beatley

Edmonton is a city that can be proud of its abundant wildlife and biodiversity. But growth and development have led to fragmentation of habitat. Edmonton is unique among cities as a leader working toward a more connected network of habitats and green areas, where the different animals that co-inhabit the city can move and travel without danger from cars. The city has been implementing this vision through the design and installation of wildlife passages.

The city's wildlife passage program began in 2007 and helped to initiate a "paradigm shift" for the city, "from focusing on the protection of isolated patches to that of an Ecological Network Approach which acknowledges the need to design a Natural Area system around ecological connections" (City of Edmonton 2015, 2). This ecological network goal has now been included in the City's Municipal Development Plan.

Since 2007 the City has designed and built 27 wildlife passages. These have included dual aquatic and mammal passages and recently passages that include significant habitat restoration. Evidence suggests the wildlife passages are working and that wildlife collisions have decreased. In 2013 wildlife collisions were 51

One of the growing number of wildlife passages in Edmonton, Alberta, Canada. Photo Credit: City of Edmonton.

percent fewer than in 2007, despite an increase in human population and development (City of Edmonton 2015).

One of the important lessons is the need to think early about wildlife passages, rather than waiting until late in the project design stage. Edmonton's Wildlife Passage Engineering Design Guidelines were prepared in 2010. This impressive document helps to establish in advance the ways in which passages can be designed into all future transportation projects and developments in the city.

Future plans include additional monitoring of the passages, and involving residents through citizen science. Edmonton has recently embarked on a new planning initiative called Breathe, that looks more holistically at the space in the city as possible habitat from rooftops to roadside verges.

## Urban National Park Planning, Nairobi, Kenya
### Green City in the Sun
*Tim Beatley*

The Nairobi National Park is a remarkable wildlife reserve in the shadow of a bustling and growing city. It is at once a remarkable story of conservation forethought and a place for urban residents to see and experience large mammals, but also a cautionary tale of the many pressures and challenges faced in protecting such urban habitat and biodiversity from all the competing pressures for this space. The park was established by the British in 1946, Kenya's first wildlife protected area. It is a relatively large park by urban standards; some 117 square kilometers (45 sq. mi.), it abuts the city on its northern boundary. It is home to remarkable nature in the form of larger iconic mammals of the African savanna, including zebras, giraffes, and around 40 lions. The park is surrounded to the north, east, and west by a fence, but open to the south and connected to the larger Athi-Kapiti plains (some 2200 square kilometers [849 sq. mi.] in size), which serve as an important zone of movement and seasonal migration for wildlife. How to prevent the encroachment of these private lands to the south has been most vexing, and efforts include a new zoning plan, which has yet to be enforced, and efforts to lease Masai pasturelands to keep them open and undeveloped (Garric 2015). The Nairobi Greenline was formed as a nonprofit organization, a collaboration of the Kenya Wildlife Society and the Kenya Association of Manufacturers, as an effort to establish a clearer, green boundary between the park and the city. Specifically, the greenline is envisioned as a "30 kilometre [18.6 mi.]

long, 50 metre [55 yd.] wide forest of indigenous trees shielding the Nairobi National Park from our growing metropolis" (NairobiGreenline.org).

Protecting the park remains a challenge, and there are a host of pressures and encroachments, notably a contentious southern bypass (for cars and trucks) that would take a small amount of land from the park. Also controversial is the proposed construction of a new rail line through the park: the Standard Gauge Railway would connect the Kenyan city Mombasa to the east and Uganda to the west. These infrastructural projects have tended, unfortunately, to pit traffic reduction and economic development against wildlife protection. Richard Leakey, the grandfather of Kenyan conservation, recently came out in favor of the rail project, which has aided design concessions, including that it will be elevated (mostly 20 meters [22 yd.] high) as it crosses the park and will allow for wildlife movement. There is also the hope that some of the funds saved by taking this railway route can be used to establish a wildlife trust fund that will flow to the benefit of the park (Leakey, as quoted in Thome 2015; see also Heyman 2013).

Nairobi is known historically as the "green city in the sun," and while its national park is its most impressive natural element, there are other urban parks and greenspaces, including a large rainforest park—Ngong Forest Sanctuary—quite close (only 6 kilometers [3.7 mi.]) to the city center (http://www.ngongforest.org/). It is not a perfect story as the city's rapid urbanization has resulted in loss of green space in the city, and much of the city's growth has happened through informal housing areas (slum areas like Kibera) with little access to nature, though there have been efforts and programs aimed at this (e.g., Trees for Cities, which has been helping to plant fruit trees here).

## Milkweeds for Monarchs, St. Louis, Missouri
### Butterflies in the City
#### Carla Jones

St. Louis may be known for the Gateway Arch and its proximity to the Mississippi River, but the city is now being recognized for creating habitats for the endangered monarch butterfly. To commemorate the city's 250th birthday in 2014, the mayor challenged citizens to plant 200 butterfly gardens in addition to the 50 gardens that the city planted. The program was so successful that it has won grants to expand the work, including the GRO1000 Gardens & Greenspaces grant from the United States Conference of Mayors (USCM) and Scotts Miracle-Gro (St. Louis-MO Gov, n.d.).

Mayor Francis Slay of St. Louis, and Sustainability Director Catherine Werner, advertising the city's Milkweeds for Monarchs program. Photo Credit: City of St Louis.

Why the monarch butterfly? Why butterfly gardens? The monarch butterfly population has declined by more than 90 percent within the last 20 years and is now categorized as "near threatened" on the World Wildlife Fund's Endangered Species List. They are perhaps the most iconic of butterfly species, and the only ones to migrate between Canada, the United States, and Mexico. Monarchs depend on milkweed plants for laying their eggs and feeding their caterpillar larvae. They are especially reliant on places like St. Louis during their annual migrations through the middle of the United States.

Catherine Werner, the sustainability director for the City of St. Louis, knows that the program is helping more than just the monarchs. She says, "I don't pretend that even if we reach our goal of 250 gardens that we will save the Monarchs. It has never been solely about that. That has been an important part, but it is just as much about encouraging people to connect with nature and beautify the city."

The Milkweeds for Monarchs Initiative evolved as a part of the city's first sustainability plan, which follows a triple-bottom-line approach (City of St. Louis Sustainability Plan n.d.). Creating strong partnerships has been crucial to the success of the Milkweeds for Monarchs Initiative. Werner says, "I know that I am not a butterfly or native plant expert. The only way that this was going to be successful was to partner with people who have the expertise, and provide them with a meaningful role."

Werner organized a brainstorming session with several dozen people, and the group considered the questions: What should we be promoting? How can we make it easy? How many plants and what are the plants? Werner explains, "We sorted through all of the comments and created the STL Monarch Mix, which includes nine species of plants. We learned that an effective garden size would be at least one square meter, and that it needed to contain both milkweed and nectar plants. The process was very collaborative."

Milkweeds for Monarchs is a public–private initiative. Werner explains, "We are committing to planting at least 50 Monarch butterfly gardens in the city, including at City Hall, parks, and fire stations. We are also challenging the people of St. Louis to plant their own gardens." The Milkweeds for Monarchs Initiative provides resources on how to plant and maintain a butterfly garden on its webpage. You can also register your garden, and then it appears on the map of the butterfly gardens.

Not only has this initiative contributed to increasing habitats for monarch butterflies and meeting the goals of the St. Louis Sustainability Plan, but Mayor Slay also sees this initiative as the start of something much bigger. Slay states, "First of all, I thought it would be something fun and something engaging in terms of getting citizens of St. Louis to band together for a common purpose to promote nature by helping to grow the monarch population. Equally as important was the positive impact that urban nature has on people generally. I know that there a lot of studies that show that the investment in green space helps reduce stress and anxiety, helps clean the air, treat storm water runoff, provides educational and learning opportunities, and raises property values. The importance can't be overstated."

Werner said she was pleasantly surprised at the number of e-mails and phone calls from other cities wanting to learn how they can replicate the program. It was recently featured in the US Mayors newsletter as a best practice.

Cities across the world can initiate unique programs in a similar way. Werner says, "It doesn't have to be a monarch butterfly or even a butterfly at all. It could be any initiative that encourages a connection to nature by doing something simple. We often hear about these large citywide initiatives, but they sometimes take millions of dollars and many staff members. While those types of initiatives are phenomenal and we should be working toward those large-scale projects, it is gratifying to have something that can be implemented easily and be successful in such a short period of time."

# I. Food and Edible Urban Landscapes

## Philadelphia Orchard Project, Philadelphia, Pennsylvania
### *Growing Fruit Trees and Building Social Capital*
Tim Beatley

The Philadelphia Orchard Project (POP) is a nonprofit working to establish fruit trees, and the capability to care for them, in needy neighborhoods in Philadelphia. It is decidedly not a city program, Phil Forsyth, the executive director of POP, says, and is intended to be very bottom-up, relying heavily on existing neighborhood and community organizations. Participating groups must have legal access to a site (this is not guerrilla gardening, Forsyth emphasizes) that must be suitable for growing fruit trees (water access and soil tests where there are concerns about soil contamination), and must have the adequate capacity to pull off the project (though building up this capacity is part of what POP does). The cost of establishing a new orchard is between $2000 and $5000, depending on size, but a relatively modest investment given the impact and the long-term potential to produce fruit (and to change lives and neighborhoods). The fruit from these orchards goes directly to the neighborhoods in which it is grown, and for the few orchards not located in low-income areas of the city POP requires a food distribution plan for how the food will contribute to community food security (with much of it going to food banks).

A fruit tree pruning workshop organized by the Philly Orchard Project. Photo Credit: Tim Beatley.

# Beacon Food Forest, Seattle, Washington
## *Designing a Food Forest*
### Tim Beatley

One of the most ambitious urban orchard projects under way in the United States is the new Beacon Food Forest, in Seattle. Here, in the Beacon Hill neighborhood, a 7-acre parcel of land, owned by the Seattle Public Utility (SPU), will eventually be transformed into a multilayered public orchard and edible park. Started by cofounders Glen Herlihy and Jacqueline Cramer, and with seed money from the City of Seattle's Office of Neighborhoods, a neighborhood steering committee was formed, and a landscape architect hired to develop a master plan for the site. Community meetings were organized to see what the neighborhood wanted, and the master plan reflects these desires. The first phase of the park was completed in 2014. The size of the orchard and the extent of the edible trees and bushes are impressive. Landscape architect Margarett Harrison (of Harrison Design) spoke with me about the project's master plan, which included a planting list of some 100 different varieties of berry bushes, and fruit- and nut-bearing trees. The orchard is  organic and planted according to the principles of permaculture (trees and bushes planted in associated guilds). There will be no straight lines she tells me. Once open, the orchard will provide edibles free for the picking, and the public nature of the urban orchard is an important and unique aspect of the project.

The master plan includes covered space for workshops and educational events, walkways, an area of P-Patch allotment gardens (what the City calls its community gardens), some designed to be wheelchair accessible, and an edible arboretum to educate about and showcase unusual varieties of fruit- and nut-bearing trees and bushes. The varieties of trees and bushes to plant were chosen by listening to what the neighborhood residents, many of them relocated to Seattle from other parts of the world, want to grow and eat. Harrison tells me about one community meeting where translators helped Chinese residents explain several varieties of berries important to them and that would do well in the Seattle climate. "The most fascinating thing to me has been the inclusion of so many different cultures and what they like to grow at home and the researching and showing that we could grow that here," Harrison says.

Harrison expects the orchard to be an important neighborhood gathering space, and the steering committee has already been planning many community events and activities for the site. There are three schools in the vicinity and a nearby Veterans Administration hospital that has already expressed interest in reserving two P-Patch gardens for use in horticultural therapy.

There have been some obstacles to overcome along the way. Notable among them was the initial resistance of the landowner, Seattle Public Utility, which was fearful that the orchard would be messy and might eventually damage the lidded water reservoir on the site. This was, Harrison notes, a "major obstacle" but one that was overcome, largely as a result of arranging for management of the orchard to be assumed by the city's P-Patch community garden program. The food forest is very much a community effort and relies heavily on volunteers (for planting, pruning, watering). Some 2000 volunteers were involved in 2014 alone. Funding has come from a mix of sources, including donations and grants. Early funding came from the City of Seattle, and it has recently provided funds through the Department of Neighborhoods for work on a Gathering Space. This has been a design/build collaboration with the University of Washington School of Architecture. The future looks bright for the Food Forest. There is much interest in the project, with the likelihood that other similar orchards will be established in other neighborhoods in the city. And in the meantime, the Beacon Food Forest is basking in the press and international attention it is being given, hosting visits from groups as far away as Norway. Proclaimed to be the largest urban orchard in the world, it is raising awareness about how cities can and should grow more than parking lots and telephone poles.

# V. Other Biophilic Urban Strategies

## A. Nature and Favelas, Disaster Recovery

### Sitie Ecological Park, Rio de Janeiro, Brazil
**From World's Largest Urban Forest to Efforts at Bringing Nature to Favelas**
*Tim Beatley*

The city of Rio de Janeiro is to many synonymous with spectacular natural beauty—sea and beaches with dramatic mountains lurching abruptly skyward, like Corcovado mountain rising more than 2300 feet. The combination of mountains, sea, and lush Atlantic Forest create the conditions for a biophilic city. But it is not a perfect story, as population growth and development have nibbled away at these qualities. More than 6 million live in the city, and more than 12 million in the Rio metropolitan area, making it Brazil's second-largest city. Pierre-André Martin, writing in the Nature of Cities blog, notes that even though the city has protected large natural areas—about one-third of the city's land area—the city continues to lose its more accessible, everyday nature. As Martin says, these larger parks "are at the edges of the city with few entrances and distant from the central cores. On the one hand they provide excellent stages for conservation, but their remoteness means that most residents have little contact with nature except for distant views. Natural landscapes in Rio are more background than foreground" (Martin 2012). As Cecilia Herzog writes, urban biodiversity and nature conservation have not been high on the list of political priorities lately (Herzog 2012).

Yet, there are impressively large parks in the city, and the City's Environment Department has been developing a strategy for connecting these existing parks and green areas. Its Green Corridors plan was issued in 2012, and the nonprofit INVERDE (which Herzog runs) has been working to help implement these ideas.

Tijuca National Park is one of the impressive large parks in Rio, and despite providing less-than-ideal access to Rio residents, it remains an important urban conservation story. Often dubbed "the largest urban forest in the world," at some 4000 hectares (9884 acres) in size it is an immense element of nature in the heart of the city. The story of its protection and revegetation goes back to the 1860s when a mostly denuded forest, a result largely of new coffee plantations, threatened the city's supply of water and led Emperor Pedro II to issue an order calling for the reforestation of the area. About 70,000 native trees were planted in roughly a 15-year period (Buckingham and Hansen 2015). The park today is a major tourist destination (some 2 million people visit annually) but also harbors a large amount of biodiversity, including a relatively large number of threatened species of plants (Pougy et al. 2014).

Favelas, or shantytowns, informal housing areas with limited facilities and services, represent another challenge for Rio, as more than 1 million residents live in the more than 700 different favela communities. The connection between urban nature and favelas has been a conflicted one, and in the mid-2000s, the city began erecting walls intended to protect remaining remnants of the Atlantic Forest from the expansion of favelas.

A more positive trend is seen in projects that seek to green and naturalize favelas by creating small parks and gardens. One such example is the Sitie Ecological Park, in the favela Vidigal. Here a former dump has been converted to a 2-acre park, through the work of residents over a number of years. Sugarcane and vegetables have been planted, and efforts at reforestation are under way, with the help of an organization called It Becomes Alive. Seedlings for reforestation have been provided by the Rio Botanical Garden. The project was the recipient of one of the Design Corps's SEED awards in 2015 (Design Corps 2015).

# Martissant Park, Port-au-Prince, Haiti
## *A Park That Is Helping a City Recover from a Devastating Earthquake*
### *Hilary Dita Beard*

Port-au-Prince, the capital of Haiti, is an overpopulated city at just below 1 million residents with a dense urban fabric. Labeled "the poorest country in the hemisphere," Haiti was hit with a massive earthquake in 2010 that devastated Port-au-Prince and left 300,000 dead and over a million homeless. The Martissant neighborhood especially faced overwhelming challenges. Considered a "red zone," it was lacking businesses or institutions, public services such as access to water and electricity, and contending with overpopulation (with 30,000 residents), lawlessness, and dangerous environmental conditions (Pierre-Louis 2014).

Before the earthquake, in 2008, the Parc de Martissant project was initiated to save the last remaining wooded area in the struggling neighborhood. Even when access to basic services was scarce and gang violence was a constant concern, the residents of Martissant threw themselves into the project. One young resident was quoted as saying, "Creating the park here in Martissant is for us a matter of dignity!" (Pierre-Louis 2014).

In order to implement the project, four previously private properties with some historically noteworthy former owners were made public by presidential decree in 2007. The park now includes 42 square acres of public space with a community center, a memorial, and multiple gardens with botanical and medicinal plants and cultural, educational, and recreational programming. Including 40 species of trees, some centuries old or rare and endangered, the park serves as a sanctuary of biodiversity and conservation in the midst of a clustered and compressed urban area. The park currently employs 200 staff, mostly local residents, giving them a sense of place, pride, and ownership over their park. With approximately 200 visitors a day and climbing, the park is a popular attraction that has had a tangible positive effect on the surrounding neighborhood, making it less dangerous and more accessible to the general public (Charles 2014).

Plans for expanded education and training programs for the environmental sciences are being developed, helping to continue to connect the people with their native botanical and natural world. The community center also currently provides resources to the residents, including waste collection, healthcare, and grants for tuition (Dreyfuss 2013).

Keith Tidball, in a chapter of the book *Greening the Red Zone: Disaster, Resilience and Community Greening* on urgent biophilia, suggests that "when humans, faced with a disaster, as individuals and communities and populations, seek engagement with nature to further their efforts to summon and demonstrate resilience in the face of a crisis, they exemplify an urgent biophilia" (Tidball 2014, 50). Examples, such as Martissant Park, may indicate that post-disaster biophilia includes an important set of human–nature interactions to address disaster and create regenerative environments as a part of the "adaptive cycle." The success of the park and its effect on the devastated, underserved, and violent neighborhood and its residents certainly point to the development and protection of the park as a community-healing effort.

# B. Nature Centers

## Eden Place Nature Center, Chicago, Illinois
### Building Connections, Awareness, and Leadership around Nature
*Carla Jones*

Chicago has numerous nature centers that help connect urban residents with the nature around and in the city. One of the most active nature centers is the Eden Place Nature Center. Eden Place Nature Center has many programs that help foster different experiences with nature. They have a farm that offers a Community Supported Agriculture program and farmers markets. When it comes to interacting with nature, they have the Wild Indigo Nature Explorations program, which includes opportunities to collect seeds, go birding, and participate in more intensive nature walks.

In addition to exploring and learning about nature, they provide opportunities for residents to participate in Monarch Propagation and Monitoring. They have been designated as an Illinois Monarch Habitat and official Illinois MonarchLIVE site. MonarchLIVE is a program that provides educational resources and habitat restoration for species that cross borders when migrating (Eden Place Nature Center, Monarch Propagation and Monitoring n.d.). Part of their work includes tagging monarchs to better understand migration patterns.

The Eden Place Nature Center is also active in training the next generation of leaders through their Leaders in Training Program. Participants in the program learn the basics of leadership and engage in nature recreation activities. These include hiking, fishing, and camping. The program is very place based and the participants complete community service projects related to nature conservation in the Fuller Park neighborhood. The program's goal is to cultivate "environmental stewardship, an appreciation for nature, and a willingness to give back to the community through nature-based service projects" (Eden Place Nature Center, Leaders in Training n.d.). The Eden Place Nature Center is home to the Dr. George Washington Carver Research Station, which fosters an appreciation for nature and involvement with the science, technology, engineering, and math disciplines for minorities.

# PART 4:
## Successes and Future Directions

We hope readers will now agree that the vision of biophilic cities is compelling, and one that fits the planetary stresses and needs of today's cities. The benefits delivered by biophilic cities are many and profound—ecological services of various kinds, mental health and well-being, not to mention meaning and wonder. But there are significant obstacles and challenges for cities working toward a biophilic agenda. This final section of the book begins a summary of what we know about what works and the key lessons from the emerging practice in some of the best biophilic cities, as described in chapter 13, but also, in chapter 14, the many challenges faced by these cities. We also provide brief profiles of some of the emerging pioneers of the biophilic cities movement. Chapter 15 speculates on the future of the biophilic cities movement, and specifically the role and promise of the new Biophilic Cities Network. In addition, we provide a list of resources (blogs, films, web pages, etc.) and references that will be useful to readers wanting to learn more and to take tangible and meaningful action.

# 13

# Lessons from the World's Emerging Biophilic Cities

The presence of nature—imagining buildings, neighborhoods, and cities immersed in nature—helps to create a positive image of places we will want to live in the future. Trees, native vegetation, food-producing gardens, and abundant contact with flora and fauna feed our need for wonder and meaning, and these are qualities and conditions at the core of biophilic design and planning. I frequently say that, in the language and practice of biophilic cities, the *philic* is as important as the *bio*; that is, the advantage of this language is that it embeds a value statement about the need for contact with the natural world, and our innate connections with and caring for it. It is not a neutral word, and not simply a factual statement about the benefits and services provided by nature (a meaning that tends to be conveyed by commonly used terms such as *green infrastructure*).

There is also embedded in the language a biocentrism which holds that nature has inherent worth and intrinsic value. While we frequently speak about the many stress-reducing and health benefits of contact with nature, we understand as well that we are imagining cities in a new way, as spaces inhabited and occupied by many different forms of life. Humans benefit in many ways through this contact (from the microbial to the mammalian), but we also acknowledge the right of these species to live and thrive in cities.

Coexistence with wildlife in cities has become an important goal and challenge in cities around the United States and the world. At the center of these efforts is a recognition of the need for humans to acknowledge humane interaction and treatment, avoidance of harm, and profound and deep respect for the many other creatures that live in cities.

Our colleagues with the Humane Society of the United States have endorsed the notion of biophilic cities as perhaps the best and most promising framework for humane coexistence, and we have been collaborating on what this means in practice. The view of cities as spaces for cohabitation, shared spaces, is growing stronger, but much more needs to be done. We see these sensibilities and priorities expressed in cities in many other ways. Examples include the adoption of bird-friendly design standards in cities like San Francisco, and new legislation aimed at humane "pest" control in cities like Washington, DC, where the Wildlife Protection Act, among other things, prohibits control practices such as glue traps and leghold traps.

There are pioneers in this struggle in many cities around the United States and the world, and they include passionate advocates, such as Camilla Fox, founder of Project Coyote, which introduces coexistence strategies for that species. Another example is the Bay Area Puma Project, founded by Zara McDonald. Her work in studying and educating the San Francisco Bay Area about pumas (mountain lions) is profiled in box 13.1.

### Promoting the Value of Centering Cities around Nature

The experiences of emerging biophilic cities begin to show the immense value of placing nature at the center of planning and design, or what we might call centering cities around nature. The benefits are many—economic, ecological, health—and together provide a compelling framework for guiding planning and decision making in cities.

Especially promising are the bold ways that cities are envisioning future urban life. In cities like Singapore and Wellington, the quality of urban life is understood to be directly and inextricably tied to experiences of nature. Singapore's reimagining itself as a city in a garden is perhaps the best expression of this new understanding of cities as places where nature is not something separate, but all around, something that residents can experience every minute of the day. The image of future cities is one where native bird songs can be heard, an aspiration in Wellington, or where it is easy to hike in and through nature, as in cities like Singapore and Oslo, that have invested in extensive networks of urban nature trails and pathways.

An easy first step in developing biophilic approaches is to look for nature already in cities. There's a lot to discover, as our case studies and partner cities demonstrate. From the spectacle of Vaux's swifts nesting in Portland, and the millions of birds migrating through cities such as San Francisco, to the ants of New York and microscopic biodiversity in the soil of Central Park, there is incredible nature there already.

There are tremendous opportunities to restore and enhance this nature, and

**Box 13.1. Biophilic Cities Pioneer Profile: Zara McDonald**

*Coexisting with Pumas and Other Wild Cats*

Zara McDonald has been a tireless champion for wild cats. From the mountain lions of the San Francisco Bay Area to the snow leopards of Mongolia, her research and advocacy have taken her around the globe. She is the founder and president of the Felidae Conservation Fund, and she started the Bay Area Puma Project in 2007. Much of her work has been in support of research and efforts to better understand the biology of wild cats. Through use of GPS collars she and her colleagues have studied the movement patterns and habitat needs of these cats. In the Bay Area Puma Project much of her effort has been focused on education, and much of it for school-aged

kids. She gives many educational lectures over the course of the year and makes many visits to Bay Area schools. Through an educational program she developed called CAT Aware she has reached some 30,000 kids. She recently unveiled a new educational video game called PumaWild and continues to look for and create ways to educate and to overcome the fear that often exists toward wild cats.

Zara McDonald, founder of the Bay Area Puma Project. Credit: Bay Area Puma Project.

to take many steps—from highly designed features, such as vertical green walls, to efforts to protect and restore existing natural areas. In different ways the steps taken in these cities are bold—from Singapore's example of viewing new projects like the Khoo Teck Puat Hospital as an opportunity to enhance bird and butterfly habitat, to Vitoria-Gasteiz's experience of restoring the Salburua wetland (previously an airport) to its former natural condition, and show what is possible when nature is a priority, demonstrating the critical role cities can and must play in global conservation.

The positive economic benefits of biophilic urbanism often seem to carry the day in policy and planning debates, reaching decision makers in ways that noneconomic reasoning does not. The example of Birmingham, in the United Kingdom, provides evidence about the power of understanding and demonstrating the economic value of the ecological services provided by biophilic cities. An urban ecology or urban nature strategy is often the most cost-effective method of achieving a desired urban or societal goal. We have seen that a small investment in office greenery delivers considerable economic benefits in the form of increased worker productivity, for instance. Integrating biophilic features into the design of schools, as a further example, delivers impressive improvements in the cognitive performance and development of children. Whether the goal is increasing test scores or reducing long-term healthcare costs, investing in more nature in the city will likely make economic sense, and is probably the most economically efficient option available.

### Connect Resilience and Biophilia

Biophilic cities can effectively address the health challenges we are facing—both planetary and human (and they are of course interconnected). Urban planners have rediscovered the importance of city design in advancing health, and in the need to pursue a more holistic notion of health.

Sometimes referred to as the "salutogenic" model, there is much value in understanding how cities and communities can provide the context for a more whole-body-and-mind form of health. Nature, and cities that are natureful, offer these kinds of benefits. We know we must walk more, be more physically active, eat more healthily, slow down, enjoy friends and family, and live in places where the air, water, and environment are recuperative, and restorative. Nature, and nature in cities where most people on this planet will be living, represents a powerful elixir and positive counterresponse to the prevailing pathogens, disease/nondisease bifurcation, and reactive (and expensive) hospital-based approaches that characterize modern American healthcare.

These more holistic perspectives on health, and goals for human health, might all be understood through the increasingly popular lens of resilience. There is certainly much value in this frame, as well, and many ways in which biophilic design and planning are helping to advance the agenda of resilient (and sustainable) cities and communities (Beatley 2009).

Several years ago Australian professor Peter Newman and I authored an academic paper entitled "Biophilic Cities Are Resilient, Sustainable Cities" (Beatley and Newman 2013). The vision of a biophilic city, and the tools, techniques, strategies for effecting this vision, accomplish many things at once. They address a variety of pressing global and local problems, including climate change, community health, and poverty reduction. If ever there was a time for a new vision of cities that sees nature at the core, it is now. How cities can build resiliency has become a major undertaking and priority and the tools, techniques, and biophilic projects of various kinds described in this book will help cities to move in this direction.

Climate change poses an especially potent set of challenges for cities. Coastal cities will experience accelerated sea level rise, more damaging coastal storms and flooding, and a need to profoundly rethink their marine and aquatic edges. A more dynamic shoreline, more flexible and adaptive, and edges that better function as ecosystems, will be needed.

Greater urban resilience is possible from just about every instance of biophilic design and planning. A major challenge in cities throughout the world will be dealing with excessive heat, and techniques such as tree planting, green roofs and walls, providing shade, and cooling through evapotranspiration must be part of the answer. Severe air pollution is a problem in many cities in the world, and again biophilic design can help significantly. Use of green walls and urban trees in cities such as Mexico City and New Delhi can be part of an effective long-term response. Modeling work at the University of Birmingham by our colleague Rob MacKenzie has shown that, at least in theory, scaling up the use of vertical green facades can have a major positive effect in controlling both particulates and nitrogen dioxide in urban street canyons (Pugh, MacKenzie , Whyatt , and Hewitt 2012). As in our example of Baltimore's Healthy Harbor Initiative it is possible to take actions, such as installing floating wetlands, that help to filter water and take up excess nutrients and also add habitat and green edges to bulkheaded and hard-surfaced urban environments.

Food-producing gardens in cities provide contact with an important form of green nature and also hold promise for addressing food insecurity. According to one recent study, one-fifth of the food produced today is grown in cities (Royte 2015). That will likely have to increase, and urban opportunities for growing food on rooftops and balconies and in backyards will help to make cities more resilient in this way.

Biophilic design features, moreover, help in important ways to enhance resource efficiency and reduce energy consumption of buildings and urban landscapes, and thus help in climate change mitigation.

## Use Many Different Tools and Strategies

Emerging biophilic cities demonstrate convincingly that there are many different tools and strategies to promote nature in cities. Context is important in selecting the best strategy, from new kinds of development permits in cities like San Francisco that permit temporary greening and the conversion of hardscapes into sidewalk gardens—to financial incentives, public education, and research and development, among others. Part of the goal of the Biophilic Cities Project is to collect and compile ordinances, codes, and program materials from cities around the world and to make these available. This is a big task because there is so much work under way, so many different ways cities are advancing biophilic urbanism.

There is no single approach, no silver bullet, but as the examples from this book show, it is best to think in terms of a suite or package of, ideally, reinforcing policies, laws, and programs. Singapore is perhaps the best example of this, combining a landscape replacement policy (a mandate) with efforts to subsidize urban greening, and to educate and celebrate innovation (as through the Skyrise Greenery Awards), as well as to support research about what works and doesn't work.

### Rewilding Our Urban Hearts

How we reconnect urbanites to the often quite abundant flora and fauna around them is a major challenge and we have provided some compelling examples in this book about ways to go about this. In Baltimore, engaging citizens (adults and school kids alike) in the active raising and caring for oysters, in oyster gardens in close proximity to that city's inner harbor promenade, represents a clever way to foster emotional connections, for instance.

Colleagues in St. Louis, a city that has been participating in the Biophilic Cities Network, have developed a very simple but informative survey for assessing environmental literacy there. They have been administering it at a neighborhood level, with interesting results.

Perhaps what we need to aspire to is what Marc Bekoff calls a "rewilding of our hearts" (Bekoff, 2014). While we have spent much energy in efforts to rewild parts of the planet, including now many cities, we may now need to concentrate on growing a new kind of citizen, one that is curious about, and cares deeply about, this nature that surrounds us.

We must undergo a similar shift in our mindset and thinking, to be open to seeing the nature around us, to caring about it, and for it, and to be interested in learning more about it. "Rewilding of Our Hearts," Bekoff says, "is about becoming reenchanted with nature. It is about nurturing our sense of wonder" (Bekoff, 2014, p.5). I've tended to summarize Bekoff's key ideas here in terms of the four C's: compassion, connection, curiosity, coexistence.

### Expand the View of Urban Nature

One important area of developing research involves the question concerning what actually constitutes "nature" and what are the many different forms it might take in cities. It is true that nature is in many ways a socially constructed idea or concept. For many of us nature is still something that conjures up a sense of the pristine, the untouched, the remote; places that we occasionally visit and that are best left without humans.

**Figure 13.1.** Wildness in cities is an important quality, and cities like Richmond, Virginia, shown here, have opportunities to highlight and celebrate this wildness. Credit: Photo by Tim Beatley.

We have now passed the 50th anniversary of the Wilderness Act of 1964, a cornerstone piece of legislation in the American environmental movement. While we increasingly recognize that "pristineness" is largely an illusion (and that humans have modified and impacted environments more profoundly and for longer periods of time than we had previously imagined), the lands that make up the American Wilderness System are important indeed, for emotional and ecological reasons, and protecting and preserving these wilderness areas far from cities remains an important goal. And wildness in cities can be experienced, increasingly, in many important and interesting ways, from urban camping in New York City (both in parks and on high-rise rooftops) to hiking to swimming and kayaking and finding other ways to directly enjoy the immensity and vastness, the unpredictability, the profound "otherness" that nature has to offer (fig. 13.1). As our many cases demonstrate, wildness is never far away, whether walking along the pipeline trail in Richmond, Virginia, or watching Vaux's swifts circle in mass to nest for the evening in Portland, Oregon. One does not need to travel hundreds of miles away to find and experience real nature.

Many of the kinds of nature in cities that we have described in this book are human designed, and human maintained, to large degrees. Nevertheless, it is our view that cities hold considerable "wildness" in their totality of flora, fauna, natural processes, and natural systems, albeit highly fractured and altered.

These kinds of nature in cities, this kind of new wildness, happens in many ways of course, big and small. And much of its wondrous quality lies beyond the physical or visual accessibility for urbanites. Our colleague Amy Savage has been doing remarkable work, for instance, understanding the diversity and biology of ant species in New York City, much of it through sampling and experiments in the median strips along Broadway! She has discovered some fascinating things, including more than 40 species of ants performing remarkable cleanup services for us (box 13.2). How to connect busy passersby on Broadway with this fascinating world so near, but emotionally distant, remains a challenge. Equally true, there is immense nature in the coastal and marine realm, for cities like Singapore and San Francisco, but hard for most residents to see and experience directly. We have stories, however, told in the preceding chapters, that give hopeful guidance about how this might be accomplished—from the low-tide walks in Singapore to the notion of bluebelts in Wellington, there is much that can be done to cultivate awareness of and connections with these harder-to-see forms of nature in cities.

As biophilic urbanism emerges, we're seeing new blendings of the natural and the built. It is sometimes hard to tell the difference in the new hybrid forms of urban nature created. Projects like Bosco Verticale—the vertical forest—in Milan, boasting some 800 trees, many of them fairly large, represents a creative fusing of actual growing nature with more conventional engineering and design principles for tall buildings.

Another open question has to do with the importance of natural shapes, forms, and materials, and the extent of the biophilic benefits they provide. I believe they are considerable (and I know that seeing and experiencing them makes me happy) but more research is needed to fully understand these effects. That said, we have some remarkable examples of blending actual, growing nature, with natural shapes and forms consider the tree-shaped beams and "forest in a clearing" design of the Credit Valley Hospital near Toronto; or projects such as Chicago's Aqua Tower that combine interesting biophilic form, (in this case, wavy facades that result in a building that looks more like an ocean, but which also help to reduce bird–building strikes), and advance the values of biophilic urbanism.

### Find Creative Ways to Engage the Public
Biophilic urbanism must include and embrace the general public; indeed this is the real promise of the vision of biophilic cities—that average individuals and families will find a life in the city that is characterized by a closeness to and profound curiosity about nature.

**Box 13.2. Biophilic Cities Pioneer Profile: Amy Savage**

*Understanding the Urban Ant*

Amy Savage teaches at Rutgers University, and is an expert on ants. She is one of the new generation of researchers in the biological sciences that are focused on cities. Savage's work has received considerable attention in the popular press for her insights about ants in urban environments. She is often found collecting ants in the median strips of New York City streets and conducting experiments that uncover new insights about ant diversity and behavior in these settings. She is also part of a larger team focused on understanding the smaller (even microscopic) forms of nature around us. She works with Professor Rob Dunn and his Wildlife of Our Homes project, and with Andrea Lucky, of Florida State, on a project called the School of Ants. The School of Ants is a clever effort both to educate citizens about ants and to engage

them in citizen science. Individuals and schools are encouraged to collect ant samples, and to send them to Lucky and her colleagues for identification, eventually adding them to an online map of ants around the United States. The School of Ants has also developed a Pictorial Key to help in identifying common ant species, not always an easy thing to do!

Amy Savage, now at Rutgers University, has done pioneering work on the biology of ants in New York City. Credit: Photo courtesy Amy Savage.

There are many creative approaches being undertaken to engage and involve the public, many utilizing new digital technologies. These efforts have included a variety of citizen science initiatives, such as Chicago Wildlife Watch, a collaboration between the Urban Wildlife Institute of the Lincoln Park Zoo and the Adler Planetarium's Zooniverse program. Here 100 motion-activated camera traps have been placed in different locations around the city, and citizens are encouraged to help identify wildlife seen in the collected photos. This is a clever way to, at once, help advance knowledge about urban wildlife and convey to the public exactly how much amazing life there is all around, near their homes and jobs.

Another example is BioSCAN, an initiative started by the Los Angeles Natural History Museum. It has enlisted 30 households to let the museum set up malaise traps in their backyards. This co-generation of new biological knowledge has resulted, remarkably, in the identification of 30 entirely new species of flies (each named after one of the families hosting a collection site (Hartop et al. 2015). The time spent engaged with electronic media and on the Internet remains a concern, especially for children (more about that in the chapter to follow) but technology also offers many new ways to engage the public in the nature around them.

There are a variety of new cell phone apps, for instance, which help in identifying flora, fauna, and fungi, and many that provide information that makes it easier to enjoy and experience nature. Some new apps can help locate parks, others can help with choosing a walk that will maximize the number of trees you will see and the amount of nature you will experience (Walkonomics), and yet other new apps that can tell you how much nature there is in your own neighborhood (e.g., treesandhealth.org).

Melbourne's efforts to plan for the expansion of its urban forest described in Section 3, show how the public can be creatively engaged and involved. By giving each of its 77,000 trees a distinct number and email address, citizens are encouraged even to send their favorite tree an appreciative e-mail. Some 3,000 e-mails have been sent to trees, though many are from people living outside Australia (Tan 2015). And you will actually get return e-mail from your tree! Whether such a strategy will help to build long-term awareness of and support for protecting and expanding urban forests is hard to say, but it is a creative, clever idea that has certainly helped to generate good buzz about the city's biophilic efforts.

Melbourne has done many other things to engage the public around trees and nature, including extensive workshops and online forums, and recently a highly successful citywide bioblitz. Melbourne sets a positive example of community engagement with nature for other cities to follow.

### Recruit Political Support and Leadership for Biophilic Cities

Thankfully there are many compelling examples of cities where biophilic design and planning have taken hold and where the qualities and conditions of living close to nature in cities is a reality. The first several years of our Biophilic Cities Project have focused on understanding, researching, and documenting this emerging body of innovative practices, largely through our partner cities. As the earlier chapters convey, cities are employing a host of tools, strategies, and techniques, many quite creatively.

The conditions (environmental, social, political, and economic) vary from city to city, so not all of the tools and ideas employed will work everywhere, but this book offers insights into a rich array of possibilities across the world. That said, there is no question that having strong political support from the top is helpful in getting things done, and in giving credibility to the biophilic frame. In cities like Wellington the mayor's unabashed enthusiasm and support for nature in the city has made a major difference. In cities from Chicago to Vancouver to London to New York, a supportive and assertive mayor often gets things done and can have a significant positive impact.

In almost all of the early leading examples of biophilic cities, strong political support, often at the mayoral level, has been critical to success. Progressive, forward-looking leadership is essential, suggesting the importance of educating and empowering the next generation of urban leaders to push the biophilic urban agenda even further.

Leadership can and must also happen at a more grassroots or neighborhood level. We have many good examples of remarkable individuals who have devoted their lives to improving their communities, undertaking tangible, meaningful steps to green the places in which they live. Growing nature and strengthening community can often happen together through inspired local leadership. An example of such a community leader is Venice Williams, director of Alice's Garden in Milwaukee (and profiled in box 13.3).

## Utilize Support from Many Groups

There is likely no single agency or government office that can be expected to do it all. Rather, the most impressive biophilic cities are places where there is a rich mosaic of organizations working to bring about living cities. They will have different agendas and different points of view, but there is considerable value in imagining a large biophilic tent.

Moreover, to make a discernible impact in greening a city an organization need not be large or financially well endowed. In cities like San Francisco, small volunteer-based organizations, such as Nature in the City, have made a significant and important impact.

Biophilic urbanism, moreover, benefits from a creative mix of top-down and bottom-up activity. Many of our most impressive stories of inserting new nature into cities, or working to protect the nature already there, involve individual activists and advocates and demonstrate what a small number of dedicated biophilic urbanists can accomplish.

**Box 13.3. Biophilic Cities Pioneer Profile: Venice Williams**

*Growing Food and Community*

Venice comes from a long line of farmers and she is extending the love of farming, gardening and cooking, through her inspiring work with Alice's Garden, an innovative community garden and urban greenspace in the Lindsay Heights neighborhood of Milwaukee, Wisconsin. Venice is the executive director of Alice's Garden, where she has worked tirelessly to enhance life opportunities there through the garden and its programming. Frequently described as a visionary, her work is fundamentally about bringing people together, and creating the spaces and opportunities for growing, learning, imagining different futures. Programs at the Garden include everything from yoga to cooking classes, and have provided jobs and income for youth in the neighborhood. Her work seeks to use gardens, food, and cooking as avenues for health and healing.

One especially innovative program, Fieldhands and Foodways, teaches about and celebrates the food and farming heritage of African Americans. Thanks to Williams's work, Alice's Garden has become an important community gathering space and through its programs a place for cultivating food but also individual and community resilience. She is also director of the Body and Soul Healing Arts Center, with its community kitchen operating in

the basement of a neighborhood church. Williams's work epitomizes the need for biophilic programs that are grown from the bottom up, and that reach lower-income and minority communities, where the power of community gardens and urban agriculture is most needed.

Venice R. Williams currently serves as the Executive Director of both Alice's Garden Urban Farm and The Body and Soul Healing Arts Center in Milwaukee, Wisconsin. Credit: Photo courtesy of Venice Williams.

## Think Multiscaled, Multifaceted

As the cases described in this book have demonstrated, there are many different ways that nature can be grown in cities. We often describe a biophilic city as a place where there is nature all around us, beginning with the home and work spaces where we spend much of our lives. There is an extensive and growing body of evidence about the power of even a small amount of nature in the workplace. It boosts worker productivity and enhances health. Natureful home and work spaces must, then, be a priority. Inserting nature into these spaces is an area where biophilic design has already made significant inroads. There are increasingly powerful examples of such efforts at the building design scales. We have profiled a number of such examples, from new residential towers that include forests, such as the Bosco Verticale in Milan; to the many examples of public institutional designs that include nature, such as the new Healy Family Center at Georgetown University; and hospitals and healthcare facilities, such as Boston's new Rehabilitation Hospital. The examples are many and growing, supporting arguments that nature can be integrated into the building scale.

These living and work spaces must be embedded, in turn, in the larger landscapes and geographies that weave them together. It is the entire geographic spectrum that must concern us—from rooftop or room to region or bioregion, and all the scales and spaces between.

## Work at Different Scales

There has been much interest in the urban planning profession recently, with the concept and idea of "tactical urbanism" (e.g., Lydon and Garcia 2015), many of the projects and initiatives we have profiled in this book would likely be labeled in this way. Grassroots, small-scale, low-cost, short-term efforts, primarily at the neighborhood level, can make a huge difference locally. They might be pop-up gardens or temporary repurposing of parking spaces, but they can effect short-term change and help to shift the perception of what is possible and desirable in a city.

On the other hand, there is significant value to putting into place a citywide biophilic planning framework, along with initiatives and regulations that can help to advance and disseminate these ideas beyond a single neighborhood or sector. Larger-scale improvements, investments, and restoration, for example, in places like the Los Angeles River, or Oslo's bold plan to restore the major rivers that connect the city's forests and fjords, set ambitious targets, goals, and visions. Adoption of citywide biophilic policies, such as Toronto's mandate for installing green rooftops, can have a huge impact across a city and may effect larger-scale, lasting change in ways that more tactical interventions can't. There is a role then for action and interventions at each end of the geographical scale and every point in between.

We will also need to harness the creative entrepreneurial energies of the many companies and enterprises working in cities, tapping into the power of the private sector. We have seen in cities like Singapore the power and influence of developers who are engaged in friendly competition about which hotel or office project can include nature in the most unusual and creative way.

Public policy can help to bolster private inventiveness, of course, as seen in the financial subsidies provided by Singapore's NParks for green projects. The Singapore story shows, moreover, how important engaging the private sector can be in biophilic design and planning. Hotel companies and office complexes, for instance, have much to reap in benefits from investing in new biophilic design. Lee Kin Seng, who is director of communications for PARKROYAL at Pickering, an exemplary office/hotel in Singapore, has been quoted highlighting the many direct benefits provided by the natural and garden elements, such as "bringing lush greenery into the guest rooms and internal spaces, enhancing the quality of life and reinforcing Singapore's tropical image" (Sustainability Leaders n.d.). These benefits are clear enough, but there is more, including improved design and public recognition and visibility. "Our green initiatives and energy features enhance the overall building performance resulting in significant cost savings and have generated much media interest and placed PARK-ROYAL on Pickering under the global spotlight" (Sustainability Leaders n.d.).

### Bring Professions Together on Behalf of Nature

Which roles and professions will we need to bring about biophilic cities? The answer is all of them!

Of course architects, landscape architects, and urban designers have had an especially important role in incorporating new forms of nature into built environments and in reimagining more living forms of buildings and urban neighborhoods. Equally true, as the vision of biophilic cities continues to take hold and gain traction in many cities, the role of planners who are able to see beyond buildings and projects will be increasingly important. It seems clear that biophilic cities are on the cusp of a shift from being seen as a design amenity to becoming a global urban movement. City planners have the ability to cast their community plans through a biophilic lens, take a more holistic and comprehensive approach to planning natureful cities, and see how all the different parts might fit together.

The biophilic cities agenda offers an unusually potent framework and mission to bring together the work of many other professions. Medicine and public health represent especially promising areas for engagement. Physicians and public health officials are becoming some of the most convincing voices on behalf of biophilic cities and lifestyles. Many physicians now regularly "prescribe nature," recognizing the great benefits of time spent outside and in experiencing nature. In Washington, DC, for example, a program called DC Parks Rx is aimed at doing just that and providing physicians and

---

**Box 13.4. Biophilic Cities Pioneer Profile: Wallace J. Nichols**

*Exploring the Blue Mind*

Perhaps the world's leading advocate for water, he is frequently heard to encourage, "get your blue mind on." Trained as a sea turtle researcher, he has emerged as an unusual voice on behalf of the power of water, in all its forms, to heal us, to enhance our lives, and its impact on our brains and on our mental and physical health. Nichols has been leading the way in helping to educate about the many powers of water. His best-selling book *Blue Mind* is the first comprehensive assessment of the research and literature surrounding water, and each year he has organized a Blue Mind conference that brings together an eclectic mix of academics, ocean and water activists, and others who have been impacted in some way by contact with water. One of Nichols's calling cards is a small blue marble, which he hands out at presentations and conferences. The marble is to symbolize the blue planet, and he encourages each person to give the

marble to someone else as a gift and as a way of giving thanks. There are some 1 million blue marbles currently in circulation.

Wallace J. Nichols, author of the bestselling book *Blue Mind*, has become a passionate advocate on behalf of the biophilic power of water. Credit: Photo by Tim Beatley.

---

patients with specific information about where in the city such prescribed nature might be experienced. Spearheaded by pediatrician Robert Zarr, the program has established a database of parks in the city, accessed by simply typing in one's zip code (Sellers 2015).

We will need scientists who are not afraid to understand (and indeed actively search out) the design and planning implications, and applications of their work: scientists who speak with scholarly authority but also speak with eloquence about the wisdom, beauty, power, and mystery of the natural world. Wallace J. Nichols (or "J" to those of us who know him) is an exceptional example: a scientist who speaks compellingly of the many emotional values of water, and its ability to heal, whether experienced as a diver, swimmer, surfer, or someone who just likes to watch and listen to oceans. (see box 13.4 for a description of this Biophilic Pioneer.).

**Box 13.5. Biophilic Cities Pioneer Profile: Natalie Jeremijenko**

*Artist and Engineer on Behalf of Nature*

Natalie Jeremijenko's official title is associate professor of art and art education, at NYU. But attaching a label to her unusual but powerful work is difficult—she is an artist, an engineer, a neuroscientist, and an inventor, among other descriptions. Her projects almost always involve a creative way of making some aspect of urban nature visible or evident, to demonstrate a new idea or technique in support of nature. Her creativity and inventiveness are her trademarks, evident in many projects she has undertaken over the years. These loosely fall within what she calls the Environmental Health Clinic. This is a virtual clinic, whereas she says "patients" are replaced with "impatients." Her projects have included the design of "ag-bags" a creative way to grow food in vertical environments; a moth cinema that highlights the presence of these insects in the city and seeks to enhance habitat for them; a Salamander Highway designed to allow

safe passage across dangerous roads; and an elevated Butterfly Bridge that similarly enhances species connectivity and mobility in urban settings, among others.

Natalie Jeremijenko is an artist and engineer at NYU and heads up something she calls the Environmental Health Clinic. Credit: Photo courtesy Natalie Jeremijenko.

Enlisting engineers in designing biophilic cities of the future is another valuable step. A desire to coexist with other forms of life in the city and to develop tangible strategies to enhance movement and viable habitat in the city will require the involvement of conservation biologists and landscape architects, but also civil engineers. The successful experience in Edmonton, Alberta, to design and construct some 27 wildlife passages (so far) was made possible in large part by the writing of an engineering manual, which made clear to all how and in what ways these structures could be viably integrated into the design and planning of more conventional roadways and road design. Without the direct involvement of these design engineers it is hard to see how the principle of ecological connectivity in that city would have been possible. Consulting, educating, and enlisting engineers in the mission and values of biophilic cities will be an important step.

But we will also need artists—painters, sculptors, poets, storytellers, photographers, and more. We are especially inspired by individuals who bring together seemingly different and disparate professions and skill sets on behalf of nature in cities. One such person is Natalie Jeremijenko, of New York University, whose work at once brings together art, engineering, and design and who herself works across the blurred lines of engineering, neuroscience, art, and advocacy. She is profiled and some of her inspiring projects are described in box 13.5.

## Conclusion

The biophilic cities agenda is a collaborative one, requiring creative, sustained partnerships. Problems of growing and restoring nature in cities, and of advancing the vision of immersive nature in cities, will require a concerted effort at working together. Indeed, some of the most successful biophilic cities described in this book are places where the public and private sectors have come together, where city agencies are communicating and collaborating, where nonprofits and other groups have joined forces to grow more nature in urban environments.

Biophilic cities will require a robust, extensive social network to help them along. Governments can do much, as the experience of Singapore shows, but there must also be an effort at developing civil society organizations and processes that allow for direct biophilic efforts and initiatives, the basis for truly collaborative efforts.

Many of the most impressive accomplishments in partner cities have occurred through nonprofits and nongovernmental organizations. The Urban Ecology Centers in Milwaukee are a good example. In 2012 they opened their third branch, and they have been able to deliver an extensive set of educational and recreational benefits to the city and especially to the specific neighborhoods in which they are located.

Nongovernmental organizations, such as Friends of the Urban Forest in San Francisco, or Portland Audubon, or Friends of the LA River in Los Angeles, are essential players in cultivating grassroots, popular support for biophilic cities, and for ensuring that what is designed, planned, and built matches the needs of ecosystems and neighborhoods alike.

# 14

# Overcoming the Obstacles and Challenges That Remain

Achieving the vision of biophilic cities will require efforts to tackle some of the major impediments and obstacles faced. These will vary from city to city, region to region, but what follows are some of the most important or common obstacles.

This book presents many strong arguments for and compelling evidence of the power of nature. For a host of reasons nature should be at the core of our design and planning and should receive priority and emphasis in our vision of cities moving forward. Yet, despite how convincing these ideas and examples are, there remain significant impediments to putting a biophilic cities agenda fully into practice.

## The Human–Nature Divide

We continue to struggle with the perceptions of being profoundly separate from nature. And even today this manifests as fear of nature, whether it is the fear of the unknown and unseeable nature around us (e.g., bacterial forms), or of the coyote or mountain lion, or even the skunk, that invades our urban and suburban neighborhoods. Part of the challenge of rewilding our hearts, mentioned previously, is that we have much work to do in shifting our mindsets to see ourselves as part of a larger natural world. Part of this challenge also involves overcoming a human hubris and narcissism that fails to see the beauty, wonder, and magic in other species and life forms.

## Competing Priorities in the Developing World

Much of the global population growth we will see in the next several decades will occur in cities in the developing world. How relevant are the biophilic design and

245

planning models we have been discussing here to the conditions in these cities? And will contact with nature be understandably seen as a luxury, in the face of poverty and poor and unhealthy living conditions of favelas, for instance?

We will need to increasingly think about how inserting and growing nature can help improve living conditions in the informal settlements where so many millions of the world's population live. We have provided some examples of how biophilia can help in these places, but probably too few. We know that nature in these settings can help to clean water, treat wastewater, grow food, and provide jobs. As the practice of biophilic design and planning continues to develop and mature, more tools, technologies, and inspiring stories will come along.

## Planning and Development Code Reform

Despite the many examples of ways that cities have reformed their planning and development management systems—from Seattle's Green Factor to Singapore's Landscape Replacement Policy—more is needed. Too often nature is secondary or an afterthought in the process of managing and regulating development. We need many more ideas for how growth and regrowth and change in cities can be effectively steered on behalf of nature. It remains unclear what a comprehensive biophilic development code might look like, or what its elements might be, but the idea holds promise. Much could be accomplished if nature figured more clearly and centrally into planning and development regulatory frameworks.

There are a variety of other areas of the local biophilic urbanism agenda where additional tools, policies, and implementation mechanisms are needed. We especially need more tools and strategies for tackling the impact cities have on nature globally. Some cities have attempted to address these impacts through green or sustainable procurement codes, and through the purchase of low-carbon, fair-trade goods and products. But this area needs more attention.

## Too Rigid Views of Aesthetics, Nature, and Professional Roles

Attitudes are certainly changing about what constitutes legitimate (and beautiful) nature in cities, but there are still perceptual obstacles. Planting spaces around urban buildings in native species still runs up against a sense of these spaces being untidy or unkempt. Richard Hassell, cofounder of the innovative Singapore architectural firm WOHA, relates that some of his architectural colleagues' reactions to his buildings, such as the natureful PARKROYAL hotel, are less than enthusiastic. They regard abundant plants and natural elements as inappropriate additions to modern architectural form.

And those in many other professions, from interior design to civil engineering,

**Box 14.1. Biophilic Cities Pioneer Profile: Lena Chan**

*Biophilia and Biodiversity Together*

Few individuals in the world have been more passionate advocates and effective leaders on behalf of urban biodiversity as Lena Chan has. As Group Director of the National Biodiversity Center, at the Singapore National Parks Board (NParks), she manages a staff of around thirty, guiding work on a variety of urban conservation programs and initiatives, many serving as innovative models for other cities around the world. She has been a key architect of the Singapore Index of Biodiversity, an international set of metrics and standards being used by a number of cities around the world. Chan is able to see the essential connections between the agenda of urban biodiversity conservation, and biophilic design and planning, something reflected in a recent (and unusual) international conference she organized in that city. With training in ecology and

parasitology, and a PhD from Imperial College, London, Chan serves as an effective bridge between the scientific community and planners, designers, and policymakers.

Lena Chan is Group Director (National Biodiversity Centre) at the National Parks Board of Singapore. Credit: Photo by Chua Ee Kiam.

who can and must participate in crafting and growing biophilic cities, are stuck in professional mindsets that make such participation difficult. Road engineers have been slow to warm to the notion of wildlife passages and the need to think as clearly about wildlife connections as they do about connections for the auto.

## Realizing and Capitalizing on the Benefits of Nature

We now have a greater sense and understanding of the many social, health, and environmental benefits associated with growing nature in cities. The economic value of ecosystem services is now well understood by planners, designers, and public officials. That said, there are still many challenges in how to tap into and steer these benefits and to harness them on behalf of growing even more nature in cities and metropolitan areas. We know that it is possible to reduce stress, and enhance mental and physical health through investments in nature, but it remains difficult to accurately estimate and take into account the health benefits, such as lowered public health costs associated with reductions in asthma, diabetes, and heart disease, to name a few, in our economic and policy frameworks (fig. 14.1). Partner cities like Birmingham are grounding much of their biophilic planning on the long-term health benefits to their residents, but finding mechanisms to measure and capture those benefits remain elusive.

## How Do We Support Biodiversity in Cities?

There also remain serious questions about the ecological effectiveness of the biophilic design strategies we are employing. We think of a biophilic city as a place that serves as a biological safe harbor, an urban ark of sorts, a place where, in the midst of global habitat loss and destruction, we can help to compensate for these losses. But do we know enough about the design of ecological roofs or vertical green walls, for example, to ensure that they contribute to biodiversity conservation? What is the ecological cumulative effect, moreover, of the smaller green additions and interventions in the city? The literature and science of urban ecology continue to grow and expand, but there remain important questions that will have major implications for guiding biophilic design and planning.

## Time-Frame Disagreements

In a number of cities exactly what types of nature are envisioned in the city becomes a point of contention and controversy. This sometimes pits local or native biodiversity against nonnative species, as seen in cities like San Francisco, where vehement debates have taken place about proposals to replace introduced species of trees like eucalyptus and Monterey pines. There are good arguments on both sides; native trees are well adapted by millennia and better support native flora and fauna, yet urban residents are often fond of and get much enjoyment from live trees, whatever their provenance. There are no easy answers.

Sometimes these debates revolve around the temporal point of reference—is the aim to repair and restore nature to what it might have been 200 or 300 years ago? or to a more recent time frame? And there are new arguments on behalf of more novel ecosystems that have blended natives and nonnatives. Differing priorities or values, even among nature advocates, can create obstacles.

## The Double-Edged Sword of Technology

Many of us have identified the growing use of, and dependence on, digital media and technologies (e.g., the Internet, smart phones, etc.), especially among young people, as a major concern and distraction, something that often seems to pull us away from nature, from the outside world (e.g., see Louv 2008, 2012).

**Figure 14.1.** It remains a challenge to overcome the bifurcation between urban settings and nature. Even when we acknowledge that there is nature in cities, we often understand that nature only to exist in certain places (such as parks) that we must travel to visit or spend time in. Singapore is one city trying to overcome this bifurcation, and assert the health benefits of nature. The Khoo Teck Puat Hospital, shown here, is an excellent example of imagining a "hospital in a garden." Credit: Photo by Tim Beatley.

Many of the obstacles identified here can also potentially be viewed as opportunities. We are accustomed to pointing our fingers at such technology and how it works against biophilia. But there is a growing sense and experience that these digital technologies can also be used to advance learning about and connecting to nature. Sue Thomas, from the United Kingdom, has coined the term *technobiophilia* to refer to the ways that the Internet and cyberspace already can be understood as reflecting biophilic sensibilities (e.g., we speak of "clouds" and "surfing" the web and "tweeting" our momentary thoughts) (Thomas 2013) (box 14.2). Thomas argues for a more balanced view of the cyberworld and suggests many ways in which connections with nature might actually be strengthened. And there is no doubt that there are now many, many new digital tools that help us in our efforts at rewilding. From iBird to iTree, from apps that help identify nearby trails and parks to new augmented reality technology that helps to enhance rather than detract from our closeness to nature. There is much potential here.

**Box 14.2. Biophilic Cities Pioneer Profile: Sue Thomas**

*Design of Technobiophilic Cities*

Sue Thomas is a former professor of new media and today a self-described "independent scholar and digital pioneer." She coined the term *technobiophilia* and is the author of a new book by the same title. Thomas's innovative work and writing argue that cyberspace and the digital world reflect many of the of the biophilic qualities we find in the real world, and she notes the references in the language of the Internet (e.g., we speak of clouds, the web, and we use social media like Twitter). She defines *technobiophilia* as "'the innate tendency to focus on life and lifelike processes as they appear in technology. It can be seen in our everyday experiences online, and found in many of the Internet's most deeply embedded stories." Moreover, while Thomas understands that we need contact with real nature, she argues that we should appreciate the many ways that the digital revolution might help to strengthen ties to nature. Her suggestions are profound and important, and she is working with others to explore, for instance, the idea of cyberparks: real park spaces that take advantage of the benefits and opportunities of digital technologies. She argues that through the use of digital technologies we might be able to reach a younger generation that sees less value in parks and nature. And there are

many ways, Thomas discusses in her book, by which even our digital lives and practices can be made more biophilic.

Sue Thomas, author of the book *Technobiophilia*, argues that the Internet and cyberspace contain important connections to biophilia that can help in many ways to foster connections to real nature. Credit: Photo courtesy Sue Thomas

There are many new opportunities to capitalize on these new digital technologies in ways that help strengthen connections to the natural world. The Internet offers the possibility of delivering nature to our work desks and home computers in wondrous ways, as long as we don't use them as a permanent substitute for direct experiences. However, peregrine falcon cams, and other wildlife cams, are highly popular and provide the chance for viewers to see kinds of nature and wildlife up close in ways that would be difficult in the wild.

## Financing Biophilic Urbanism

Many, if not most, of the biophilic design and planning measures and strategies we have discussed in this book make good economic sense, and indeed represent the best possible investments even from a narrow economic return point of view. But there is still work to be done in creatively working out the financial aspects of nature in cities.

There are now many impressive stories of how groups in biophilic cities are raising capital to fund projects. On the public sector side, new taxation and public finance tools are being developed. Stormwater utility fees, for instance, are helping to fund some biophilic investments. In Colorado, state lottery funds are used almost entirely to fund parks and trails (largely through Great Outdoors Colorado), to the tune of more than $2.5 billion in funds since 1983. In other places there are creative efforts to utilize tax increment financing and other forms of benefit assessment that recognize the increase in property values that investments in nature often bring about. Los Angeles is utilizing a version of this idea (an enhanced infrastructure district) to fund the habitat enhancements and restoration work planned along the LA River.

The emergence of crowd-funding platforms, such as Kickstarter or Indiegogo, represent another opportunity for securing support for biophilic projects. One especially promising model can be seen in IOBY, a Brooklyn-based crowd-funding organization that has already raised some $1.3 million for a variety of mostly small green projects. IOBY's innovation is that it is neighborhood focused, with funders living in or near the neighborhood in which a project is proposed, and encouraged to volunteer and become active participants in these projects.

## Ensuring a "Just Biophilia"

A major challenge remains ensuring that there is a fair distribution of both the benefits of nature and the burdens of nature-deficient environments. We might call it *just biophilia*, and it must receive more attention as the biophilic cities movement advances. There is often a profoundly unjust or inequitable distribution of nature in cities, by race and income. Recent studies showing that tree canopy coverage is strongly associated with income underscore this challenge (Schwarz et al. 2015).

In recent years some high-profile urban greening projects, such as High Line Park, in New York City, have been criticized for setting in motion unintended consequences for the Chelsea neighborhood—displacement and increasing housing prices (fig. 14.2). This dynamic has been variously referred to as environmental gentrification, or ecological gentrification (Dooling 2009; Haffner 2015). Much more

**Figure 14.2.** The High Line Park, in New York City, is the story of how an abandoned elevated rail line has been converted to a popular linear park. Despite the undeniable value of this unusual park, concerns have been raised about the gentrification and displacement associated with the project. Planners and biophilic city advocates will need to develop new tools to ensure that green projects like this do not have unintended economic and social consequences, and that their benefits are widely and fairly distributed. Credit: Photo by Tim Beatley.

attention needs to be given to such problems, and more thinking and creative practice is needed to advance the agenda of biophilic urbanism, but in ways that do not unfairly or unjustly impact the least-advantaged members of society.

A healthy new discussion is emerging about techniques and strategies, with some now arguing for more bottom-up and more decentralized approaches, for instance, smaller green spaces, more evenly distributed, and new ideas, such as "just green enough" (approaches that link nature improvements to jobs and industrial cleanup in a neighborhood), and generally efforts to moderate and minimize gentrification impacts (Wolch, Byrne, and Newell 2014). There are a range of tools and mechanisms that could be better used to ensure that the benefits of projects like the High Line Park are more evenly distributed (e.g., community benefit agreements, tax increment financing where the benefits flow to affordable housing), but other tools and strategies need to be developed and tested. In short, a biophilic city must be a natureful city and also a just city.

## Concluding Thoughts

The foregoing are serious challenges and ones that will be faced by any city and any group of advocates of urban biophilia in that city. The good news is that the movement is robust and that cities around the world are working hard and creatively to address them. New and innovative funding and governance strategies have been developed, as well as new ways of thinking about and designing-in nature of all sorts. Many cities are recognizing the serious equity issues in the access to and enjoyment of nature and taking steps to address them. In very practical ways cities are experimenting and creatively exploring ways to address these new challenges, and that is to be expected. Many of these experiments and innovations are described in the cases—short and long—in this book, and, although these challenges remain, there are emerging new ideas, stories, and examples for cities to learn from and be inspired by.

# 15

# Conclusions:
## *Reimagining Cities of the Future*

As Planet Earth lunges forward toward a higher and higher percentage of world population living in cities, it is timely to rethink how these cities function and feel to those living in them. It is a fundamental premise of this book that nature is not something optional, but, rather, absolutely essential to living healthy, interesting, and meaningful lives. There has been a virtual explosion of research and literature connecting nature, and contact with nature, with a host of positive mental and physical conditions—nature has the power to calm us, to reduce stress, to put us in a better mood, as well as to enhance our cognitive performance. In a world of otherwise diminishing resources and where conflict and strife seem endemic we can use some additional empathy and generosity. We are facing a host of health- and environmental-related conditions and calamities from overharvesting ocean fisheries to abysmal air quality in many cities of the South, to of course the overarching concerns of climate change. As the ideas and cases presented here suggest, returning to nature, and returning nature to cities, will help on all of these fronts. And from an economic calculation there are few investments that will deliver a greater, more substantial and long-lasting payoff than those that involve nature and natural systems.

That said, many obstacles remain. Some of the challenges moving forward have been outlined in the previous chapter—social equity, for example, and concerns about how individual urban greening interventions can add up to a coherent, well-functioning urban ecosystem, to name a couple. Other larger cultural obstacles remain—how we continue to understand nature as something "away," a remote and pristine place that one visits occasionally to seek solace and restore one's spirit.

Cultivating some new and powerful ways of understanding nature and wildness—an urban notion of concepts—will be necessary. But the good news from the research is that the human brain does indeed seem to respond to and appreciate nature in all its forms—from the green rooftop to the urban stream to the single street tree. Nature need not be remote and distant, and in fact it must be nearby.

Biophilic cities efforts must be concerned with species and nature wherever they are found on Planet Earth. Invoking the broadest translation of *biophilia*—"love of nature"—reinforces the value that conservation, restoration, and protection of nature are key values of a biophilic city. Here the tack must be severalfold: protecting and expanding the nature locally, but also important, working on behalf of nature globally. This includes efforts to reduce a city's global footprint (something Canadian cities like Vancouver and Edmonton have established as goals in their plans) and to rethink and moderate urban metabolism in ways that reduce damage to nature and natural systems. It is also about finding ways to demonstrate global leadership in support of global nature. How to give tangible meaning to a biophilic city's commitment to global nature remains open to further exploration and is one of the most important areas of future work.

We live in a time when urban planners like myself employ different terms and terminology, different frames for cities—sustainability, or sustainable cities, has been one potent frame, and more recently resilience, or resilient cities, another powerful frame. These ways of thinking about cities remain important, and these languages need not be discarded. Few cities could currently be considered either sustainable or resilient, and there is herculean work remaining on these fronts. But biophilic cities offers a powerful and necessary additional frame. As I have argued elsewhere a biophilic city is a sustainable, resilient city (Beatley and Newman 2013). But perhaps more important, this frame conveys things that are missing from the others—as often said, the *philic* is as important as the *bio*; that is, there is an essential element of affect and affection—and that we need to explicitly acknowledge the value of the care we hold about nature and the sense of duty toward the many other forms of life we share the world with. It is about giving priority to nature in our design and planning, but also making room for other forms of life and recognizing their inherent worth. It gives space for celebrating the wonder and awe we experience (or should) in cities and the compassion and empathy we hold toward others writ large.

It is tempting to offer nature as an antidote to many of our more vexing social problems, and the evidence does seem to move us in that direction. We know that hospitals and medical facilities of various kinds are increasingly designed to enlist nature and the natural world in the healing process (e.g., think of the many examples in this book: Khoo Teck Puat Hospital in Singapore, Spaulding Rehab Hospital in Boston, Credit Valley Hospital in Toronto, among many others). Nature propels us outside and has the ability to create healthier, more productive, and enjoyable office and work environments. Nature has remarkable power to engage elders and children alike, addressing especially the challenge of a graying society where nature can provide meaning and connection and health in the waning years of life. Nature and biophilic cities can be part of the answer, as we have seen, in addressing poverty reduction, providing meaningful work for troubled youth, and reducing tendencies toward violence and crime. I must be careful not to overstate the benefits, but frankly this seems increasingly hard to do. As cities and urban societies struggle with so many interconnected problems and challenges the vision of biophilic cities, of cities of abundant nature where care for and curiosity about nature are at the core of their DNA, represents an unusually powerful and potent way forward.

How the goals and vision of a given biophilic city are expressed, and their specific look, feel, and practical meaning will vary from place to place. Clearly differences in culture, climate, urban history, and other factors will suggest different ways that cities can expand, restore, and integrate nature—green roofs work not so well in desert environments; local species of plants, birds, and trees will vary radically from place to place. What works in one city may not work in another. Perhaps accident, experimentation, and serendipity may explain how a particular ordinance or tool or project gains traction. We must be creative, resourceful, and collaborative to address these complex issues.

## The Role of the Global Biophilic Cities Network

For these reasons, and others, we have been working to organize a global Biophilic Cities Network (information about it can be found at www.biophiliccities.org) (fig. 15.1). Launched in late 2013, and with a series of partner cities (many described herein) serving as the initial inspiration, we have unveiled a set of guidelines for new cities wishing to join the Network. The Network is gaining visibility and traction, which we hope will continue. Individuals and groups can join the Network by simply signing an online pledge; participating partner cities must do a bit more, by, for instance, adopting (by a city council or other local elected body) a resolution or proclamation indicating intent to join the Network and to work toward becoming a biophilic city.

There are many challenges remaining as we advance forward globally the concept and practice of biophilic cities. Many policy and research questions remain unanswered, and there is much left to do. But we need not wait for all of these questions

**Figure 15.1.** A picture taken at the end of a 4-day meeting of biophilic partner cities, and the formal launch of the global Biophilic Cities Network. Credit: Photo by Tim Beatley.

to be answered, and we know for certain that cities can do much more to create experiences of immersive nature for their residents. We know as well that there is much nature in cities to celebrate and steward and many, many opportunities to further support and grow this nature.

How the Network will function, and what tasks and activities it will take on, remain open questions. It will hopefully continue to serve as a vehicle for sharing insights and information about what works, and doesn't, and about the many successful (and sometimes not) efforts under way to integrate nature. It will provide opportunities for sharing information and good design and planning practices, will establish a set of peer cities and professionals who will help each other moving forward, and will serve as a political and social force in arguing for a more proactive, assertive role for cities in relation to nature. We encourage others (as individuals, as an organization, as an official partner city) to become involved. The resources section to follow provides some places where additional information can be found. We are also finding that there is as much of a need to connect individuals, groups, and enterprises *within* a city or metropolitan area as *between* them; thus we are seeing the emergence of grassroots groups in cities such as Washington, DC (Biophilic DC) and Philadelphia (BioPhilly), and we are doing what we can to assist these efforts.

We have already told the stories of many cities—through books, case studies, blogs, and film—and we will do more in the future. We hope as well that the Network will become a force to aid in the advancement of the biophilic cities movement, to provide support for citizens, groups, and government officials in cities seeking to give nature greater importance in urban planning and urban management. We need help in this cause and hope that readers will explore the different ways that they might be able to give a hand and apply their skills and energy.

These are daunting times globally, but exciting times as well, as we reimagine a life in cities profoundly connected to the natural world. We invite you, the reader, to join us in this journey and to put your energy, compassion, and bright ideas to work in shaping the future of biophilic cities!

# Resources

We have included a list of resources that you may find helpful as you continue to explore biophilic cities.

## Web Pages and Web Materials

The Biophilic Cities Project http://biophiliccities.org/

Children and Nature Network http://www.childrenandnature.org/

European Green Capital City http://ec.europa.eu/environment/europeangreencapital /about-the-award/index.html

Harvard School of Public Health Program in Nature, Health, & the Built Environment http://www.chgeharvard.org/category/nature-health-built-environment

TKF Foundation/Nature Sacred http://naturesacred.org/

Therapeutic Landscapes Network http://www.healinglandscapes.org/

Wellington—A Biophilic City. https://www.youtube.com/watch?v=7HqCfyjstyo.

WILD Cities/WILD Foundation http://www.wild.org/where-we-work/wild-cities/

## Blogs

The Dirt: Uniting the Built and Natural Environments http://dirt.asla.org

The Nature of Cities http://www.thenatureofcities.com/

## Books

Beatley, Timothy. 2011. *Biophilic Cities: Integrating Urban Design and Nature*. Washington, DC: Island Press.

Beatley, Timothy, 2014. *Blue Urbanism: Connecting Cities and Oceans*. Washington, DC: Island Press.

Bekoff, Marc. 2014. *Rewilding Our Hearts: Building Pathways of Compassion and Coexistence*. Novato, CA: New World Library.

Cooper Marcus, Clare, and Naomi Sachs. 2013. *Therapeutic Landscapes: An Evidence-Based Approach to Designing Healing Gardens and Restorative Outdoor Spaces*. New York: Wiley.

Kaplan, Stephen, and Rachel Kaplan. 1989. *The Experience of Nature: A Psychological Perspective*. Cambridge: Cambridge University Press.

Kellert, Stephen. 2014. *Birthright: People and Nature in the Modern World*. New Haven, CT: Yale University Press.

Kellert, Stephen. and E. O. Wilson. 1995. *The Biophilia Hypothesis*. Washington, DC: Island Press.

Kellert, Stephen R., Judith Heerwagen, and Martin Mador. 2008. *Biophilic Design: The Theory, Science and Practice of Bringing Buildings to Life*. Hoboken, NJ: Wiley.

Louv, Richard. 2008. *Last Child in the Woods: Saving Our Children from Nature-Deficit Disorder*. Chapel Hill, NC: Algonquin Books.

Louv, Richard. 2012. *The Nature Principle: Reconnecting with Life in a Virtual Age*. Chapel Hill, NC: Algonquin Books.

Nichols, Wallace J. 2014. *Blue Mind*. New York: Little, Brown and Company.

Sampson, Scott D. 2015. *How to Raise a Wild Child: The Art and Science of Falling in Love with Nature*. New York: Houghton Mifflin Harcourt.

Selhub, Eva M., and Alan C. Logan. 2012. *Your Brain On Nature: The Science of Nature's Influence on Your Health, Happiness, and Vitality*. New York: Wiley Press.

Stoner, Tom, and Carolyn Rapp. 2008. *Open Spaces, Sacred Places*. Baltimore: TKF Foundation.

Tova Bailey, Elizabeth. 2010. *The Sound of a Wild Snail Eating*. Chapel Hill, NC: Algonquin Books.

Thomas, Sue. 2013. *Technobiophilia: Nature and Cyberspace*. New York: Bloomsbury Academic.

Wilson, E. O. 1984. *Biophilia*. Cambridge, MA: Harvard University Press.

Wilson, E. O. 2007. *The Creation: An Appeal to Save Life on Earth*. New York: Norton.

## Articles

Aspinall, P., P. Mavros, R. Coyne, and J. Roe. 2013. "The Urban Brain: Analysing Outdoor Physical Activity with Mobile EEG." *British Journal of Sports Medicine* (March): 1–6.

Beatley, Timothy. 2014. "Launching the Global Biophilic Cities Network." http://www.thenatureofcities.com/2013/12/04/launching-the-global-biophilic-cities-network/.

Beatley, Timothy, 2014. "The Need for and Vision of Biophilic Cities." http://humanspaces.com/2014/10/17/on-the-need-for-and-vision-of-biophilic-cities/.

Beatley, Timothy, and Peter Newman. 2013. "Biophilic Cities Are Sustainable, Resilient Cities." *Sustainability* 5(8): 3328–3345. http://www.mdpi.com/2071-1050/5/8/3328.

Blaustein, Richard. 2014. "Urban Biodiversity Gains New Converts: Cities around the World Are Conserving Species and Restoring Habitat." *BioScience* 63 (2): 72–77. http://bioscience.oxfordjournals.org/content/63/2/72.full.

Hanscom, Greg. 2014. "Why Our Cities Need to Be Ecosystems Too." http://grist.org/cities/habitats-for-humanity-why-our-cities-need-to-be-ecosystems-too/.

Patel, Neel V. 2014. "Migrating to the City: How Researchers Are Beginning to Think Differently about Urban Biodiversity." http://scienceline.org/2014/06migrating-to-the-city/.

Schwartz, Ariel. 2013. "Why We Need Biophilic Cities." http://www.fastcoexist.com/1679821/why-we-need-biophilic-cities.

van der Wal, Ariane J., Hannah M. Schade, Lydia Krabbendam, and Mark van Vugt. 2013. "Do Natural Landscapes Reduce Future Discounting in Humans?" *Proceedings of the Royal Society B* 280 (1773): 2295–. doi:10.1098/rspb.2013.2295.

Weinstein, N., A. K. Przybylski, and R. M. Ryan. 2009. "Can Nature Make Us More Caring? Effects of Immersion in Nature on Intrinsic Aspirations and Generosity." *Personality and Social Psychology Bulletin* 35(10): 1315–1329.

## Reports

Browning, William. 2014. "The 14 Patterns of Biophilic Design." http://www.terrapinbrightgreen.com/report/14-patterns/.

Terrapin Bright Green. The Economics of Biophilia: Why Designing with Nature in Mind Makes Financial Sense. http://www.terrapinbrightgreen.com/report/economics-of-biophilia/.

## Film and Video

*Biophilic Design: The Architecture of Life.* http://www.biophilicdesign.net/film-trailer.html.

*The Nature of Cities.* http://topdocumentaryfilms.com/nature-cities/.

*Singapore: Biophilic City.* https://www.youtube.com/watch?v=XMWOu9xIM_k.

# References

2012-Vitoria-Gasteiz. 2012, January 1. http://ec.europa.eu/environment/europeangreen capital/winning-cities/2012-vitoria-gasteiz/.

Agencia de Gestión Urbana de la Ciudad de México. 2014, January 15. "Arma tu azotea verde y obtén descuento en predial." http://www.agu.df.gob.mx/sintesis/index.php /arma-tu-azotea-verde-y-obten-descuento-en-predial/.

Alday, I., M. Jover, and C. Dalnoky. 2008. El Parque del Agua Luis Buñuel =: Le parc de l'eau Luis Buñuel = The Water Park Luis Buñuel. Zaragoza: Expoagua Zaragoza.

Anchorage Park Foundation. n.d. "Anchorage Trails Initiative." http://anchoragepark foundation.org/programs/trails-initiative/.

Arch Daily, 2015. "Bosco Verticale / Boeri Studio" found at: http://www.archdaily.com /777498/bosco-verticale-stefano-boeri-architetti, November 23.

Architect's Newspaper. 2013. "Unveiled> 300 Lafayette." *Architect's Newspaper* (November 11).

Architectural Review, 2011. "Stacking Green House by Vo Trong Nghia, Daisuke Sanuki and Shunri Nishizawa, Saigon, Vietnam," July 27. http://www.architectural-review .com/today/stacking-green-house-by-vo-trong-nghia-daisuke-sanuki-and-shunri nishizawa-saigon-viet nam/8617710.fullarticle.

Aspinall, Peter, Panagiotis Mavros, Richard Coyne, and Jenny Roe. 2013. "The Urban Brain: Analysing Outdoor Physical Activity with Mobile EEG." *British Journal of Sports Medicine*. 49(4): 72–76.

Atchley, R. A., D. L. Strayer, P. Atchley. 2012. Creativity in the Wild: Improving Creative Reasoning through Immersion in Natural Settings. *PLoS ONE* 7(12): e51474. doi:10.1371/journal.pone.0051474.

Audubon Society of Portland. 2015. "Swift Watch." http://audubonportland.org/local-bird ing/swiftwatch.

Bahl, V. 2014, December 8. "Revolutionising the Factory." http://www.newindianexpress .com/education/student/Revolutionising-the-Factory/2014/12/08/article2560123.ece.

Barrett, Tom, 2012. "A plan to knit the city back to the land", *Milwaukee Sentinel Journal*, September 22. http://www.jsonline.com/news/opinion/a-plan-to-kint-the-city-back-to -the-land-md6tom5170774146.html.

Barton, Jo, and Jules Pretty. 2010. "What Is the Best Dose of Nature and Green Exercise for Improving Mental Health? A Multi-Study Analysis." *Environmental Science and Technology* 44:3947–3955.

Beatley, Timothy. 2009. *Planning for Coastal Resilience*. Washington, DC: Island Press.

Beatley, Timothy. 2011. *Biophilic Cities: Integrating Nature into Urban Design and Planning*. Washington, DC: Island Press.

Beatley, Timothy. 2012. "Exploring the Nature Pyramid." Nature of Cities blog. http://www .thenatureofcities.com/2012/08/07/exploring-the-nature-pyramid/.

Beatley, Timothy, and Peter Newman. 2013. "Biophilic Cities Are Sustainable, Resilient Cities." *Sustainability* (June). http://www.mdpi.com/2071-1050/5/8/3328.

Biografía Julio Carlos Thays. n.d. http://www.buenosaires.gob.ar/jardinbotanico/biografia -julio-carlos-thays.

BirdNote. 2013. "The Aqua Tower—Architecture with Birds in Mind." http://birdnote.org /show/aqua-tower-architecture-birds-mind.

Boeri, Stefano. 2015. "The Brief." http://www.architectsjournal.co.uk/buildings/bosco-verti cale-by-stefano-boeri-architetti/8679088.article.

Bratman, Gregory N., J. Paul Hamilton, and Gretchen Daily. 2012. "The Impacts of Nature Experience on Human Cognitive Function and Mental Health." *Annals of the New York Academy of Sciences* 1249:118–136.

Bratman, Gregory N., J. Paul Hamilton, Kevin S. Hahn, Gretchen C. Daily, and James J. Gross. 2015. "Nature Experience Reduces Rumination and Subgenual Prefrontal Cortex Activation." *Proceedings of the National Academy of Sciences* 112(28): 8567–8572. doi: 10.1073/pnas.1510459112.

Buckingham, Kathleen, and Craig Hanson. 2015. "The Restoration Diagnostic: Case Example: Tijuca National Park, Brazil." Washington, DC: World Resources Institute. http://www.wri.org/sites/default/files/WRI_Restoration_Diagnostic_Case_Example _Brazil.pdf.

*Buffalo Bayou and Beyond: Visions, Strategies, Actions for the 21st Century*. 2002. https://issuu .com/buffalobayou/docs/2002masterplan.

Bullen, James. 2015. "More Trees on Your Street Help You Feel Younger." www.smh.com.

Cape Town. 2012. "City Statistics." https://www.capetown.gov.za/en/stats/Documents /City_Statistics_2012.pdf.

Catlow, Agnes. 1851. *Drops of Water: Their Marvelous and Beautiful Inhabitants Displayed by the Microscope*. London: Reeve and Benham.

Cave, Damien. 2012. "Lush Walls Rise to Fight a Blanket of Pollution." *New York Times* (April 9). http://www.nytimes.com/2012/04/10/world/americas/vertical-gardens-in -mexico-a-symbol-of-progress.html?_r=2&partner=rss&emc=rss&.

Charles, W. 2014. "Parc Natural de Martissant: A Project Model to Be Replicated." *Lakay Weekly—Le nouvelliste en anglais* (October 30). http://lenouvelliste.com/lenouvelliste /articleprint/137566.

Chengdu Planning and Management Bureau. 2003, October. *Ecological Chengdu Green Tiangfu: A Briefing on the Ecological Belt around Chengdu*. Chengdu: Author.

Chiang, Kelly, and Alex Tan, eds. 2009. *Vertical Greenery for the Tropics*. Singapore: NParks.

Chicago Green Roofs. 2016. http://www.cityofchicago.org/city/en/depts/dcd/supp_info/chicago_green_roofs.html.

Chicago Wilderness. n.d. http://www.chicagowilderness.org.

City and County of San Francisco, Planning Department. 2011. Standards for Bird-Safe Buildings, adopted July 14. http://sf-planning.org/standards-bird-safe-buildings.

City of Birmingham, UK, 2013. "Green Living Spaces Plan." http://www.birmingham.gov.uk/greenlivingspaces.

City of Edmonton. 2015. "Designing for Wildlife Passage in an Increasingly Fragmented World." Edmonton, AB: Author.

City of Philadelphia, Department of Public Works. 2011, June 1. "Green City, Clean Waters." Philadelphia, PA: Author.

City of Portland, Oregon. 2001. "Portland's Willamette River Atlas." http://www.portlandoregon.gov/bps/47531.

City of Portland, Oregon. Parks and Recreation. 2016a. "History, 1852–1900." https://www.portlandoregon.gov/parks/article/95955.

City of Portland, Oregon. Parks and Recreation. 2016b. "Eastbank Esplanade." http://www.portlandoregon.gov/parks/finder/index.cfm?&propertyid=105&action=viewpark.

City of Portland, n.d. "Green Streets." https://www.portlandoregon.gov/bes/45386

City of Richmond. 2009. "Richmond Downtown Plan." Richmond, VA: Author.

City of Richmond. 2012. "Richmond Riverfront Plan." Richmond, VA: Author.

City of St. Louis. n.d. "Sustainability Plan." https://www.stlouis-mo.gov/sustainability/plan/.

City of Vancouver. 2010. "Greenest City Action Plan." http://vancouver.ca/files/cov/greenest-city-action-plan.pdf.

City of Vancouver. 2012. "Grants from Greenest City Fund Top $500,000 in First Year." http://vancouver.ca/news-calendar/grants-from-greenest-city-fund-top-500-000-in-first-year-.aspx.

Columbia Slough Watershed Council. 2016. "Slough School Overview." http://columbiaslough.org/index.php/slough_school/.

Cracknell, Deborah, et al. 2015. "Marine Biota and Psychological Well-Being: A Preliminary Examination of Dose–Response Effects in an Aquarium Setting." *Environment and Behavior*. http://eab.sagepub.com/content/early/2015/07/27/0013916515597512.full.pdf.

Crompton, John, and Marsh Darcy Partners. 2011. "Bayou Greenways—A Key to a Healthy Houston." (August).

Curbed. 2013. "From Gas Station to Glass Station at Houston and Lafayette." *Curbed* (April 2). http://ny.curbed.com/archives/2013/04/02/from_gas_station_to_glass_station_at_houston_and_lafayette.php.

Daly, John, Margaret Burchett, and Fraser Torpy. 2010. "Plants in the Classroom Can Improve Performance." http://www.wolvertonenvironmental.com/Plants-Classroom.pdf.

Daugherty, Charles. 2013. "Growing the Halo." www.visitzealandia.com/growing-the
-halo/.

Design Corps. 2015. "Urban Park and Institute Sitie." https://designcorps.org/2015-seed
-award-winners/.

dlandstudio, n.d. "Gowanus Canal Sponge Park," found at: http://www.dlandstudio.com
/projects_gowanus.html.

Donovan, Geoffrey, and David T. Butry. 2010. "Trees in the City: Valuing Street Trees in
Portland, Oregon." *Landscape and Urban Planning* 94:77–83.

Donovan, Geoffrey, et al. 2011. "Urban Trees and the Risk of Poor Birth Outcomes."
*Health and Place* 17:390–393.

Dooling, Sarah. 2009. "Ecological Gentrification: A Research Agenda Exploring Justice in
the City." *International Journal of Urban and Regional Research* 33(3): 621–639.

Dreyfuss, J. 2013. "FOKAL and Parc de Martissant: An Urban Success." *Haiti Cultural
Exchange* (December 10). http://haiticulturalx.org/archive-fokal-and-parc-de-martis
sant-an-urban-success-written-by-joel-dreyfuss.

Eden Place Nature Center. n.d. "Leaders in Training." http://www.edenplacenaturecenter
.org/leaders-in-training.html.

Eden Place Nature Center. n.d. "Monarch Propagation and Monitoring." http://www
.edenplacenaturecenter.org/monarch-propagation-and-monitoring.html.

Education Outside, n.d."About." https://www.educationoutside.org/.

Elzeyadi, Ihab M.K., 2011. "Daylighting-Bias and Biophilia: Quantifying the Impact of
Daylighting on Occupants Health." http://www.usgbc.org/sites/default/files/OR10
_Daylighting%20Bias%20and%20Biophilia.pdf.

Faggi, A. 2012, October 26. "Botanical Gardens: More Than Places at Which the Plants Are
Labelled."    http://www.thenatureofcities.com/2012/10/26/botanical-gardens-more
-than-places-in-which-the-plants-are-labelled/.

Farrow, Tye. 2007/2008. "Designing Strong LInks to Nature." *International Hospital Fed-
eration Reference Book*. http://farrowpartners.ca/images/stories/articles/05-sustainable
-design/IntlHospitalFedReview_TBRHSC.pdf.

Feda, D. M., A. Seelbinder, S. Baek, S. Raja, L. Yin, and J. N. Roemmich. 2015. Neighbour-
hood Parks and Reduction in Stress among Adolescents: Results from Buffalo, New
York. *Indoor and Built Environment* 24(5): 631–639.

Feinberg, J. A., et al. 2014. "Cryptic Diversity in Metropolis: Confirmation of a New Leopard Frog Species (Anura: Ranidae) from New York City and Surrounding Atlantic Coast
Regions." *PLOS One* (October 29). doi: 10.1371/journal.pone.0108213.

Forest Park Conservancy. 2016. "Hikes and Events." http://www.forestparkconservancy
.org/forest-park/events/.

Freeman, David. 2015. "Bright Lights Bring More Bad News for Urban Bats." *Huffing-
ton Post* (June 8). http://www.huffingtonpost.com/2015/06/08/bats-light-bad-news
_n_7521274.html.

Garric, Audrey. 2015. "WIldlife Pushed Back as City Encroaches on Nairobi National
Park." *Guardian* (March 8). http://www.theguardian.com/world/2015/mar/08/nai
robi-national-park-endangered-city-wildlife-lions.

Gaston, K. J., et al. 2007. "Urban Domestic Gardens: Improving Their Contributions to Biodiversity and Ecosystem Services." *British Wildlife* 18:171–177.

Goertzen, M. 2015, March 22. "Envisioning a More Walkable Anchorage." *Alaska Dispatch News*. http://www.adn.com/61degnorth/article/envisioning-more-walkable -anchorage/2015/03/22/.

Goodyear, Sarah. 2013. "Liking Your Neighbors Could Help Prevent You from Having a Stroke." CityLab. http://www.citylab.com/housing/2013/09/liking-your -neighbors-could-help-prevent-you-having-stroke/6951/.

Government of Cape Town. n.d. "Cape Town's Unique Biodiversity and Plant and Animals." http://www.capetown.gov.za/en/EnvironmentalResourceManagement/publica tions/Documents/Biodiv_fact_sheet_08_ThreatenedSpecies_2011-03.pdf.

Greater London Authority. n.d. "All London Green Grid." https://www.london.gov.uk /priorities/environment/greening-london/improving-londons-parks-green-spaces /all-london-green-grid.

Greater London Authority. n.d. "Big Green Fund." https://www.london.gov.uk/priorities /environment/greening-london/improving-londons-parks-green-spaces/big-green -fund.

Greater London Authority. 2014. "The GLA Releases a Green Roof Map of London." http://climatelondon.org.uk/articles/the-gla-releases-a-green-roof-map-of-london/.

Greater London Authority. n.d. "More Trees for a Greener London [RE:LEAF Prospectus]." https://www.london.gov.uk/sites/default/files/RELEAF%20prospectus.pdf.

Guenther, Robin, and Gail Vittori. 2013. *Sustainable Healthcare Architecture*. New York: John Wiley.

Haffner, Jeanne. 2015. "The Dangers of Eco-gentrification: What's the Best Way to Make a City Greener?" *Guardian* (May 6). http://www.theguardian.com/cities/2015/may/06 /dangers-ecogentrification-best-way-make-city-greener.

Harless, John. 2013. "A Tree Spat Grows in San Francisco: Plans to Replace Nonnative Varieties with Indigenous Ones Have Run Into Opposition from Residents. *Wall Street Journal*. http://www.wsj.com/articles/SB10001424127887323300004578558103268015398.

Harper, Margaret, John Patterson, and John Harper. 2009. "New Diatom Taxa from the World's First Marine Bioblitz Held in New Zealand." *Acta Botanica Croatica* 68(2): 339–349.

Hartop, Emily A., Brian V. Brown, R. Henry, and L. Disney. 2015. "Opportunity in Our Ignorance: Urban Biodiversity Study Reveals 30 New Species and One New Nearctic Record for *Megaselia* (Diptera: Phoridae) in Los Angeles (California, USA). *Zootaxa* 3941(4). http://biotaxa.org/Zootaxa/article/view/zootaxa.3941.4.1.

Hawthorne, Christopher. 2010. "Jeanne Gang Brings Feminine Touch to Chicago's Muscled Skyline." *Los Angeles Times* (January 17). http://articles.latimes.com/2010/jan/17 /entertainment/la-ca-aqua17-2010jan17.

Hedblom, Marcus, Erik Heyman, Henrik Antonsson, and Bengt Gunnarsson. 2014. "Bird Song Diversity Influences Young People's Appreciation of Urban Landscapes." *Urban Forestry and Urban Greening* 13(2014): 469–474.

Hero MotoCorp Garden Factory and Global Parts Center–William McDonough Partners. n.d. http://www.mcdonoughpartners.com/projects/hero-motocorp-garden-factory -and-global-parts-center/.

Herzog, Cecilia. 2012. "A Green Dream to Counter 'Greenwashing' in Brazilian Cities." The Nature of Cities blog. http://www.thenatureofcities.com/2012/12/02/a-green-dream-to-counter-greenwashing-in-brazilian-cities/.

Heschong Mahone Group, Inc. 2003. "Windows and Offices: A Study of Office Worker Performance and the Indoor Environment." Prepared for the California Energy Commission. http://www.energy.ca.gov/2003publications/CEC-500-2003-082/CEC-500-2003-082-A-09.PDF.

Heyman, Glen. 2013. "Reimagining Nairobi National Park: Counter-Intuitive Tradeoffs to Strengthen This Urban Protected Area." The Nature of Cities Collective blog. http://www.thenatureofcities.com/2013/04/03/reimagining-nairobi-national-park-counter-intuitive-tradeoffs-to-strengthen-this-urban-protected-area/.

Hickman, Matt. 2015. "Urban Pollinators Fly High along Oslo's Flower-Lined Highway." www.mnn.com.

Hoh, Fadian. 2013, May 23. "Over 100 New Marine Species Discovered in Singapore." *Strait Times.* http://www.straitstimes.com/singapore/over-100-new-marine-species-discovered-in-singapore.

Holling, Crawford Stanley (Buzz). 1973. "Resilience and Stability of Ecological Systems." *Annual Review of Ecology and Systematics* 4:1–23.

Houston Wilderness. 2007. *Houston Atlas of Biodiversity.* College Station, TX: Texas A&M University Press.

Huang, Danwei, et al. 2009. "An Inventory of Zooxanthellate Scleractinian Corals in Singapore, Including 33 New Records." *Raffles Bulletin of Zoology* (Suppl. 22): 69–80.

Inhabitat. n.d. "VERDMX's Soaring Vertical Gardens Clean Mexico City's Air." http://inhabitat.com/verdmx-vertical-gardens-scour-mexico-city-air/verdmx-mexico-city-vertical-garden-2/?extend=1.

Jane, J. n.d. "Seoul Urban Renewal: Cheonggyecheon Stream Restoration." http://policytransfer.metropolis.org/case-studies/seoul-urban-renewal-cheonggyecheon-stream-restoration.

Jha, aLok. 2009, June 2. "City Birds Sing Higher than Country Cousins, Scientists Find." *Guardian.* http://www.theguardian.com/environment/2009/jun/03/great-tit-city-bird-song.

Journee, Stephen. 2014. *Wellington Down Under,* Wellington, NZ: Grantham House Publishing.

Kadas, Gyongyver. 2006, December. "Rare Invertebrates Colonizing Green Roofs in London." *Urban Habitats.* http://www.urbanhabitats.org/v04n01/invertebrates_full.html.

"Kaka Numbers Recovering in Wellington." n.d. http://halo.org.nz/kaka-numbers-recover-wellington/.

Kamin, B. 2011, May 9. "A Mayor Who Left His Mark on Chicago's Cityscape." http://articles.chicagotribune.com/2011-05-09/news/ct-met-kamin-daley-0508-20110509_1_mayor-richard-j-daley-cityscape-millennium-park.

Kaplan, Rachel, and Stephen Kaplan. 1989. *The Experience of Nature: A Psychological Perspective.* Cambridge University Press.

Kardan, Omid, Peter Gozdyra, Bratislav Misic, Faisal Moola, Lyle J. Palmer, Tomáš Paus and Marc G. Berman. 2015. "Neighborhood Greenspace and Health in a Large Urban Center." *Scientific Reports* 5 (article number: 11610). http://www.nature.com/articles/srep11610?utm_source=tech.mazavr.tk&utm_medium=link&utm_compaign=article.

Karlovitis, Bob. 2014. "Sounds of Nature Get a 'Remix' for Phipps Project." http://triblive.com/aande/music/6196763-74/says-sounds-aresty.

Kellert, Stephen. 2002. *Children and Nature: Psychological, Sociocultural, and Evolutionary Investigations.* Cambridge, MA: MIT Press.

Kellert, Stephen. 2005. *Building for Life: Designing and Understanding the Human–Nature Connection.* Washington, DC: Island Press.

Kellert, Stephen R., and Elizabeth F. Calabrese. 2015. "The Practice of Biophilic Design." http://www.biophilic-design.com/.

Kellert, Stephen R., Judith Heerwagen, and Martin Mador, 2008. *Biophilic Design: The Theory, Science and Practice of Bringing Buildings to Life.* Hoboken, NJ: Wiley.

Keltner, Dacher, and Jonathan Haidt. 2003. "Approaching Awe—A Moral, Spiritual, Aesthetic Emotion." *Cognition and Emotion* 17(2): 297–314.

Kenward, Alyson, Daniel Yawitz, Todd Sanford, and Regina Wang. 2014. *Summer in the City: Hot and Getting Hotter.* Climate Central. http://www.climatecentral.org/news/urban-heat-islands-threaten-us-health-17919.

Khanna, Parag. 2010, August 6. "Beyond City Limits." *Foreign Policy.* http://foreignpolicy.com/2010/08/06/beyond-city-limits/.

Kim, Eric S., Nansook Park, and Christopher Peterson. 2013. "Perceived Neighborhood Social Cohesion and Stroke." *Social Science and Medicine* 97: 49–55.

Kim, E.S., A.M. Hawes, and J. Smith, 2014. "Perceived Neighborhood Social Cohesion and Myocardial Infarction," J Epidemiol Community Health. Nov; 68(11): 1020–1026.

Kim, E.S., Park, N., Peterson, E., 2013. "Perceived neighborhood social cohesion and stroke", Soc Sci Med. 97: 49-55, Aug.

Kowarik, Ingo, and Andreas Langer. 2005. "Natur-Park Südgelände: Linking Conservation and Recreation in an Abandoned Railyard in Berlin." In *Wild Urban Woodlands: New Perspectives for Urban Forestry*, ed. Ingo Kowarik and Stefan Körner, 287–299. New York: Springer.

Lay, B. 2014, May 9. "Otter Makes Bishan Park Its New Home, Causes Everybody to Say 'Awww'." http://mothership.sg/2014/05/otter-makes-bishan-park-its-new-home-causes-everybody-to-say-awww/.

Lee, Kate E., Kathryn Williams, Leisa Sargent, Nicholas Williams, and Katherine Johnson. 2015. "40-Second Green Roof Views Sustain Attention: The Role of Micro-breaks in Attention Restoration," *Journal of Environmental Psychology* 42:182–189.

Lichtenfeld, Stephanie, Andrew J. Elliot, Markus A. Maier, and Reinhard Pekrun. 2012. "Fertile Green: Green Facilitates Creative Performance." *Personality and Social Psychology Bulletin* 38(6): 784–797.

Logan, Jason. 2009, August 29. "Scents and the City." *New York Times.* http://www.nytimes.com/interactive/2009/08/29/opinion/20090829-smell-map-feature.html.

Los deportes extremos tienen su lugar en el Parque Costanera Norte. 2013, October 9. http://www.buenosaires.gob.ar/noticias/macri-presento-el-parque-costanera-norte-para-la-practica-de-skate.

Louv, Richard. 2008. *Last Child in the Woods: Saving Our Children from Nature-Deficit Disorder.* Chapel Hill, NC: Algonquin Press.

Louv, Richard. 2012. *The Nature Principle: Reconnecting with Life in a Virtual Age.* Chapel Hill, NC: Algonquin Books of Chapel Hill.

Lydon, Mike, and Anthony Garcia. 2015. *Tactical Urbanism: Short-Term Action for Long-Term Change.* Washington, DC: Island Press.

Lynch, Yvonne. 2015. "Enhancing Urban Ecology for the City of Melbourne." Webinar presentation, Biophilic Cities Webinar Series. https://www.youtube.com/watch?v=W6tpNXXUmow.

Maas, J., R. A. Verheij, P. P. Groenewegen, S. de Vries, and P. Spreeuwenberg. 2006. "Green Space, urbanity and Health: How Strong Is the Relation?" *Journal of Epidemiology and Community Health* 60(7): 587–592.

Maas J., R. A. Verheij, S. de Vries, P. Spreeuwenberg, F. G. Schellevis, P. P. Groenewegen. 2009. "Morbidity Is Related to a Green Living Environment," *Journal of Epidemiology and Community Health* 63(12): 967–973.

MacKerron, George, and Susana Mourato. 2013. "Happiness Is Greater in Natural Environments." *Global Environmental Change.* doi:10.1016/j.gloenvcha.2013.03.010.

Magellan Development Group. 2010. "Aqua Apartments's Awards." http://www.magellandevelopment.com/Aquas-awards-peta-proggy-award-given-to-jeanne-gangs-eco-friendly-Aqua-design/.

Martin, Pierre-André. 2012. "Putting Nature Back into the Natural Beauty of Rio de Janeiro." The Nature of Cities blog. http://www.thenatureofcities.com/2012/11/10/putting-nature-back-into-the-natural-beauty-of-rio-de-janeiro/.

Marzluff, John M., et al, 2010. "Lasting recognition of threatening people by wild American crows, " Animal Behavior, Vol 79, Issue 3, March 2010, Pages 699–707.

Metro. 2014. "Metro News: Community Nature Project Gets $5.2 Million Boost from Metro Grants." http://www.oregonmetro.gov/news/community-nature-projects-get-52-million-boost-metro-grants.

Metro. 2016. "Nature in Neighborhoods Grants." http://www.oregonmetro.gov/tools-partners/grants-and-resources/nature-grants.

Miles, Irene, with William C. Sullivan and Frances E. Kuo. 2000. "Psychological Benefits of Volunteering for Restoration Projects." *Ecological Restoration* 18(4): 218–227.

Mooney, Chris. 2015, May 26. "Just Looking at Nature Can Help Your Brain Work Better, Study Finds." *Washington Post.* https://www.washingtonpost.com/news/energy-environment/wp/2015/05/26/viewing-nature-can-help-your-brain-work-better-study-finds/.

Mordas-Schenkein, L. 2014, October 4. "The World's Tallest Vertical Garden Lives and Breathes in Sydney." http://inhabitat.com/the-worlds-tallest-vertical-garden-lives-and-breathes-in-sydney/one-central-park-facades/.

Municipalidad de la Ciudad de Buenos Aires. n.d. "Costanera Sur—Parque Natural y Reserva Ecológica—Ciudad Buenos Aires." http://www.patrimonionatural.com/html/provincias/cba/costanerasur/descripcion.asp.

Muschamp, Herbert. 2000, April 29. "R. L. Zion, 70, Who Designed Paley Park Dies."

*New York Times.* http://www.nytimes.com/2000/04/28/arts/r-l-zion-79-who-designed -paley-park-dies.html.

Ng, Peter K. L., Richard T. Corlett, and Hugh T. W. Tan, eds. 2011. *Singapore Biodiversity: An Encyclopedia of the Natural Environment and Sustainable Development.* National University of Singapore.

Nichols, Wallace J. 2014. *Blue Mind.* New York: Little, Brown.

NParks. 2009. *Trees of Our Garden City.* Singapore: Author.

"Oregon Field Guide: Forest Park BioBlitz." 2012. YouTube video, 9:00, May 18, 2012. http://www.youtube.com/watch?v=7hV_tvnbWJ8.

Orive, L., and R. Dios Lema. 2012. "Vitoria-Gasteiz, Spain: From Urban Greenbelt to Regional Green Infrastructure." In *Green Cities of Europe: Global Lessons on Green Urbanism,* 155–180. Washington, DC: Island Press.

Osgood, Melissa. 2014. "Daylight Is the Best Medicine, for Nurses." mediarelations.cornell.edu.

Oslo City Council, 2008. Oslo Towards 2025: The 2008 Municipal Master Plan, Oslo, Norway.

Oslo City, n.d. "Oslo Application for the European Green Capital City," Oslo Norway.

Oslo Kommune, 2007. *Grantplan for Oslo,* Plan-og bygningsetaten, Oslo Kommune.

Park Royal Hotels and Resorts, 2013. "PARKROYAL ON PICKERING NOW OPEN," found at: https://www.parkroyalhotels.com/en/news-room/news-listing/global/2013 /prsps-parkroyal-on-pickering-now-open.html#.V6imClUrLnA.

Perinotto, Tina. 2015, "Green and Wellbeing Are the New Black, Sitting Is the 'New Smoking'." The Fifth Estate. http://www.thefifthestate.com.au/innovation/design /green-and-wellbeing-are-the-new-black-sitting-is-the-new-smoking.

Perkins and Will. 2013, April 24. "Perkins and Will Defines Inclusive Design at New Spaulding Rehabilitation Hospital." http://perkinswill.com/news/new-spaulding -rehabilitation-hospital.html.

Phipps Conservatory. n.d. "Center for Sustainable Landscapes." https://phipps.conserv atory.org/green-innovation/at-phipps/center-for-sustainable-landscapes.

Pierre-Louis, M. D. 2014. "A Daunting Challenge: Creating an Urban Park in an Impoverished Neighborhood of Port-au-Prince, Haiti." In *Greening in the Red Zone: Disaster, Resilience and Community Greening,* ed. K. G. Tidball and M. E. Krasny, 45–50. Dordrecht, Netherlands: Springer.

Pougy, Nina, et al. 2014. "Urban Forests and the Conservation of Threatened Plant Species: The Case of the Tijuca National Park, Brazil." *Natureza & Conservação* 12(2): 170–173.

Project for Public Spaces. n.d. "Paley Park." http:/placemaking.pps.org/great_public _spaces/.

PUB. 2016, March 20. "ABC Waters Makes the Next Big Leap with 20 More Projects." http://www.pub.gov.sg/mpublications/Pages/PressReleases.aspx?ItemId=464.

Pugh, Thomas A. M., A. Robert MacKenzie, J. Duncan Whyatt , and C. Nicholas Hewitt. 2012. "Effectiveness of Green Infrastructure for Improvement of Air Quality in Urban Street Canyons." *Environmental Science and Technology* 46(14): 7692–7699. doi: 10.1021/es300826w.

Ramirez, Kelly S., et al. 2014. "Biogeographic Patterns in Below-Ground Diversity in New York City's Central Park Are Similar to Those Observed Globally." *Proceedings of the Royal Society B* 281(1795). doi: 10.1098/rspb.2014.1988.

Raven-Ellison, Daniel. 2014, May 27. "Why Greater London Should Be Made Into an Urban National Park." *Guardian.* http://www.theguardian.com/local-government -network/2014/may/27/greater-london-national-park-city.

Reserva Ecológica Costanera Norte: Biodiversidad. n.d.. http://recostaneranorte.blogspot .com/p/biodiversidad.html.

Reynolds, Gretchen. 2015, July 22. "How Walking in Nature Changes the Brain." http:// well.blogs.nytimes.com/2015/07/22/how-nature-changes-the-brain/?_r=0.

River Revitalization Foundation. n.d. "Greenway." http://riverrevitalizationfoundation .org/greenway/.

River Revitalization Foundation. 2010, June. Milwaukee River Greenway Master Plan. http://riverrevitalizationfoundation.org/wp-content/uploads/2014/10/100622_Final -Report_WEB.pdf.

Roe, Jenny, and Peter Aspinall. 2011. "The Restorative Outcomes of Forest School and Conventional School in Young People with Good and Poor Behavior." *Urban Forestry and Urban Greening* 10:205–212.

Rogers, Shannon H., John M. Halstead, Kevin H. Gardner, and Cynthia H. Carl-son. 2011. "Examining Walkability and Social Capital as Indicators of Quality of Life at the Municipal and Neighborhoods Scales." *Applied Research Quality Life* 6:201–213.

Royal Forest and Bird Protection Society. 2007. "Marine Bioblitz Uncovers Biodiversity Bonanza." www.scoop.co.nz/.

Royte, Elizabeth. 2015. "Urban Farms Now Produce 1/5 of the World's Food. GreenBiz. http://www.greenbiz.com/article/urban-farms-now-produce-15-worlds-food.

Sabatini, Joshua. 2016, April 19. "SF to Require Rooftop Solar Installations on New Buildings." *SF Examiner.* http://www.sfexaminer.com/san-francisco-require-rooftop -solar-installations-new-buildings/.

Sable-Smith, B. 2013, November 1. "What's the Great Rivers Greenway District?" https:// www.stlbeacon.org/#!/content/33431/greenway_explainer_102813.

San Francisco Great Streets Project. 2011. "Parklet Impact Study, San Francisco." http:// nacto.org/docs/usdg/parklet_impact_study_sf_planning_dept.pdf.

San Francisco Permaculture Guild. n.d. "Beekeeping Apprenticeship Program." http:// www.permaculture-sf.org/beekeeping-apprenticeship-program/.

San Francisco Recreation and Parks Department. 2016. "WIld Habitat Conserva-tion." http://sfrecpark.org/parks-open-spaces/natural-areas-program/wild-habitat -conservation/.

Saw, Le E., Felix K. S. Lim, Luis R. Carrasco. 2015, July 29. "The Relationship between Natural Park Usage and Happiness Does Not Hold in a Tropical City-State." *PLOS One.* http://journals.plos.org/plosone/article?id=10.1371/journal.pone.0133781.

Savvage AM, Hackett B, Guénard B, Youngsteadt EK, Dunn RR. Fine-scale heterogene-ity across Manhattan's urban habitat mosaic is associated with variation in ant composition and richness. Insect Conservation and Diversity. 8: 216-228. doi: 10.1111/icad.12098.

Schwarz, Kristen, et al. 2015. "Trees Grow on Money: Urban Tree Canopy Cover and Environmental Justice." *PLOS One.* http://journals.plos.org/plosone/article?id=10.1371/journal.pone.0122051.

Science News. 2012. "City Birds Adapt to Their New Predators." https://www.sciencedaily.com/releases/2012/11/121107073044.htm.

Seggelke, L. 2008, April 23. "Green Building and Climate in Chicago." http://www.sustainable-chicago.com/2008/04/23/green-building-and-climate-in-chicago/.

Sellers, Frances Stead. 2015, May 28. "D.C. Doctors Rx: A Stroll in the Park Instead of a Trip to the Pharmacy." *Washington Post.* https://www.washingtonpost.com/national/health-science/why-one-dc-doctor-is-prescribing-walks-in-the-park-instead-of-pills/2015/05/28/03a54004-fb45-11e4-9ef4-1bb7ce3b3fb7_story.html.

Shanahan, Danielle, et al., 2016. "Health Benefits from Nature Experiences Depend on Dose," Scientific Reports, June 23. http://www.nature.com/articles/srep28551

Siemens. 2011. "International Green City Index." http://www.siemens.com/entry/cc/features/greencityindex_international/all/en/pdf/report_africa_en.pdf.

Slobodchikoff, C. N., B. Perla and J. L. Verdolin. 2009. "Prairie Dogs: Communication and Community in an Animal Society." Harvard University Press, Cambridge, MA.

Soumya, Elizabeth. 2015, July 31. "The Night-Time Hunt for the Secretive Urban Slender Loris of Bangalore." *Guardian.* http://www.theguardian.com/cities/2015/jul/31/urban-slender-loris-bangalore-india-animal.

Spaulding Rehabitation Hospital. 2013. "Spaulding Rehabilitation Hospital Unveils Its State-of-the-Art New Hospital to the Public." www.spauldingrehab.org/asdf.

Stanley Park Ecology Society. n.d.(a). "The Coyote Shaker." http://stanleyparkecology.ca/wp-content/uploads/2012/02/The-Coyote-Shaker-July-2011.pdf.

Stanley Park Ecology Society. n.d.(b). "Co-Existing with Coyotes." http://stanleyparkecology.ca/conservation/co-existing-with-coyotes/.

Stephens, Suzanne. n.d. "Aqua Tower." GreenSource. http://greensource.construction.com/green_building_projects/2010/1001_Aqua-Tower.asp.

Stewart, Barbara. 2002, July 24. "A New Kind of New Yorker, One with 82 Legs." *New York Times.* http://www.nytimes.com/2002/07/24/nyregion/a-new-kind-of-new-yorker-one-with-82-legs.html.

Stewart, Matt. 2013. "Bird-Safe Havens Morgan's New Halo." http://www.stuff.co.nz/environment/8799333/Bird-safe-havens-Morgans-new-halo.

St. Louis-MO Gov. n.d. "Milkweeds for Monarchs." https://www.stlouis-mo.gov/monarchs/.

Sustainability Leaders. n.d. "Singapore Sustainability Leaders: PARKROYAL on Pickering," http://sustainability –leaders.com.

Tan, Monica. 2015, July 15. "Leaf Letters: Fan Email for Melbourne's Trees Pours in from around the World." *Guardian.* http://www.theguardian.com/australia-news/2015/jul/15/leaf-letters-fan-mail-melbourne-trees-pours-in-around-the-world.

Tempelhof. n.d. "An Overview of Pioneer Projects." http://www.thf-berlin.de/en/get-in volved/pioneer-projects/.

Terrapin Bright Green LLC. 2012. *The Economics of Biophilia: Why Designing with Nature in Mind Makes Financial Sense*. New York: Terrapin Bright Green.

Thomas, Sue. 2013. *Technobiophilia: Nature and Cyberspace*. London: Bloomsbury Academic.

Thome, Wolfgang. 2015. "Conservation Godfather: Why Rail Will Run through Nairobi National Park." http://www.eturbonews.com/62100/conservation-godfather-why-rail -will-run-through-nairobi-nationa.

Tidball, K. 2014. "Urgent Biophilia: Human–Nature Interactions in Red Zone Recovery and Resilience." In *Greening in the Red Zone: Disaster, Resilience and Community Greening*, ed. K. G. Tidball and M. E. Krasny, 50. New York: Springer.

Transbay Transit Center. n.d. "City Park." http://transbaycenter.org/project/transit-center /transit-center-level/city-park.

Troy, Austin, J. Morgan Grove, and Jarlath O'Neill-Dunne. 2012. "The Relationship between Tree Canopy and Crime Rates across an Urban–Rural Gradient in the Greater Baltimore Region." *Landscape and Urban Planning* 106(3):262–270.

Trust for Public Land (TPL). 2014, October. *The Economic Benefits of San Francisco's Park and Recreation System*. https://www.tpl.org/sites/default/files/files_upload/San%20 Francisco%20Economic%20Value%20Study%20report%20final%20low-res.pdf.

UNESCO. 2015. "Cape Floral Region Protected Areas." http://whc.unesco.org/en/list/1007.

United Nations. 2014. *World Urbanization Prospects: The 2014 Revision*. Highlights (ST/ESA/ SER.A/352). https://esa.un.org/unpd/wup/Publications/Files/WUP2014-Highlights.pdf.

United States National Park Service. n.d.. "Chain of Rocks Bridge: Madison, Illinois to St. Louis, Missouri." https://www.nps.gov/nr/travel/route66/chain_of_rocks_bridge_illi nois_missouri.html.

University of Birmingham, n.d. "About BIFoR," *Birmingham Institute for Forest Research*. http://www.birmingham.ac.uk/research/activity/bifor/about/index.aspx.

University of Birmingham, 2015. "Minding the gap . . . city bats won't fly through bright spaces." http://birmingham.ac.uk/new/latest/2015/06/03Jun15Mindingthegap%E2 %80%A6Citybatswontflythroughbrightspaces.aspx.

Urban Ecology Center. n.d. "Neighborhood Environmental Education Project (NEEP)." http://urbanecologycenter.org/what-we-do/neep.html.

Urban Ecology Center. 2014. "2013–2014 Annual Report." http://urbanecologycenter.org/.

Urban Park Rangers Weekend Adventures. n.d.. https://www.nycgovparks.org/programs /rangers/explorer-programs.

Usborne, Simon. 2014, September 25. "47 Per cent of London Is Green Space: Is It Time for Our Capital to Become a National Park?" *Independent*. http://www.independent .co.uk/environment/47-per-cent-of-london-is-green-space-is-it-time-for-our-capital -to-become-a-national-park-9756470.html.

van der Wal, A. J., H. M. Schade, L. Krabbendam, M. van Vugt. 2013. "Do Natural Landscapes Reduce Future Discounting in Humans?" *Proceedings of the Royal Society B* 280: 20132295. http://dx.doi.org/10.1098/rspb.2013.2295.

Vertical Garden Patrick Blanc. n.d. http://www.verticalgardenpatrickblanc.com/realisa tions/sydney/one-central-park-sydney.

Villagran, Lauren, 2012. "Bidding Farewell to Mexico City's Green Mayor," Next American City, April 30, 2015. https://nextcity.org/daily/entrybidding-farewell-to-mexico-citys -gree-mayor.

Wang, Hui, Yuko Tsunetsugu, and Julia Africa. 2015. "Seeing the Forest for the Trees." *Harvard Design Magazine*. http://www.harvarddesignmagazine.org/issues/40/seeing -the-forest-for-the-trees.

Ward Thompson, C., J. Roe, P. Aspinall, R. Mitchell, A. Clow, D. Miller. 2014. "More Green Space Is Linked to Less Stress in Deprived Communities: Evidence from Salivary Cortisol Patterns." *Landscape and Urban Planning* 105:221–229.

Weinstein, N., A. K. Przybylski, and R. M. Ryan. 2009. "Can Nature Make Us More Caring? Effects of Immersion in Nature on Intrinsic Aspirations and Generosity." *Personality and Social Psychology Bulletin* 35: 1315–1329.

Wellington City Council. 2015. "Our Natural Capital: Wellington's Biodiversity Strategy and Action Plan, 2015, Wellington, New Zealand. Urban Ecology Center. 2013–2014 Annual Report. http://wellington.govt.nz/your-council/plans-policies-and-bylaws /policies/biodiversity-strategy-and-action-plan.

Wellington Zoo. 2014, December 3. "Wellington Zoo Celebrates Five Years of the Nest Te Kōhanga." Media release. http://www.scoop.co.nz/stories/AK1412/S00104/wellington -zoo-celebrates-five-years-of-the-nest-te-kohanga.htm.

Wells, Nancy M. 2000. "At Home with Nature: Effects of 'Greenness' on Children's Cognitive Functioning." *Environment and Behavior* 32(6): 775–794.

Wheeler, B. W., M. White, W. Stahl-Timmins, and Michael Depledge. 2012, "Does Living by the Coast Improve Health and Wellbeing?" *Health Place* 18(5): 1198–1201. doi: 10.1016/j.healthplace.2012.06.015. Epub 2012 Jul 1.

Wilson E. O. 1984. *Biophilia*, Cambridge, MA: Harvard University Press.

Wohlforth, Charles. 2015, June 5. "History of Anchorage's Trails and Greenbelts." http:// www.alaskapublic.org/2015/06/05/history-of-anchorages-trails-and-greenbelts/.

Wolch, Jennifer R., Jason Byrne, and Joshua P. Newell. 2014. "Urban Green Space, Public Health, and Environmental Justice: The Challenge of Making Cities 'Just Green Enough.'" *Landscape and Urban Planning* 125:234–244.

Wolf, K. L., and K. Flora 2010. "Mental Health and Function: A Literature Review." In *Green Cities: Good Health*. Seattle: College of the Environment, University of Washington. www.greenhealth.washington.edu.

Woodman, Ellis. 2015. "Bosco Verticale by Stefano Boeri Architetti." *Architect's Journal*. http://www.architectsjournal.co.uk/buildings/bosco-verticale-by-stefano-boeri-ar chitetti/8679088.article.

World Landscape Architecture. n.d. "Kallang River Bishan Park." http://worldlandscape architect.com/kallang-river-bishan-park-singapore-atelier-dreiseitl/.

Wright + Associates. n.d. "Waitangi Park." http://www.waal.co.nz/our-projects/urban/wai tangi-park/.

Wyland Foundation, n.d. "Wyland Walls" http://www.wylandfoundation.org/community.php?subsection=wyland_walls.

Yeang, K., and T. R. Hamzah. n.d. "Solaris Fusionopolis." http://www.greenroofs.com/content/articles/126-SOLARIS-at-Fusionopolis-2B-From-Military-Base-to-Bioclimatic-Eco-Architecture.htm#.V1zWRab2aUk.

Yu, Kongjian. 2010. "Qiaoyuan Park, Tianjin—An Ecosystem Services–Oriented Regenerative Design." *Topos* 70:28.

Zealandia. n.d. "Forest Restoration." http://www.visitzealandia.com/what-is-zealandia/conservation-restoration/forest-restoration/.

Zealandia. n.d. "Our Groundbreaking Fence." http://www.visitzealandia.com/what-is-zealandia/conservation-restoration/our-groundbreaking-fence/.

Zealandia. n.d. "Progress to Date." http://www.visitzealandia.com.

Zelenski, John, Raelyn L. Dopko, and Colin Capaldi, 2015. "Cooperation is in Out Nature: Nature Exposure May Promote Cooperation and Environmentally Sustainable Behavior" Journal of Environmental Psychology. 42: 24-31.

# Index